Praise 1

Some time ago, I .... eisler
presenting his und................... .... Calvinism. The errors in
the tape were simply breathtaking, and so I was very glad to hear that
James White had undertaken a book-length response to Dr. Geisler's
Chosen But Free. This response is outstanding. *The Potter's Freedom* is
firmly, pointedly, and charitably written. For someone of Dr. Geisler's
stature to go into print with his misunderstandings was simply inexplicable. The easy thing would have been to simply let the whole thing go
in an embarrassed silence, but in this book, James White has assumed
the role of a biblical friend to Dr. Geisler. It deserves a wide reading.
    —Douglas Wilson, Pastor; Editor of *Credenda Agenda* Magazine

We are in debt to Norman Geisler for displaying once again just how
unpalatable the truth of the Scripture can be, even for those who know
its contents well. His screed against Calvinism has provided the occasion for James R. White to give us *The Potter's Freedom*, a book that not
only reveals the poverty of Geisler's argument but also provides us with
a refreshing presentation of the glorious truths of salvation by grace
alone as set forth by authentic Calvinism. The so-called "moderate
Calvinism" which Geisler embraces and presents in *Chosen But Free* is
no more useful than a moderate fire department.
    —Joel Nederhood, Pastor; Host of *The Back to God Hour*

The Potter's Freedom is a more than adequate response to the misleading
and erroneous book, *Chosen But Free* by Norman Geisler. Indeed, it is a
fresh and helpful statement of true Calvinism over against a system
purporting to be "Calvinistic" which is really nothing more than a brand
of Arminianism. This book should be widely disseminated and read as it
will clarify much that is often misunderstood about Calvinism.
    —Jay Adams, Ph.D., Westminster Seminary, Escondido, California

James White's *The Potter's Freedom* is a modern "Antidote to
Arminianism." His devastating rebuttal to Geisler's *Chosen But Free* is a
clearly expressed alternative to a theology which halts between two opinions. White not only effectively presents the case for the absolute sovereignty of God, but demonstrates Geisler's tendency to faulty research,
partial citations, and fallacious argumentation. If you desire to better
understand the ways of God with man, this book is for you.
    —Kenneth L. Gentry, Jr., Th.D.; Bahnsen Theological Seminary

Many of us, who have otherwise profited from the writings of Dr. Norman Geisler, have been grieved by his hapless attempt to harmonize Calvinism and Arminianism. With the skill of a surgeon, Dr. James R. White dissects Geisler's arguments and reveals them to be based on convoluted thinking, inconsistencies, and misinterpretations of Scripture. I pray that this book shall have a wide audience, not just as a definitive rebuttal to Geisler, but also as a helpful exposition of the Calvinisim/Arminianism debate.
　　—Dr. Erwin W. Lutzer, Senior Pastor, Moody Church, Chicago

Piece by piece, James White dissects the flawed arguments of Geisler's misnamed "moderate Calvinism," which is in fact a very common breed of Arminianism. I am under no illusion that Geisler will wave the white flag on this one, but every honest reader of this book will know that he should.
　　—Jim Elliff, President, Christian Communicators Worldwide

James White's response to *Chosen But Free* arises from a personal knowledge of Dr. Geisler and an appreciation for his positive impact on the broader evangelical community. This sincere appreciation, however, does not cause him to downplay the seriously flawed presentation Geisler gives of the issue of divine determination and human responsibility. White's work is an incisive and, in my opinion decisive response to the specific fallacies of Geisler, and provides a positive exposition of the issue that is valuable even apart from its polemical context.
　　—Dr. Tom J. Nettles, Author of *By His Grace & For His Glory*

The popular view of divine sovereignty which Geisler advocates is a serious departure from the self-revelation of God in the Scriptures. Indeed, White's strongest suit is his demonstration that Geisler's argument is entirely indefensible at the exegetical level. Some may read White and continue to hold Geisler's opinions, but they will no longer be comfortable with those opinions.
　　—Fred G. Zaspel, Pastor, Author of *The Theology of Fulfillment*

There can hardly be a topic more important or relevant than the one James White tackles in this superb book. Who is free? Man or God? Which is sovereign? These are the issues at stake in this timely rebuttal of error and demonstration of biblical truth. This book deserves a careful reading by all who truly seek clarity and genuine biblical light.
　　—Rev. Richard D. Phillips, Assoc. Minister, Tenth Presbyterian Church, Philadelphia, PA; V. P., Alliance of Confessing Evangelicals

This vigorous defense of the Reformation exposes the widening gap, and the growing hostility, between "evangelicalism" and classic confessional Protestant Christianity. Synergism may wear a happy face, but it proclaims a hollow "gospel." Written in the context of high-profile rapprochement between evangelicals and Catholics, and between Lutherans and Romanists, Dr. White turns up the lights to show us the real struggle, namely, the fundamentally religious contest between divine sovereignty and human ability. Our salvation comes either from God or from man. And in terms of both Bible teaching and human experience, this is where everything starts—and ends.

> **—Nelson D. Kloosterman, Th.D., Professor of Ethics and New Testament, Mid-America Reformed Seminary**

James White combines sound biblical exegesis, theological erudition, and a deep passion for truth in his able rebuttal to Norman Geisler's *Chosen But Free*. I am grateful that *The Potter's Freedom* powerfully exposes Geisler's inconsistencies and shows that his self-labeled "moderate Calvinism" is no Calvinism at all. *The Potter's Freedom* has far-reaching consequences for any serious student of Reformed theology, for Geisler is not a lone ranger in promoting historic Reformed theology as "extreme Calvinism" and Semi-pelagianism as "moderate Calvinism." I pray that God may use this book abundantly to remove many caricatures about the Reformed faith and to move many to embrace unabashedly solid, Reformed convictions.

> **—Dr. Joel R. Beeke, Author, President of Puritan Reformed Theological Seminary, Grand Rapids, Michigan**

The Reformed community has given Norman Geisler a "free" pass for too long with respect to his pronouncements on God's sovereignty and free will. James White's book, *The Potter's Freedom*, is the much-needed antidote to his flawed (and failed) attempt, in typical Thomistic fashion, to synthesize what cannot be synthesized. As soon as he insists that "God's grace works synergistically on free will," and that the "one condition" for receiving grace, namely, faith, "is logically prior to regeneration" (pp. 233-34), he falls away from the thought of the sixteenth-century Reformation and stands in concert with the synergism of Rome. It is high time that he who has warned the members of the Evangelical Theological Society to "beware human philosophy" should heed his own warning and listen less to Aquinas and more carefully to Holy Scripture.

> **—Robert Reymond, Ph.D., Knox Theological Seminary, Ft. Lauderdale, FL, Author of *A New Systematic Theology of the Christian Faith***

A comparison of Norman Geisler's book, *Chosen But Free*, with James White's book, *The Potter's Freedom*, reveals two observations. First, Geisler's book is one of demagoguery, propaganda, and an embarrassing lack of accurate scholarship, while White's book is one of careful and scholarly exegesis of the Bible, coupled with a convincing exposition and defense of the Reformed Faith (i.e., the Biblical Faith) from misrepresentation and caricature. Second, James White effectively distinguishes Norman Geisler's theology from Calvinism by pointing out this difference: Geisler believes in a God who tries to save all the sinners He can, and Calvinism believes in a God who saves all the sinners He will.
—Dr. Joseph C. Morecraft, III; Author, Pastor of Chalcedon Presbyterian Church, Cumming, GA; Publisher of *The Counsel of Chalcedon*

White's work evidences unusually good exegetical and theological insight into some of the greatest themes of the Bible touching our Lord's work of salvation, themes that Geisler has abused, maltreated and generally misunderstood (for example, Geisler attempts to make a case for a conditional unconditional election!), such as the biblical doctrines of man under sin, divine election and the sovereignty of God in salvation. With a keener grasp of systematic theology and exegesis of the text of Scripture White has taken Geisler to the theological woodshed!
—S.Lewis Johnson, Jr., AB, ThM, ThD, Former Prof. of New Testament & Systematic Theololgy at Dallas Theological Seminary; Former Prof. of Bible & Systematic Theology at Trinity Evangelical Divinity School

There are few authors today who are able to write with a burning passion for truth, tempered by a charitable spirit towards those with whom one disagrees. Having achieved that balance, Dr. White's contribution to the defense of Reformed soteriology is both sound and timely. His biblical exegesis of all the relevant passages, together with the misrepresentations he corrects, is secured by detailed analysis and demonstrates convincingly to the fair-minded reader that every true believer in the Lord Jesus Christ has nothing of which to boast but in the freedom of the Potter.
—David King, Pastor, Dayspring Presbyterian Church, Forsyth, GA

(see end-pages of this book for additional endorsements)

The
Potter's
Freedom

A Defense of the Reformation
and a Rebuttal of Norman Geisler's
Chosen But Free

James White

CALVARY PRESS PUBLISHING
PO BOX 805 · AMITYVILLE, NY 11701
WWW.CALVARYPRESS.COM

Calvary Press Publishing
2005 Merrick Rd., #341
Merrick, N.Y. 11566
U.S.A.
1 (800) 789-8175 / calvarypress.com

Unless otherwise noted, the Bible quotations contained in this manual
are from the New American Standard Bible, © by the Lockman Foundation 1960, 1962, 1963, 1968, 1971, 1972, 1973, 1975, 1977, 1995. Used
by permission. Verses marked KJV are taken from the King James Version
of the Bible. Verses marked NKJV are taken from the New King James
Version of the Bible. Verses marked NIV are taken from the New Interna-
tional Version of the Bible.

Book & Cover Design: Anthony Rotolo

White, James R., 1962-
        The Potter's Freedom / James R. White.
        Includes index.
ISBN: 978-1-879737-43-3
Recommended Dewey Decimal Classification: 234
Suggested Subject Headings:
1. Justification 2. Evangelicalism—Controversial literature.
3. Evangelicalism—Doctrines 4. Church—Contemporary Issues
I. Title

Manufactured in the United States of America
6th Printing 2007

I have had the great blessing of introducing many brothers and sisters in the Lord to the doctrines of grace. Nothing is more encouraging than to see those who have come to know these divine truths growing in grace and maturing in the faith.

———————

It is with great love and thankfulness that I dedicate this work to my close friend, Greek student, lifting partner, and fellow Reformed Baptist, Simon Escobedo III.

Acknowledgements

I am deeply grateful to the many brothers and sisters in the Lord who have provided encouragement and assistance in this work. Especially I wish to note Richard Pierce, Mike Porter, Simon Escobedo III, Larry Vondra, Chris Jenkins, Pastor David King, Jeff Niell, Kevin Johnson and all the kind folks in #prosapologian, especially NIna ^'^ (Han vet ikke mer enn katten!). Special thanks go to Keith Plummer and Mark Ennis for their help in research. I am grateful to the wonderful people of the Phoenix Reformed Baptist Church and my fellow elders Don Cross and Don Fry. My thanks as well to Chris Arnzen and the folks at Calvary Press. And of course I am thankful for the patience and support of my wife Kelli and my children, Joshua and Summer.

CONTENTS

Preface by Phillip R. Johnson

A blurb on the back cover of Norman Geisler's *Chosen But Free* boasts that it is "the definitive work on the relationship between divine election and human choice." One would not have expected anything less from a seminary professor of Dr. Geisler's stature and reputation.

Unfortunately, *Chosen But Free* is a disappointment. More than a mere letdown, actually. It is a stunningly inept treatment of the subject it undertakes. Dr. Geisler manages to misrepresent his friends and foes alike. He utterly mangles the doctrines of divine sovereignty, election, and free will—and in the process he obscures and redefines the historical positions of both Calvinism and Arminianism. The reader who has the regrettable persistence to follow Dr. Geisler to the last page of his work is certain to be hopelessly befuddled at the end of the effort.

The fact is, if Dr. Geisler were not a teacher of such stature, there would be no reason at all to pay any attention to his book. It is a bad book by any measure.

Nevertheless, it is obvious that the book is having a widespread impact among evangelicals—especially lay readers. Hardly a week goes by that someone doesn't ask me about Geisler's book, and especially Geisler's fatuous claim that the position set forth in his book deserves the label "moderate Calvinism."

That's why I am very grateful for James White's careful, patient, and thorough response to Geisler in *The Potter's Freedom* . Dr. White meticulously unravels the near-hopeless tangle Geisler has made of these doctrines, skillfully employing both Scripture and his solid grasp of historical theology to make the truth unmistakably clear.

In answering Geisler, Dr. White has produced one of the finest explanations of the doctrines of grace and the sovereignty of God that has seen publication in recent years. I hope this important book will reach a wide audience.

Phillip R. Johnson
Executive Director of John MacArthur's *Grace To You* Ministry
Elder of Grace Community Church, Sun Valley, CA

Foreword by R.C. Sproul, Jr.

I often find myself baffled as I consider the state of the church in our day. People often ask me, in light of the radical unbelief that infests the pulpits of so many mainline churches, why these "pastors" bother to pretend to be Christian. What benefit do wolves get from masquerading as shepherds? But such questions betray a misunderstanding. The men and women who embrace theological liberalism operate under the premise that words have no meaning. They are not pretending to be Christians, they are re-imagining the meaning of the term "Christian." People who have no respect for the history of the church will not have respect for the history of words. In our post-modern world if a word still carries the scent of goodness, all the baddies will claim it for their own. Thus the homosexual crowd lobbies for gay marriage, even though marriage has *always* been defined as a union between a man and a woman.

When the Roman religion codified a false gospel at the Council of Trent, dogmatically teaching that those who affirm justification by faith alone are worthy of damnation, the true church had a problem. We had two groups, each claiming the word "Christian." The two sides taught mutually exclusive views of a cardinal tenet, the doctrine of salvation. So the Protestants, instead of just holding onto the name "Christian," added the terms "Protestant" or "evangelical" as qualifiers to their understanding of what a Christian was. To be sure, they af-

affirmed that there were no non-Protestant, or non-evangelical Christians, just non-Protestant, non-evangelical people and
institutions who wrongly claimed the word, "Christian."

J. Gresham Machen made much the same argument when
he titled his monumental work *Christianity and Liberalism*. He
took great pains to argue that theological liberalism was not a
variety of the Christian faith, but another faith altogether. The
liberals, however, did not give up the term.

Within that group which took the name Protestant there
are sub-groups. There were Lutherans, and there were Reformed people; there were Mennonites, and there were Angli-
cans. There were Calvinists, and there were Remonstrants.
Many of the terms have faded from use, but some remain.
And one of the oddities is how the term Calvinist has come to
be used in the modern American church.

For many in the modern visible church to identify someone as a "Calvinist" is akin to saying that such a person is
worthy of the death penalty. The ghost of Servetus still haunts
us. Just as in our age of hyper-sensitivity no one can make fun
of any other group (unless, of course, that group is comprised
of evangelical Christians), so it seems that within
evangelicalism political correctness decrees that we speak ill
of no one else (with the possible exception of those Calvinists). We (for alas, in the sovereign outworking of God's decrees, I am one of *them*) are presented in caricature. We are
the dour crowd, pinched lips, plain clothes, ready to burn our
enemies at the stake. Calvinists, for good or for bad, have a
reputation for being smart. We are the ones ever so adept at
crossing our theological "t's," and dotting our soteriological
"i's." We are the proud owners of cold, dead orthodoxy, with
minds aflame, and hearts of coal, or so it is said.

This consideration might help us to understand a rather
curious phenomenon in the modern church. We now are having to deal with "moderate Calvinists." It is my suspicion that
a "moderate Calvinism" is the theological equivalent of a "compassionate conservative" in the political realm. That is, it can

involve an element of double speak. The "compassionate conservative" candidate for public office wants you to see him as a person who wants to cut your taxes while at the same time raising your benefits. "Compassion" speaks to the benefits, "conservative" to the taxes, and in all the confusion we forget that we're talking about only one pile of money. Place your bets on "compassion" not on "conservative," and remember, they're compassionate with *your* money.

I believe those who describe themselves as "moderate Calvinists" are playing the same game. "Moderate" means not so mean-spirited, not given to hard rhetoric on the sovereignty of God, not quite so stingy on free will, while "Calvinist" maintains the air of intellectual rigor and respectability.

Dr. Norman Geisler (perhaps having grown weary of his previous oxymoronic self-description as a "Cal-minian") has not only taken to calling himself a moderate Calvinist, but has weighed in with a book, *Chosen but Free*, designed to lay out for the reader this "you can have your cake and eat it too" system. As so often happens, "moderate" eats up "Calvinism."

Apart from mislabeling his own views, Geisler makes a spirited defense of historic Arminianism, and in the process seeks to paint historic Calvinism as not only "extreme," but false. Dr. Geisler is no intellectual lightweight. His book however carries no punch. One makes little progress when battling the rock that is the Word of God.

Martin Luther argued that we are all Pelagians by nature: We have a natural propensity to see ourselves as having a propensity for good. And so, we should not be surprised if Dr. Geisler's book will find a welcome audience. Which is perhaps why Dr. White took up the challenge of answering Dr. Geisler. In *The Potter's Freedom*, Dr. White follows in the tradition of Augustine, Luther, Calvin, and Edwards, fighting for the angels, and more importantly, for the unassailable sovereignty of God in our salvation. He works his way by moving between two important books, the error filled work of Dr.

Geisler, and the inerrant Word of God. Point by point, paragraph by paragraph, Dr. White shines the light of Scripture on
Chosen But Free. Along the way he shows us that the views
espoused in *Chosen But Free* are not only not Calvinism of any
stripe, but not biblical, and therefore not true.

It seems that while we are all born Pelagians, most of us are
reborn as semi-Pelagians. That is, we come into the kingdom
as Arminians. Dr. White will, God willing, help many progress
to what Spurgeon said was but a nickname for biblical Christianity: Calvinism.

R.C. Sproul, Jr.
Editor-in-Chief of *TableTalk* Magazine

INTRODUCTION

Dr. Norman Geisler is a nationally-known and well-respected apologist. The head of Southern Evangelical Seminary, Dr. Geisler has written dozens of books and countless articles. Many of his works have been tremendously useful to the evangelical Christian community. He has spoken widely on a variety of topics. He is a wonderfully personable man, and I can say I have enjoyed more than one lunch and dinner with him over the years.

When Dr. Geisler warns the Christian community about a dangerous belief, many listen. Therefore, when he uses particularly strong language about a popular and widespread theological viewpoint, the wise person will consider well what he has to say. In particular, in his book, *Chosen But Free,* he seeks (in the majority of the text) to dissuade his readers from embracing one particular viewpoint that is widely represented in the modern day. He describes this viewpoint's adherents as presenting conclusions that are "unsupported by the many texts they employ."[1] In establishing whether embracing this system is important or not, Geisler warns us that "Belief affects behavior, and so ideas have consequences....Likewise, false doctrine will lead to false deeds."[2] And this system seems particularly pernicious in Dr. Geisler's view. It can lead to failure to take personal responsibility for our actions.[3] It can "have a devastating effect on one's own salvation, to say nothing of one's enthusiasm to reach others for Christ."[4] This belief even lays the ground for universalism,[5] undermines trust in the love of God,[6] and in so doing has even been the "occasion for disbelief and even atheism for many."[7] The God presented by adherents of this system "is not worthy of worship" and "does not represent God at all."[8] Indeed, those who follow this line of thought are in danger of moving from their current viewpoint "into being a universalist—from one unfortunate belief to another."[9] So "unfortunate" is this viewpoint that it even undermines the motivation for evangelism as well as the motivation for intercessory prayer![10]

But that is not all. Dr. Geisler insists that this system is "contradictory."[11] The proponents of this view "go through exegetical contortions in order to make a text say what their preconceived theology mandates that it must say."[12] He says the Bible is "seriously lacking" in verses that support some of the main elements of this system.[13] These people "misuse" texts of Scripture,[14] and he bluntly says that the God worshipped by these people "is not all-loving."[15] He describes central aspects of this belief as "shocking."[16] And in the strongest terms he insists that the very heart of this system's belief is a "hideous error,"[17] and that this system is at its heart "theologically inconsistent, philosophically insufficient, and morally repugnant."[18]

To what theological system is Dr. Geisler referring? Is this a new review of Mormonism, the Watchtower Society, or possibly Roman Catholicism? No, all of the above phrases are used by Dr. Geisler to describe the system of belief that historically has been called Calvinism. All of these phrases are used of simple Reformed theology, the theology of Calvin, the Westminster Confession of Faith, the 1689 Baptist Confession of Faith, Francis Turretin, the Puritans, John Owen, John Bunyan, Jonathan Edwards, George Whitefield, William Cunningham, Charles Haddon Spurgeon, Charles Hodge, J. Gresham Machen, B.B. Warfield, Hermann Bavinck, Abraham Kuyper, John Murray, Edwin Palmer, John Gerstner, John Piper, and R.C. Sproul.

Surprised? I certainly was when I first read *Chosen But Free* (hereafter *CBF*) in June of 1999. I knew the book was coming out, and in fact had discussed two elements of the book with

Dr. Geisler while the book was being written.[19] But I was in no way prepared for the fact that *CBF* would take the direction it does, nor that it would have such *strong* anti-Reformed conclusions. I immediately recognized that a response was needed. *CBF* will cause great confusion for those examining these vital topics. As an elder in a Reformed Baptist Church I am always blessed to be able to introduce men and women to the great truths of the Reformation: truths directly challenged by *CBF*. And as an apologist, I firmly believe that the *only* consistently biblical response to the challenges made to the Christian faith is that offered by Reformed theology.

Reinventing the Wheel?

There are many tremendous works in print defining and defending the great biblical faith of the Reformation. God has been most gracious in raising up men like Calvin,[20] Edwards,[21] Turretin,[22] Warfield,[23] Palmer,[24] Sproul,[25] and Piper[26] who have been gifted to communicate His truth to their generations in a unique fashion. These works really need no defense, for any person reading them can see their internal consistency and depth of exegetical insight. These are *profoundly biblical* works written by men who are deeply committed to the authority of the Scriptures as the Word of God.

So why offer this small volume to the Christian church? I have already written an introduction to the doctrines of grace,[27] and will not seek to repeat what I have written there. This work is prompted solely by the publication of Dr. Norman Geisler's *Chosen But Free*. *CBF* seeks to present what it calls "moderate Calvinism" as a "balanced perspective" regarding the tremendously important concept of God's sovereignty and man's will. Given that Dr. Geisler is a prolific author who has addressed a tremendously wide variety of topics,[28] his work automatically carries the weight of his previous experience and scholarship. As a result, many will take his conclusions at face value. But it is my firm conviction that *CBF* will be a source of great confusion, not enlightenment, on the subject of the sovereignty of

of God and the will of man. Why do I say this? I offer five
sources of confusion that I believe are created by the discussion in *CBF.*

Redefinition of the Terms of the Debate

The first thing that any informed reader discovers in reading *CBF* is that it presents a complete revision of the historic
set of terms that have been used by theologians to frame and
explain the debate. This is one of the most disturbing aspects
of this work in that it cannot possibly do anything else than
cause tremendous confusion on the part of those who are attempting to understand the Reformed/Arminian debate. For
some reason Dr. Geisler chose arbitrarily to identify his position as "moderate Calvinism" and historic Reformed theology
becomes "extreme Calvinism." The problem becomes clear
when we consider for just a moment that Dr. Geisler: 1) denies Calvin's doctrine of God's sovereignty and decrees; 2)
denies Calvin's doctrine of the total depravity of man and his
enslavement to sin; 3) denies Calvin's belief that God's electing grace is given without any condition whatsoever to a particular people (the elect); and 4) denies, vociferously, Calvin's
doctrine of the grace of God that brings new life to dead sinners. One could even argue that Dr. Geisler disagrees with
Calvin's doctrine of atonement and with the very *foundation*
of Calvin's doctrine of perseverance as well. If that is true, *why
should Dr. Geisler wish to be called any kind of Calvinist at all?* I
honestly do not understand the desire to take a theological
moniker that does not in the slightest represent one's fundamental beliefs.

Dr. Geisler's "moderate Calvinism" will be shown to be
merely a modified form of historic Arminianism. In fact, there
are really only two elements of the viewpoint of *CBF* that are
in fact "borrowed" from Calvinism: the concept of a substitutionary atonement (alien to Arminianism) and "eternal security," likewise utterly inconsistent with Arminian beliefs. Beyond these two issues, *CBF* presents a thoroughly *non*-Re-

formed position under the name "moderate Calvinism." And such is simply indefensible.

Poor Representation

CBF takes no pains to accurately or adequately represent the Reformed position that it so strongly denounces. While some mention is made of a small number of Reformed works, even these are normally quoted in such a brief fashion as to make their citation less than useful. A person reading CBF would see a straw-man view of the reality, not the real thing.

Of course, immediately someone will say, "That's what *everyone* says." Possibly so: however, through the text of this work we will document the repeated instances where CBF, *even while admitting what Reformed writers assert*, rejects this and substitutes a more easily defeated enemy. For example, CBF will cite Reformed writers speaking of the human will, but, on the same page, will insist that it is their view that the will is "destroyed." All through the book the Reformed view of God's sovereign regeneration of the sinner, where God graciously grants spiritual life, faith, and repentance to a person who was spiritually dead, condemned, and incapable of doing anything pleasing in God's sight, is inaccurately portrayed as "force" and "coercion," all in an attempt to make Calvinism look like something it is not. Such inaccuracies only add to the confusion produced by the redefinition of terms.

Most frustrating to the Reformed believer who has provided a reasoned and Scripturally-based defense of his or her beliefs is the *utter lack* of serious interaction on the part of CBF with such works. There is simply no attempt to interact *on a meaningful level* with the many Reformed works that provide in-depth, serious biblical exegesis and argumentation in defense of the Reformed position. While some works, such as Owen's *The Death of Death in the Death of Christ* and Piper's *The Justification of God*, are mentioned, and even cited, the responses are so surface-level that they amount to nothing more than a dismissal, not a rebuttal. And even here, the Reformed material is handled in such a cavalier manner as to make even the effort of citing it worthless. This is clearly seen in the way in which *CBF* will quote as little as a single sentence, and on the basis of this, accuse Reformed writers of "changing" Scripture. For example, Dr. Geisler "quotes" from John Owen and writes:

> Arguably, the best defense of extreme Calvinism on limited atonement comes from John Owen. His response to this passage is a shocking retranslation to: "God so loved his elect throughout the world, that he gave His Son with this intention, that by him believers might be saved"! This needs no response, simply a sober reminder that God repeatedly exhorts us not to add to or subtract from His words (Deut. 4:2; Prov. 30:6; Rev. 22:18-19).[29]

This citation is from page 214 of Owen's work. Was this great Christian scholar suggesting that we should "retranslate" John 3:16? Is this a fair representation of Owen's position? Not in the slightest. This citation comes toward the end of a *lengthy* discussion of the passage (a discussion, I note, that is significantly longer and in more depth than *any* discussion of *any* passage in all of *CBF*). There is no attempt whatsoever on the part of *CBF* to address the actual argument and the reasoning set forth. Here, in context, is what Owen said:

> First, If this word *whosoever* be distributive, then it is restrictive of the love of God to some, and not to others,—to one part of the distribution, and not the other. And if it do not restrain the love of God, intending the salvation of some, then it is not distributive of the forementioned object of it; and if it do restrain it, then all are not intended in the love which moved God to give his Son. Secondly, I deny that the word here is distributive of the object of God's love, but only declarative of his end and aim in giving Christ in the pursuit of that love,—to wit, that all believers might be saved. So that the sense is, "God so loved his elect throughout the world,

that he gave his Son with this intention, that by him
believers might be saved." And this is all that is by any
(besides a few worthless cavils) objected from this place
to disprove our interpretation....[30]

As anyone reading the passage in context can see, to charge
Owen with alteration of the Word of God is quite simply ri-
diculous. He not only specifically says, "the *sense* is..." (a phrase
that would *have* to be cited on the basis of mere honesty *if*
CBF is serious in accusing Owen of "adding" to the Word of
God), but it is painfully obvious that Owen is interpreting the
passage in the light of the preceding ten pages of argumentation he had provided. One cannot avoid noting that aside from
this allegedly "sober reminder" offered by Geisler, *there is not
a single word of meaningful argumentation or refutation provided.*

The same thing is true of CBF's treatment of John Piper's
The Justification of God. While CBF acknowledges the existence of the work, and recognizes the high place it holds in the
thinking of Reformed exegetes and apologists, there is almost
nothing in it that smacks of the first attempt to seriously respond to the conclusions so soberly and masterfully presented
by Piper. For example, Piper spends many pages (pp. 56-73)
fairly, carefully, and most importantly, *exegetically* examining
the issue of whether Romans 9 is addressing *individuals* and
their *personal* salvation, or merely addressing *nations.* In so
doing he provides forty-one footnotes, addresses numerous
issues regarding both the Hebrew and Septuagint texts, and
cites many (in full contexts) who present a viewpoint *other*
than his own. His conclusion, then, is *exegetical* in nature. Note
his words:

> The interpretation which tries to restrict this predesti-
> nation or unconditional election to nations rather than
> individuals or to historical tasks rather than eternal des-
> tinies must ignore or distort the problem posed in Rom.
> 9:1-5, the individualism of 9:6b, the vocabulary and logi-

cal structure of 9:6b-8, the closely analogous texts elsewhere in Paul, and the implications of 9:14-23. The position is exegetically untenable.[31]

What is truly amazing is that there is not *the first attempt to
deal with anything presented by Piper in this section on the part
of CBF.* The only citation of this section by CBF reads,

> Even Piper, who holds that the Romans passage is speak-
> ing of *individual* election to eternal salvation admits of
> modern scholars that "the list of those who see no indi-
> vidual predestination to eternal life or death is impres-
> sive."[32]

The footnote goes on to cite Piper's quotation of those who
disagree with his position, *but the entire book never once attempts to deal with Piper's refutation of the viewpoints he cites!*
And, to be fair, Dr. Geisler *should have* likewise cited, *from the
same page,* this statement, "The list of modern scholars on the
other side is just as impressive." To cite only this passage, *and
ignore the exegesis that follows that utterly undermines Geisler's
position,* is simply unacceptable. This is only exacerbated by
the fact that on page 83 of CBF Piper is again cited and said to
be mistaken in his view of God's eternal predestination of Jacob
and Esau, *but nowhere is an attempt made to even begin to interact with the pages and pages of exegetical argumentation provided by Piper in support of his position.* While Geisler is content to simply cite secondary sources regarding Romans 9,
Piper does original exegetical work. It is not sufficient response
on Geisler's part to simply allege an error while ignoring the
counter-evidence.

R.K. Wright experienced a very similar situation that he
relates concerning his studies at Trinity Evangelical Divinity
School under Clark Pinnock in the early 1970s. Pinnock directed him to Arminian writers for "balance" in his research.
Wright comments:

This material only confirmed my suspicion that
Arminian writers had no understanding of the questions
I was struggling with and showed no willingness to interact seriously with Calvinist exegesis. In fact, they wrote
as if they were in a historical vacuum. Apart from a passing nod toward Calvin or a reference to Augustine, they
wrote as if no Calvinist had ever dealt with these issues
in detail before. They made no attempt, for example, to
answer the meticulous demonstration by John Gill that
the Arminian exegesis of key passages (such as 2 Pet 3:9
and 2 Tim 2:4-6 [sic: 1 Tim 2:4-6]) is fallacious. I did
not see then, and do not see now, why Gill should be
treated with contempt simply because he is so detailed
and writes in the labored and finicky style so common to
the 1700s. Pinnock made derogatory remarks about Gill,
but showed no concern to answer Gill's painstaking treatment of Matthew 23:37, which I raised as an example of
a solid Calvinist response to careless Arminian exegesis.[33]

The parallels to *CBF* are striking. *CBF* offers no substantial
refutation of Reformed exegesis. Indeed, if all one read was
CBF, one would not be aware that there *was* substantial Reformed exegetical defense of the Calvinistic position. In the
same way, Geisler's work makes no attempt to respond to Gill's
comments on Matthew 23:37 despite the fact that he makes
use of the passage *eleven times* in *CBF*. The Arminian understanding is assumed *but nowhere defended*. It seems, then, that
CBF falls into the same category of Arminian writings as those
examined by Dr. Wright.

Knowingly Predetermining?

The third source of confusion comes from Dr. Geisler's
rather unique, yet, I believe, completely unworkable concept
of God's foreknowledge and man's "free will." The concept is
confusing because it allows Dr. Geisler to use mutually exclusive terms in the same sentence as if they actually "fit" to-

gether. In reality, as we will see, the terms have been redefined from their historical or biblical usages to allow them to "fit" together, but without a knowledge of the background of Geisler's position, most will not see how the position simply does not survive examination. What is most troubling is the only conclusion that can be drawn from an analysis of the position espoused in *CBF*: there is no positive, free decree of God that determines what takes place in this, God's creation. We will carefully unpack all of this particular aspect of *CBF* in chapter two.

Silence Speaks Volumes

In what is advertised to be the "definitive" work on the subject of divine sovereignty and personal responsibility one would expect to find full and fair discussions of *all* of the key passages that have been used to press the claims of both sides. Additionally, in a work that is obviously coming from one of the two perspectives (in this case, *CBF* is plainly non-Reformed and seeks to undermine that position in the majority of its argumentation), it can be logically expected that the key passages pressed by Reformed advocates would be addressed in at least somewhat of a comprehensive manner. But such is surely not the case with *CBF*. Instead, not only are vitally important passages utterly passed over, but in the majority of instances, key and definitional passages are dismissed (*not* exegeted) without any effort to interact with the texts at all. The Reformed advocate who finds his beliefs under constant attack cannot help but feel tremendous frustration at this constant element of *CBF*.

For example, one of the strongest passages in all the New Testament that plainly asserts the Reformed belief in the sovereignty of God is John 6:37, where the Lord Jesus says, "All that the Father gives Me will come to Me, and the one who comes to Me I will certainly not cast out." The words are so clear and compelling that surely there must be some lengthy attempt in *CBF* to explain how the Lord can assert that *all* that the Father gives Him will come to Him. Such words present both the sovereignty of God (the Father gives men to the Son) as well as the certainty of His work of salvation (*all* that the Father gives *will* come to the Son). But there is barely one short paragraph in all of *CBF* on the passage. It is found in a section where Dr. Geisler is speaking of the "twin pillars" of sovereignty and human responsibility. Here is the entire commentary on John 6:37 in all of *CBF*:

> Another example of both God's sovereignty and our responsibility being found in the same scriptural text is found in Jesus' statement from John 6:37: "*All that the Father gives me will come to me*, and *whoever comes to me* I will never drive away." On the one hand, only those the Father preordains to do so will come to Christ (John 6:44). On the other hand, it is also true that "whoever" chooses to come will be saved (Rom. 10:13).

This is *all CBF* has to say about John 6:37, a passage that teaches "extreme Calvinism" if there ever was one. Likewise, when addressing the subject of "limited atonement," the key passages presenting this vital truth are lumped into a single paragraph (page 76) and provided with a handful of almost irrelevant sentences in reply. A serious Reformed theologian can only shake his head at the firm anti-Reformed conclusions offered upon such shallow argumentation. *Every* aspect of the biblical evidence treated in *CBF* suffers from this kind of problem.

Poor Exegesis

The Reformed position is nothing if not rich in the most in-depth exegetical work of generations of men who have labored diligently at the task of fairly and honestly dealing with the Scriptures in their original tongues. Calvinists are known for writing entire books on short passages of Scripture, and preaching entire series of sermons on just a few verses. The Reformed person is exhorted to handle the text of Scripture with great care and concern to listen to the words of Scripture in their own context, constantly seeking to *draw out from Scripture* its meaning rather than *pressing onto Scripture* a meaning that is not a part of the original context. Even Calvin's detractors are forced to admit the value of his commentaries on the Bible even to this day.

But exegesis is not the forte of *CBF*. Very few passages are addressed in a truly exegetical fashion, and in most cases, mere assertion takes the place of meaningful consideration of the important elements of the task of biblical interpretation. Unfortunately, *CBF* provides far more examples of *eisegesis* than it does of *exegesis*. Since this book will focus upon a *biblical* defense of the Reformed position, example after example will be offered in the text itself. But just one brief citation that is related to John 6, mentioned above: In mustering a few citations in defense of the idea that anyone can believe and that true, saving faith is *not* a gift from God, Geisler cites John 3:16 and 18, and then writes, "And, '*Whoever comes* to me I will never drive away' (John 6:37)." Even a cursory glance at the text reveals that this partial citation is the second half of a full sentence; that there is no indefinite relative pronoun here ("whoever"), but instead it literally reads, "and the one coming." The sentence defines who this "coming" one is: "All that the Father gives Me will come to Me." The one coming to Christ in John 6:37b is the one of the entire body of the elect given by the Father to the Son in 6:37a. The text literally contradicts Geisler's thesis, yet, by not taking it in its own context, the verse is cited to present the exact opposite of its intended meaning. This kind of eisegetical procedure marks the entirety of *CBF*.

Clearing the Confusion

Christ's sheep hear His voice. Despite all the distracting noises of the world, Christ quietly teaches His people His truth. At times we hold so tenaciously to our traditions, to our self-importance, to our misconceptions, that the process is a long and arduous one. Deep-seated traditions are hard to dislodge, as the Apostle Peter discovered. But God is patient with His people.

There is great confidence in trusting in God's sovereignty, especially when it comes to the fact that even Christians are willing to place their own supposed freedom and autonomy over the true freedom and autonomy of God. I have seen many precious souls struggle through these foundational issues and emerge changed, strengthened, with a new and lasting appreciation of the holiness and love of God along with a passion for His grace that cannot be erased. While I am grieved at the confusion that books like *CBF* cause, I am confident that the Word is so clear, so plain, and so compelling, that the mere presentation of its truths is sufficient for the child of God. And it is to that we now turn.

The Format

In past days it was common for theologians to write volumes in response to someone else. They did so expecting that their audience had read and assimilated the information in their opponent's work. Publishers are hesitant to present such works today, preferring merely a "positive presentation" rather than a direct response.

The Reformed tradition is rich in honest dialogue and debate. Those who love truth will not be offended by honest, direct refutation and interaction. The "politically correct" culture we live in should not be allowed to silence meaningful theological debate. Dr. Geisler himself has written:

> Third, what about those who insist that drawing lines will divide Christians? In response it must be lovingly but firmly maintained that it is better to be divided by truth than to be united by error. There is an unhealthy tendency in evangelical Christianity to hide under the banner of Christian charity while sacrificing doctrinal purity.[34]

In the spirit of these words I offer a rebuttal of Dr. Geisler's work. This is not meant to be a presentation of the Reformed view so ably accomplished by others: my positive presentation will be limited to establishing facts that are not in evidence from a reading of *CBF*. Instead, I will be demonstrating that the biblical argumentation provided by Norman Geisler is in error. It is my hope that the reader will be edified by the consistent focus upon biblical exegesis, for this is, truly, the heart and soul of Reformed theology.

Notes

1 Norman Geisler, *Chosen but Free* (Bethany House, 1999), p. 100.
2 Ibid., p. 131.
3 p. 132.
4 p. 134.
5 Ibid.
6 p. 135.
7 Ibid.
8 Ibid.
9 p. 136.
10 pp. 136-137.
11 p. 21
12 p. 28.
13 p. 35.
14 p. 82.
15 p. 85.
16 p. 86.
17 p. 205.
18 p. 242.
19 Specifically, I had asserted, in response to his claim that Calvin did not embrace particular redemption (limited atonement), that there are a number of excellent works on the subject that come to the opposite conclusion. I had also objected to his use of the phrase "extreme Calvinist."
20 There are a number of Calvin's works that are useful here, including, of course, his *Institutes of the Christian Religion* as well as his *Concerning the Eternal Predestination of God*.
21 Many of Edwards' sermons are focused upon this doctrine. See *The Works of Jonathan Edwards* (Banner of Truth, 1984).
22 Turretin is not easy reading, but incredibly thorough. See his *Institutes of Elenctic Theology* (Presbyterian and Reformed, 1992).
23 See *The Works of Benjamin B. Warfield* (Baker Book House, 1981), Volume 5, "Calvin and Calvinism."
24 Edwin Palmer, *The Five Points of Calvinism* (Baker Book House, 1972).
25 Dr. Sproul's works are especially important as they figure prominently in this work, since Dr. Geisler especially focuses on him and cites from his works in *Chosen But Free*. See *Chosen by God* (Tyndale House Publishers, 1986) and *Willing to Believe* (Baker Book House, 1997).

26 Most importantly is Piper's tremendous exegesis of Romans 9
    found in *The Justification of God* (Baker Book House, 1993).
27 James White, *God's Sovereign Grace* (Crowne Publications, 1991)
    and *Drawn by the Father* (Crowne Publications, 1991).
28 And many in a tremendous way. For example, I heartily recom-
    mend his work with Nix, *A General Introduction to the Bible*
    (Moody Press, 1986).
29 *Chosen But Free*, p. 193.
30 John Owen, *The Death of Death in the Death of Christ* (The Banner
    of Truth Trust, 1985), p. 214.
31 John Piper, *The Justification of God* (Grand Rapids: Baker Book
    House, 1993), p. 73.
32 *Chosen But Free*, p. 82, footnote 7.
33 R.K. Wright, *No Place For Sovereignty: What's Wrong with Freewill
    Theism* (InterVarsity Press, 1996), pp. 38-39.
34 Norman Geisler, *The Battle for the Resurrection* (Thomas Nelson
    Publishers, 1992), p. 171.

Chapter 1

The Vital Issue

The Society of Jesus (the Jesuits) was founded by the industry and endeavor of Ignatius of Loyola. This fiery Roman Catholic zealot dedicated his life to the defense of the Roman Church against the "heresies" of the Protestant Reformation. Toward the end of his life he wrote the following:

> Seeing the progress which the heretics have made in a short time, spreading the poison of their evil teaching throughout so many countries and peoples, and making use of the verse of the Apostles to describe their progress, 'And their speech spreadeth like a canker', it would seem that our society [i.e., the Jesuits], having been accepted by Divine Providence among the efficacious means to repair such great damage, should be solicitous to prepare the proper steps, such as are quickly applied and can be widely adopted, thus exerting itself to the utmost of its powers to preserve what is still sound and to restore what has fallen sick of the plague of heresy, especially in the northern nations.
>
> The heretics have made their false theology popular and presented it in a way that is within the capacity of the common people. They preach it to the people and teach it in the schools, and scatter booklets which can be bought and understood by many, and make their influence felt by means of their writings when they cannot do so by their preaching. Their success is largely due to the negligence of those who should have shown some interest;

and the bad example and the ignorance of Catholics,
especially the clergy, have made such ravages in the vine-
yard of the Lord.[1]

One of the charges Loyola made to his followers involved
the danger of allowing the Protestants to so emphasize the
power of God that the "freedom of man" would be eclipsed.
One of his followers, Luis de Molina, dedicated many years
attempting to fulfill the vision of Loyola. He finally produced
an entire philosophical theory of divine knowledge called
scientia media (the concept of "middle knowledge"): the idea
that God knows what free agents will do given certain circumstances, but their actions are still "free" in the sense that they
are not fixed. The entire reason why the concept was devel-
oped was to "get around" the preaching of the Reformers that
emphasized the sovereignty of God, the freedom of God, as
ultimate in all things. The "heretics" were preaching that God
is the Potter, men are the clay, formed as He wills, not as *they*
will. Such a teaching was devastating to the Roman concept of
the Church as the mediator and dispenser of graces. Such a
system could speak often of grace *as long as that grace was
merely a necessary aid* but *never an efficient power that saves*. As
long as the ultimate "control" of salvation was kept out of God's
hands, all would be well. Sadly, to this very day, nominal "Protestants" embrace Molina's desperate attempt to get around
God's freedom.

Loyola was not the first to see the Reformed emphasis upon
the freedom of God and the creatureliness of men as a deadly
threat to Roman Catholic theology. In fact, the first written
debate of the Reformation itself was focused on the very same
issue.

As Martin Luther closed his monumental response to the
Roman Catholic scholar and theologian, Desiderius Erasmus,
titled, *The Bondage of the Will*, he made it plain how he believed that the issue of God's absolute freedom and man's
absolute dependence is, in fact, the very central issue of the
entire Reformation. He affirmed, with clarity you will only rarely

hear in modern Lutheran preachers or theologians, the utter
dependence of man upon God:

> For if we believe it to be true, that God fore-knows and
> fore-ordains all things; that He can be neither deceived
> nor hindered in His Prescience and Predestination; and
> that nothing can take place but according to His Will,
> (which reason herself is compelled to confess;) then, even
> according to the testimony of reason herself, there can
> be no "Free-will"—in man,—in angel,—or in any crea-
> ture![2]

But take careful note of how this great Reformer understood
the *absolute centrality of God's freedom and man's bondage in
sin:*

> In this, moreover, I give you (Erasmus) great praise,
> and proclaim it—you alone in pre-eminent distinction
> from all others, have entered upon the thing itself; that
> is, the grand turning point of the cause; and have not
> wearied me with those irrelevant points about popery,
> purgatory, indulgences, and other like *baubles*, rather than
> *causes*, with which all have hitherto tried to hunt me
> down,—though in vain! You, and you alone saw, what
> was the grand hinge upon which the whole turned, and
> therefore you attacked the vital part at once; for which,
> from my heart, I thank you.[3]

A more modern translation of the passage goes like this:

> Moreover, I give you hearty praise and commendation
> on this further account—that you alone, in contrast to
> all others, have attacked the real thing, that is, the essen-
> tial issue. You have not wearied me with those extrane-
> ous issues about the Papacy, purgatory, indulgences and
> such like—trifles, rather than issues—in respect of which
> almost all to date have sought my blood (though with-
> out success); you, and you alone, have seen the hinge on
> which all turns, and aimed for the vital spot.[4]

Do not allow Luther's words to pass you by. We must understand what Luther meant by "the thing itself" or "the real thing."
What is "the cause," "the whole," "on which *all* turns"? To
what does he refer? *To the very Reformation itself!* Luther is
speaking to his Roman Catholic opponent about the very essential and definitional issue of the entire Reformation. What,
then, is the "grand turning point of the cause," the "essential
issue," the "grand hinge upon which the whole turned," and
"the vital part"? *The truth of predestination (God's freedom) and
man's depravity (his will in bondage)!* Here at the very *inception*
of the Reformation the definitional issue is laid out: God is
the absolutely free Creator, the Potter, who has complete sovereignty over the pots, humans, who, as fallen creatures, find
their wills enslaved to sin, in bondage and unable to "cooperate" with any offered grace.

This is the soil from which springs the Reformed emphasis
upon *sola fide*, "faith alone," the truth that one is justified not
by any meritorious action or work but by faith in Jesus Christ
alone. *One cannot claim to be faithful to the Reformation by
crying "sola fide" when the foundation of that call is abandoned.*
The truth that *God saves* by Himself, by His *own* power, on the
basis of His *own* will, *defines* the message of the Reformers.
Those who follow their lead are convinced that their faith is
founded firmly upon the consistent interpretation of Scripture
alone (sola scriptura) and *all* of Scripture *(tota scriptura)*. One
cannot claim to stand in harmony with Luther, Zwingli, Bucer,
or Calvin without believing *both* in the doctrine of justification
by faith *as well as* the truth of God's absolute freedom and
man's bondage in sin.

Few have had the ability to speak with the clarity and force
of Charles Haddon Spurgeon, the great Baptist evangelist of
London. Regarding this issue he wrote:

> There is no attribute of God more comforting to His
> children than the doctrine of Divine Sovereignty. Under
> the most adverse circumstances, in the most severe
> troubles, they believe that Sovereignty hath ordained their

afflictions, that Sovereignty overrules them, and that Sovereignty will sanctify them all. There is nothing for which the children of God ought more earnestly to contend than the dominion of their Master over all creation — the kingship of God over all the works of His own hands — the throne of God, and His right to sit upon that throne.

On the other hand, there is no doctrine more hated by worldlings, no truth of which they have made such a football, as the great, stupendous, but yet most certain doctrine of the Sovereignty of the infinite Jehovah. Men will allow God to be everywhere except upon His throne. They will allow Him to be in His workshop to fashion worlds and to make stars. They will allow Him to be in His almonry to dispense His alms and bestow His bounties. They will allow Him to sustain the earth and bear up the pillars thereof, or light the lamps of Heaven, or rule the waves of the ever-moving ocean; but when God ascends His throne, His creatures then gnash their teeth; and when we proclaim an *enthroned God*, and His right to do as He wills with His own, to dispose of His creatures as He thinks well, without consulting them in the matter, then it is that we are hissed and execrated, and then it is that men turn a deaf ear to us, for God on His throne is not the God they love. They love Him anywhere better than they do when He sits with His scepter in His hand and His crown upon His head. But it is God upon the throne that we love to preach. It is God upon His throne whom we trust.[5]

The Christian loves God *as He reveals Himself.* The non-Christian seeks to conform God to an image that is less threatening to him in his rebellion. It is a work of grace in the heart that allows a person to love God *as God really is*, not as we wish He would be. The Christian desires to love God truly.

This is the single issue that separates the supernatural religion of Christianity from the man-centered religions that surround us. Whether the work of salvation is *perfectly accomplished by God for His own glory* or is dependent upon man's cooperation and assistance is the watershed issue that separates biblical Christianity from everything else. The specifics of the debate revolve around what it means to confess that "salvation is of the Lord." What does this necessarily mean with reference to man's abilities (or inabilities)? What does this tell us about the atoning work of Christ, or the perfection of Christ's work of salvation? These are the issues of the debate.

The Thrust of This Work

The writer of this work has absolute confidence that the Reformed proclamation of the Gospel will never pass from this world, and that the work of Christ's kingdom represented by that proclamation will continue until He rules and reigns. Why? Because God's Word will never fall. As long as the Holy Scriptures exist and the Holy Spirit brings regeneration in the hearts of men, the message of God's free and glorious grace will continue.

The message of the gospel of grace is, first and foremost, a *biblical* message. It is not philosophy that leads the Reformed believer to his or her conclusions: it is *biblical exegesis* that does so. And for this reason the firm ground upon which the true Calvinist stands in defense of his belief in the absolute freedom of God is the text of Holy Writ. Because of this conviction, this work will focus primarily upon biblical issues. The argumentation provided by Dr. Geisler, and other proponents of a non-Reformed position, fails upon *exegetical* examination.

A Necessary Definition

What are the "doctrines of grace," and why do they matter? Such is like asking, "What does the Bible teach about the very heart of the gospel, and does it matter one way or the other?" The doctrines of grace are the biblical teachings that define the *goal* and *means* of God's *perfect* work of redemption. They tell us that God is the one who saves, for His own glory, and freely. And they tell us that He does so only through Christ, only on the basis of His grace, only with the perfection that marks everything the Father, Son, and Spirit do. The doctrines of grace separate the Christian faith from the works-based religions of men. They direct us away from ourselves and solely to God's grace and mercy. They destroy pride, instill humility, and exalt God. And that's why so many invest so much time in the vain attempt to undermine their truth. The religions of men maintain authority over their followers by 1) limiting God's power, 2) exalting man's abilities, and 3) "channeling" God's power through their own structures. A perfect salvation that is freely bestowed by God for His own glory is not a "system" that can be controlled by a religious body or group. And even more importantly, such a system is destructive of any sense of pride in the creature man, and if there is anything man's religions must safeguard, it is man's "self-esteem."

In our modern setting the debate is normally framed by the famous "Five Points of Calvinism." These have historically been defined as follows:

T = Total Depravity: Man is dead in sin, completely and radically impacted by the Fall, the enemy of God, incapable of saving himself. This does not mean that man is as evil as he could be. Nor does it mean that the image of God is destroyed, or that the will is done away with. Instead, it refers to the *all pervasiveness of the effects of sin*, and the fact that man is, outside of Christ, the enemy of God.

U = Unconditional Election: God elects a specific people unto Himself without reference to *anything they do*. This means the basis of God's choice of the elect is *solely* within Himself: His grace, His mercy, His will. It is not man's actions, works, *or even foreseen faith*, that "draws" God's choice. God's election is unconditional *and final*.

L = Limited Atonement: Since it is God's purpose to save a special people for Himself, and He has chosen to do so *only* through the perfect sacrifice of Jesus Christ, Christ came to give His life "a ransom for many" so as to "save His people from their sins" (Matthew 1:21). The *intention* of Christ in His cross-work was to save His people *specifically*. Therefore, Christ's sacrifice is *perfect and complete*, for it actually *accomplishes* perfect redemption.

I = Irresistible Grace: This is the belief that God is able to raise the spiritually dead sinner to life. This is an act of *efficient* grace. When God chooses to bring one of His elect to spiritual life, it is an act similar to when Jesus raised Lazarus from the dead: just as Lazarus was incapable of resisting the power of Christ in raising him from the dead, so too the dead sinner is incapable of resisting the power of God that raises him to spiritual life. This is *not* to say that men have not resisted God's grace. This doctrine speaks specifically to the grace that brings regeneration, not to individual acts of sin committed by believers or unbelievers.

P = Perseverance of the Saints: Some prefer saying "the preservation of the saints" to emphasize that this is the work of God: others use the phrase "eternal security" to emphasize the impossibility of God's perfect work of salvation being undone. But whatever one calls it, it is the belief that when Christ saves one of His elect, He will not fail to keep that saved person throughout life and bring them safely into His presence. It is, in short, the belief that Christ is able to save perfectly.

Historically, the debate goes back long before the Reformation, however. One can trace the argument back through the centuries, through men such as Gottschalk of Orbais, all the way back to Augustine and Pelagius in the fifth century. But really the issue can be found clearly addressed in the New Testament itself, so we should not be surprised that it remains an ever-new issue with each generation that comes along. Sin causes man to constantly seek to insert himself into the work of God in salvation, so every generation has to be reminded of their complete dependence upon Him and of His perfect freedom.

That is one reason why I do not believe the common "five points" listed above is enough for today. There is a sixth point, one that lies at the head of the list, that must be firmly proclaimed and defended today: the freedom of God. While it may have been taken for granted a few centuries ago, today it is surely a belief under fire. But since it lies at the very heart of the debate, we need to begin with a discussion of what it means.

The Free and Proper Kingship of God

I believe one of the reasons modern men struggle with some of the plain biblical truths of old is because so few of us any longer have a "king." Royal power and authority was fundamental when the Scriptures were written, and often the power of God to properly rule over His own creation is likened to the power of a king to rule over his realm. Since most of us do not bow to a king, we see little reason why we should bow to God.

The phrase "the free and proper kingship of God" is a rather verbose means of saying "God's sovereignty." So why do I use the longer phrase? Because it has become "fashionable" to confess belief in "the sovereignty of God." How can anyone read the Bible and not hear its constant testimony to the unfettered, unlimited, undiminished authority of God to do as He wishes with His creation? So many are quick to say, "Oh yes, I believe in the sovereignty of God." Yet, when pressed to believe consistently that God truly can do as He pleases *without getting permission from anyone, including man*, we discover that many who in fact confess such a belief in practice deny it. Just a few passages that testify to this are as follows:

> Whatever the LORD pleases, He does,
> In heaven and in earth, in the seas and in all deeps.
> (Psalm 135:6)

"For the LORD of hosts has planned, and who can frustrate *it*? And as for His stretched-out hand, who can turn it back?" (Isaiah 14:27)

"Remember the former things long past,
For I am God, and there is no other;
I am God, and there is no one like Me,
Declaring the end from the beginning,
And from ancient times things which have not been done,
Saying, 'My purpose will be established,
And I will accomplish all My good pleasure.'"
(Isaiah 46:9-10)

Let all the earth fear the LORD;
Let all the inhabitants of the world stand in awe of Him.
For He spoke, and it was done;
He commanded, and it stood fast.
The LORD nullifies the counsel of the nations;
He frustrates the plans of the peoples.
The counsel of the LORD stands forever,
The plans of His heart from generation to generation.
(Psalm 33:8-11)

"Present your case," the LORD says.
"Bring forward your strong *arguments*,"
The King of Jacob says.
Let them bring forth and declare to us what is going to take place;
As for the former *events*, declare what they *were*,
That we may consider them and know their outcome.
Or announce to us what is coming;
Declare the things that are going to come afterward,
That we may know that you are gods;
Indeed, do good or evil, that we may anxiously look about us and fear together.
(Isaiah 41:21-23)

The king's heart is *like* channels of water in the hand of the LORD;

He turns it wherever He wishes.
(Proverbs 21:1)

"But at the end of that period, I, Nebuchadnezzar, raised
my eyes toward heaven and my reason returned to me,
and I blessed the Most High and praised and honored
Him who lives forever;
For His dominion is an everlasting dominion,
And His kingdom *endures* from generation to genera-
tion. All the inhabitants of the earth are accounted as
nothing, But He does according to His will in the host of
heaven And *among* the inhabitants of earth;
And no one can ward off His hand
Or say to Him, 'What have You done?'
(Daniel 4:34-35)

The biblical testimony could be expanded almost indefinitely.
God is king over all the earth. As the Creator, it is His to do
with as *He* chooses. This concept is brought out with striking
clarity in the analogy of the Potter and the clay. A number of
times in Scripture God likens Himself to a Potter and we as
clay or as pots, formed and fashioned as He wishes. This sovereign power is seen in God's dealings with Israel. He sent
Jeremiah the prophet to the potter's house, and recorded this
incident in Jeremiah 18:4-6:

But the vessel that he was making of clay was spoiled in
the hand of the potter; so he remade it into another vessel, as it pleased the potter to make. Then the word of
the LORD came to me saying, "Can I not, O house of
Israel, deal with you as this potter *does?*" declares the
LORD. "Behold, like the clay in the potter's hand, so are
you in My hand, O house of Israel."

God could refashion and remake Israel as He pleased. He did
not have to ask permission, seek advice, or in any way consult
anyone or anything outside of Himself. The entire nation was
as the clay in the potter's hand. Clay has no inherent "rights,"

no basis upon which to complain about the potter's decisions, no say in what the potter does.

The vast gulf that separates the created from the Creator is highlighted in these words from Isaiah 29:16 (NIV):

> You turn things upside down, as if the potter were thought to be like the clay! Shall what is formed say to him who formed it, "He did not make me"? Can the pot say of the potter, "He knows nothing"?

The very idea of "what is formed" *speaking* to the one who formed it is supposed to strike within us the absurdity of man, the creature, thinking that God is to be thought of as existing on the same plane, the same level, as man. Man's every thought of God should be marked with reverential awe, with true fear of the One who formed us and gives us every breath we take. The sheer *stupidity* of man arguing with his Maker comes up yet again a little later in Isaiah 45:9:

> "Woe to *the one* who quarrels with his Maker — An earthenware vessel among the vessels of earth! Will the clay say to the potter, 'What are you doing?' Or the thing you are making *say*, 'He has no hands'?

Sarcasm and irony are tools the Lord uses to emphasize the utter foolishness of man arguing with God. "Will the clay say to the potter, 'What are you doing?'" Clay by nature is under the sovereign power of the potter. It is a thing to be formed and used as the potter desires. In comparison with the potter, the clay is utterly powerless. *There can be no clash of wills between the Potter and the pots.* The Potter's will is free and unfettered by any considerations the clay may present. What is more, the pot is forced to recognize the *active involvement of the potter*. This is seen in the *argumentum ad absurdum*, "Or the thing you are making say, 'He has no hands.'" The thing "being made" cannot deny the very hands that are forming and fashioning its very shape! And yet this is the very attitude of

man today: there is no Creator, and all evidence of His existence must be immediately dismissed. And even amongst those
who embrace the Christian faith, there is a hesitance to confess God as Creator, God as *determiner* of my shape *and my
destiny.*

The people of God gladly confess that they are "God's pots,"
creatures made by His hand. Hear these words:

> But now, O LORD, You are our Father,
> We are the clay, and You our potter;
> And all of us are the work of Your hand. (Isaiah 64:8)

The renewed heart *rejoices* in knowing that God is our Father,
our Creator, the Potter who has formed us by His own hand.
But such a thought is utter *terror* to the unregenerate person,
and completely *anathema* to the religions of men who seek to
control God and His power through the exercise of man's will.

The Decrees of the King

The conjunction of God's absolute freedom and His
Creatorship results in the doctrine of God's decrees: the soul-
comforting truth that God has wisely and perfectly decreed
whatsoever comes to pass in this universe. Nothing is outside
His control, nothing is without purpose. There are no "renegade atoms" in the universe, nothing that is beyond the positive decree of God. This extends not only to inanimate objects
(galaxies, stars, planets, earthquakes, hurricanes, landslides,
etc.) but to every aspect of human history, personal relationships, and most importantly, to the life of every man, woman,
and child. While many are content to allow God to control the
"big things" like hurricanes and the natural realm, it is the assertion that God's freedom extends to the actions of men,
even to their choices, that meets with immediate rejection. But
the Bible is clear on the matter. Three scriptural witnesses will
testify to this truth.

One of the most striking evidences of God's sovereign control over the affairs of men is hidden from a cursory reading of the Scriptures. It is buried in some of the history of the Old Testament. Think carefully about these words:

> Woe to Assyria, the rod of My anger
> And the staff in whose hands is My indignation,
> I send it against a godless nation
> And commission it against the people of My fury
> To capture booty and to seize plunder,
> And to trample them down like mud in the streets.
> Yet it does not so intend,
> Nor does it plan so in its heart,
> But rather it is its purpose to destroy
> And to cut off many nations.
> (Isaiah 10:5-7)

Here God reveals that *He* is sending Assyria "the rod of His anger" against His people Israel, a "godless nation." God is specifically bringing this ravaging nation against Israel "to capture booty and to seize plunder, and to trample them down like mud in the streets." Obviously, this results in great suffering and distress among the rebellious Israelites. But, God is clear: the woe He is announcing is on the very instrument He is using to punish Israel! Assyria is not a willing party to the punishment of Israel: they do not intend to be involved in doing God's work, "but rather it is its purpose to destroy and to cut off many nations." Assyria had one purpose, God another, and all in the same historical events. While God says He is using Assyria, He likewise says He will punish them for their *intentions*. Note these words:

> So it will be that when the Lord has completed all His work on Mount Zion and on Jerusalem, *He will say,* "I will punish the fruit of the arrogant heart of the king of Assyria and the pomp of his haughtiness." For he has said,

"By the power of my hand and by my wisdom I did *this*,
For I have understanding;
And I removed the boundaries of the peoples
And plundered their treasures,
And like a mighty man I brought down *their* inhabit-
ants, And my hand reached to the riches of the peoples
like a nest,
And as one gathers abandoned eggs, I gathered all the
earth;
And there was not one that flapped its wing or opened *its*
beak or chirped."
Is the axe to boast itself over the one who chops with it?
Is the saw to exalt itself over the one who wields it?
That would be like a club wielding those who lift it,
Or like a rod lifting *him who* is not wood.
Therefore the Lord, the GOD of hosts, will send a wast-
ing disease among his stout warriors;
And under his glory a fire will be kindled like a burning
flame.
And the light of Israel will become a fire and his Holy
One a flame,
And it will burn and devour his thorns and his briars in
a single day.
(Isaiah 10:12-17)

When God completes "His work" in Jerusalem He will punish
the arrogance of the Assyrians. He points out the foolishness
of the Assyrian thinking that he is operating separately from
God's sovereign decree. This is the essence of the rhetorical
questions concerning the axe, the saw, the club, and the rod:
all instruments in the hand of another. Assyria has one purpose in heart: but it is God's purpose that prevails. Yet, *God is
perfectly just to judge on the basis of Assyria's sinful intentions.*
Assyria acts *in accordance with its desires*, and yet, what is done
is the fulfillment of God's decree.

Joseph knew this truth as well. After the death of Jacob,
Joseph's brothers were fearful of reprisals due to their treatment of Joseph years before. As they cowered before their

powerful sibling, Joseph wept, realizing that his brothers still did not understand how he had forgiven them, nor how God had worked in the circumstances. So he says to them,

> "Do not be afraid, for am I in God's place? As for you, you meant evil against me, *but* God meant it for good in order to bring about this present result, to preserve many people alive. So therefore, do not be afraid; I will provide for you and your little ones." So he comforted them and spoke kindly to them. (Genesis 50:19-21)

These are the words of one who has come to see the sovereign plan of God in his own life. Joseph well knew the motivations of his brothers when they sold him into slavery. But, in the very same event he saw the over-riding hand of God, guiding, directing, and ultimately meaning *in the same action* to bring about good. One might ask, "But, if God decreed that this event would take place, how can He still hold Joseph's brothers personally accountable for their actions?" Even if we did not have an answer to this question, it would not matter: God makes it clear that He *does* hold men accountable. But it is clear that they are judged on the basis of the *intention of their hearts*. We dare not think that Joseph's brothers were *forced against the desires of their hearts* to commit the evil of selling their brother into slavery. They desired to do this: indeed, if God had not intervened it is sure they would have killed him outright, so great was their hatred toward their brother. But God preserved Joseph's life, and sent him to Egypt to preserve life and accomplish His will.

But by far the greatest example of this is found in the pinnacle of God's work of redemption, the cross of Jesus Christ. Surely no one can suggest that the cross was an after-thought, a desperate attempt to "fix" things after all had gone awry. Jesus taught His disciples that it was *necessary* that He go to Jerusalem and die (Mark 8:31, Luke 9:22). The early church had the proper understanding of the relationship of God's sovereign decree and the evil men showed in the act of nailing the sinless Son of God to a tree. As they prayed to God in the face of the persecution of the religious authorities, this truth came out with striking clarity:

> "For truly in this city there were gathered together against Your holy servant Jesus, whom You anointed, both Herod and Pontius Pilate, along with the Gentiles and the peoples of Israel, to do whatever Your hand and Your purpose predestined to occur. And now, Lord, take note of their threats, and grant that Your bond-servants may speak Your word with all confidence, while You extend Your hand to heal, and signs and wonders take place through the name of Your holy servant Jesus." (Acts 4:27-30).

The Church prays to the Sovereign of the universe, the one who rules and reigns over all authorities, including those who were persecuting the Church. Just as Herod, and Pontius Pilate, the Gentiles and even the people of Israel had gathered against Christ, so too the early Church faced the wrath of the governing authorities. Yet, these Christians knew something that many today have forgotten: what took place at Calvary had been predestined by the sovereign decree of God. No human being had the power to raise a hand against the Savior unless God so determined. But again, is it not true that what Herod and Pilate and the Jews and the Romans did was *evil?* Most assuredly. Man had never shown himself more evil than on Mount Calvary. Yet, what they did was predestined by God, and that to His glory. No event in history will bring more glory, honor and praise to God than the atoning sacrifice of Jesus Christ in the place of His people. Yet again we find one single act, freely engaged in by evil men for evil motives, yet, at the same time, eternally predestined for good by God. The Potter is indeed free. He can, and does, decree whatsoever comes to pass, for His own glory (Ephesians 1:11). And yet the Potter is the righteous judge of all the earth who always does right.

The Vital Conclusion

"Salvation is of the Lord" (Jonah 2:9). The most funda-mental difference between the God-centered Gospel of the Apostles and of the Reformers and *all other viewpoints* is summed up in these few words. Is salvation a work of God *and* man, a cooperative effort? Is it something that God "sets up" like a cosmic multi-level marketing program where we "work the numbers" and gain eternal life as the final prize? Is it a grand and beautiful design that simply awaits man's turning of the key, so to speak, to work? Is salvation of the Lord, of men, or a mixture of both?

Salvation is of the Lord. Does this simply mean that the plan comes from His hand, so that without Him, there would be no salvation? Is that all it means? The Apostle Paul did not view it that way:

> For consider your calling, brethren, that there were not many wise according to the flesh, not many mighty, not many noble; but God has chosen the foolish things of the world to shame the wise, and God has chosen the weak things of the world to shame the things which are strong, and the base things of the world and the de-spised God has chosen, the things that are not, so that He may nullify the things that are, so that no man may boast before God. But by His doing you are in Christ Jesus, who became to us wisdom from God, and righ-teousness and sanctification, and redemption, so that, just as it is written, "LET HIM WHO BOASTS, BOAST IN THE LORD" (I Corinthians 1:26-31).

No man can boast before God. God has chosen the weak things, the base things, the foolish things, so that He might destroy the wisdom of the wise. It is by "His doing" that any person is in Christ. It is not by His doing *and* our doing, a cooperative effort, but by His *alone*. Now, one might object to the use of the term "alone," but the passage bears this out. Christ has become to us everything we need: wisdom, righteousness, sanc-tification and redemption. None of this comes from ourselves. None of this is dependent upon us. The result, Paul says, is that if anyone is to boast, he can boast *solely* in the Lord.

The Christian heart is glad to confess, "Salvation is of the Lord." All of it. In completeness. In perfection. The God who decrees all things saves perfectly. Salvation is a divine act, a divine work. It is centered upon *God*, not upon man. It is God's glory, not man's, that is at stake. The God-centeredness of the gospel is what makes the biblical teaching so fundamentally different than all the religions of men.

Many, including Dr. Geisler, speak of the sovereignty of God. But what do they mean? Dr. Geisler's position is unusual—almost unique. Since he claims it is in harmony with a "moderate Calvinistic" view, we need to understand his presentation and how it differs from the historic Reformed position.

Notes

1   13th August 1554, *Letters of St. Ignatius of Loyola*, p. 345 as cited in Hans Hillerbrand, ed., *The Reformation* (Grand Rapids: Baker, 1987), pp. 446-447.

2   Martin Luther, *The Bondage of the Will*, Henry Cole, trans., (Baker, 1976), p. 390.

3   Ibid., pp. 390-391.

4   Martin Luther, *On the Bondage of the Will: A New Translation of De Servo Arbitrio (1525) Martin Luther's Reply to Erasmus of Rotterdam*, trans. J.I. Packer and O.R. Johnston (Fleming H. Revell Company, 1957), p. 319.

5   "Divine Sovereignty," a sermon delivered May 4, 1856.

Chapter 2

Determinately Knowing

Chosen But Free begins with an affirmation of the sovereignty of God, for which we can all be thankful. But what does *CBF mean* when it speaks of the "sovereignty of God"? Are we in fact reading about the same emphasis upon the absolute freedom, power, and will of God that is part of classic Reformed writings when we read the first chapter of *CBF*?

One of the most confusing aspects of Dr. Geisler's presentation in *CBF* flows from his rather unique emphasis upon the idea that we simply can't ask (or answer) the question, "Does God's foreknowledge[1] determine what He decrees or does God's decree determine what He foreknows?" While theologians down through the centuries have taken one side to the exclusion of the other, Dr. Geisler's presentation[2] essentially says that the question should not be asked. I believe his system *does*, in fact, end up favoring one side against the other, but as far as embracing either of the historic sides in this great theological battle, *CBF* seeks a different conclusion.

It is vital to understand this concept in Geisler's theology, for it is the key to unlocking the problem of his use of terminology. That is, we can read in *CBF* of God's "sovereignty" yet at the same time read of man's absolute freedom.[3] How can one affirm both equally? *CBF* does so by presenting a unique understanding of what "predetermined" or "determined" means. But to get a "running start" at understanding *CBF*, we can go back a number of years to previous writings of Dr. Geisler to see his position stated in even stronger terminology.

Walvoord: A Tribute

In 1982, Moody Press published a tribute to Dallas Seminary professor John Walvoord.[4] Dr. Geisler wrote an essay for this work titled "God, Evil and Dispensations" (pages 95-112). We here begin to pick up the outline of the position that comes to full expression philosophically in *CBF* and that explains the biblical exegesis and theology that is presented therein. Most importantly, we here encounter the phrase "determinately foreknew" which becomes central to the understanding of Geisler's position:

> Finally, since God knows the end from the beginning (Isa. 46:10), He determinately foreknew (cf. Acts 2:23) that He would bring a greater good out of evil, namely, the redemption of all who will believe. In short, what brings glory to God also brings good to mankind. Good and glory cannot be separated. God is interested in bringing good to men—the greatest good possible.[5]

Throughout Dr. Geisler's discussions of "determination" one will find a constant emphasis upon God's *knowledge*. We will see how vital this is below. For now, *since* God knows, *then* He "determinately foreknew."

> God will achieve the greatest number in heaven that He possibly can. He does not love just some men; He loves all and will do everything within His loving power to save all He can....
>
> When the statement is made that God will achieve the greatest good "possible," it does not mean the greatest number of people will be saved that is *logically possible* (that would be 100 percent). What is meant by that statement is that God will save the greatest number of people that is *actually achievable* without violating their free choice. A loving God will not force anyone against their

will to love Him or to worship Him. Forced love is not love; forced worship is not worship. Heaven will not be composed of robots. God is not a kind of "Cosmic B. F. Skinner" who believes in manipulating people into certain behavior patterns which are pleasing to Himself. God does not, as Skinner wishes, go "beyond freedom and dignity." In short, God will not save people at all cost—not if it is at the cost of their freedom and dignity—for that would mean at the cost of their humanity. God will not dehumanize in order to save. To dehumanize is to de-create, since that is what God created—a human....God is love, and love works persuasively but not coercively. Those whom God can lovingly persuade have been foreordained to eternal life. Those whom He cannot, are destined in accordance with their own choice to eternal destruction (2 Thess. 1:7-9, Rev. 20:11-15).[6]

Here in brief scope is a summary of what Dr. Geisler will say in full in *CBF*: God will save as many as *possible*, but He will do so not on the basis of a positive decree of personal election (i.e., God elects a *particular* people) but instead will make salvation *available* but leave it to man's "free will." Geisler's concept of "freedom" insists that man, to be man, must be absolutely free. To violate man's "freedom" is to "dehumanize" or "decreate" man, and this cost is too high. It should be noted that these sentiments are not Calvinistic: no Calvinist believes God "dehumanizes" when He regenerates; no Calvinist speaks of God as merely "persuading" the elect, nor do they speak of God "coercing" the elect (neither term, logically, can be attached to the concept of regeneration, which is being raised from spiritual death to spiritual life). These are Arminian descriptions, not Calvinistic ones.

Four Views

Three years after the publication of the Walvoord tribute InterVarsity Press released *Predestination & Free Will*, edited by David and Randall Basinger. Here John Feinberg, Norman

Geisler, Bruce Reichenbach, and Clark Pinnock contributed essays which were then reviewed by the other three writers. The focus is directly on the very issue at hand, that being the relationship between God's sovereignty, knowledge, and the will of man. One will find that this essay is repeated, sometimes almost verbatim, throughout *CBF*, so its importance in grasping Geisler's most recent presentation is clear.

Fundamentally, Dr. Geisler presents a concept of God's predetermination that he asserts is *"according to"* not *"contrary to"* foreknowledge. Here are his words:

> Perhaps God's predetermination is neither *based on* his foreknowledge of human free choices nor done *in spite of* it. The Scriptures, for example, declare that we are "chosen *according to* the foreknowledge of God" (1 Pet 1:2). That is to say, there is no chronological or logical priority of election and foreknowledge. As a simple Being, all of God's attributes are one with his indivisible essence. Hence, both foreknowledge and predetermination are one in God. Thus whatever God knows, he determines. And whatever he determines, he knows.[7]

Right here we run directly into the most problematic element of Geisler's paradigm: "there is no chronological or logical priority of election and foreknowledge." That means that in his system one cannot ask the question that has been asked by generations of theologians before him: it has always been recognized that God either bases His election and decrees on what he *foresees* in the free actions of creatures, or, His decree and election determines what takes place in time. In the first scenario, the creatures are by default the sovereigns of the universe, since their wills and actions are ultimate; God becomes a mere servant of the creature, reacting rather than reigning. In the second, God is absolutely free and man, the creature, acts in accordance with his created nature. But Geisler (it seems) attempts to chart a different course, in essence saying that one cannot ask which one gives rise, logically, to the other.

Geisler bases this assertion on the statement that "all of God's attributes are one with his indivisible essence. Hence, both foreknowledge and predetermination are one in God." It is somewhat startling that generations of Christian theologians could have missed such a simple truth and as a result have needlessly argued over this issue for centuries. But does the simplicity of the Being of God necessitate that there really is no logical relationship between foreknowledge and predetermination?

It is at this very point that Geisler's thesis is subject to devastating criticism. John Feinberg was quite right to respond:

> But, granting God such knowledge does *not* mean that he does not know the logical sequence and relations among the items that he knows. Moreover, granting that God foreordains all things simultaneously does not mean that there is no logical order in what he foreordains. For example, God always knew that Christ would be born and would also die. But he also understood that logically (as well as chronologically) one of those events had to precede the other. That does not mean that God knew one of those events before he knew the other. It only means that in *knowing* both simultaneously, he knows the logical and chronological relation between the two events.[8]

Indeed, one can point to the fact that God is fully *just* and fully *merciful*. Yet, even these two aspects of God's character bear a logical relationship to the other: one cannot define *mercy* without logical reference to *justice*. Hence, the mere assertion that God's Being is simple and one does not logically entail accepting the idea that there is no logical relationship between God's act of decreeing, His election, His foreordination, and his knowledge of future events. We *must* agree with Feinberg when he summarizes the question Geisler (and everyone else) must answer: "does God foreknow because he foreordains or does he foreordain because he foreknows?"[9] The fact is we will

see that Dr. Geisler *does* take a *de facto* position on this topic.
Geisler continues:

> More properly, we should speak of God as *knowingly*
> *determining* and *determinately knowing* from all eternity
> everything that happens, including all free acts....In other
> words, all aspects of the eternal purpose of God are equally
> timeless. For if God is an eternal and simple Being then
> his thoughts must be coordinate and unified.
>
> Whatever he forechooses cannot be *based on* what he
> foreknows. Nor can what he foreknows be based on what
> he *forechose*.[10] Both must be simultaneous and coordi-
> nate acts of God. Thus God knowingly determined and
> determinately knew from all eternity everything that
> would come to pass, including all free acts. Hence, they
> are truly free actions, and God determined they would
> be such. God then is totally sovereign in the sense of
> actually determining what occurs, and yet humans are
> completely free and responsible for what they choose.[11]

It is very difficult to understand these words, given that they
are based upon the assertion that there is no logical priority of
foreordination to foreknowledge, for they are "one." But given
that in point of fact there is no reason to accept this assertion,
we are still left with the classical conundrum of how God can
be sovereign over all things on one hand, and man "completely
free" on the other. Using phrases like "determinately knowing"
or "knowingly determining" does not in reality solve the problem, it only confuses it.

At this point it is good to note that there is a real danger in
misunderstanding the use of the term "predetermined" or just
"determined." Most people upon reading this term think of a
positive, volitional action on the part of God: i.e., in the sense
of decreeing that something is going happen, such as the crucifixion of Christ (Acts 4:28) which took place, we are told, as
God's power and will had decided beforehand. Most people
understand these terms to speak to something *active* on the
part of God. But we will see this is not Geisler's meaning.

When he speaks of "knowingly determining," the *active* element is gone. "Determined" here refers to the *passive recognition of the actions of free men*, not the sovereign *decree* that the action would take place *through* the instrumentality of creatures.

In other words, what Geisler means is that God "determines" what will take place *through* His perfect knowledge. It would be like my saying that "I determined the water in the pool was very cold by putting my toe in the water." "Determined" here is passive: I did not *make* the water hot or cold, I just passively took in knowledge that it was, in fact, cold. We could contrast this with my saying, "I installed a heating system in my pool, and determined the temperature would stay at 76 degrees." Here, "determined" is active because I am actually making the water a particular temperature. When Geisler speaks of God "determining" things he is saying that since God has perfect, complete, and instantaneous knowledge of all events, past, present, and future, then He *determines* those actions—but this is solely in the passive sense. The grand issue of whether God *actively* decrees whatsoever comes to pass is, in fact, directly denied. In this sense, Geisler's position, despite all the theological terminology and discussion of sovereignty, is very much the same as the Arminian who says that God merely looks into the future and elects on the basis of what He sees. While Geisler repeats his assertion that one cannot logically determine the relationship between foreknowledge and predetermination, his constant emphasis upon the *absolute freedom* of the creature betrays the reality of his system. This comes out with clarity in these words:

> This being the case, there is no problem of how an act can be truly free if God has determined in advance what will take place. God's foreknowledge is not foreordaining anything which will *later* occur to him. All of time is present to God's mind from all eternity. God does not really foreknow it; he simply knows it in his eternal presence. Hence, God is not foreordaining from his vantage

point, but simply ordaining what humans are doing freely.
God *sees* what we are freely doing. And what he sees, he
knows. And what he knows, he determines. So God *de-terminately* knows and *knowingly determines* what we are
freely deciding.[12]

It is important to follow this closely: God simply "knows" all
of time and the *free choices* of humans that take place within
time. God is not *determining* this actively, but passively. And
this comes out in the final sentences: humans are "doing" things
"freely." God "sees" what they are "freely doing." What God
sees, He must know, and what He knows, He knows perfectly.
Now here is the key: "And what he knows, he determines."
Knowing the free actions of men results in his "determining"
those actions: passively, of course, not actively. This then is
the meaning of "knowingly determining" what humans are
"freely deciding."

What is really being said here needs to be kept in mind: the
decisions or "decreeing" that takes place is done by man. God
perfectly knows what man does, and passively "determines" it
simultaneously as He knows it (in Geisler's view). But there is
one major problem here: who is actually deciding what takes
place in time? Feinberg saw this in reviewing Geisler's position and asked the question this way: "Does the agent act because of causal factors which decisively incline the will or does
he act without any factors decisively inclining the will?" In plain
language, do men do what they do because God has decreed
all things (including the actions of men) or do men act autonomously, and God simply has perfect knowledge of the results? It seems Dr. Geisler's position leads inevitably to the
latter: that in the final analysis, man is the one that actively,
willfully, freely determines what takes place in the human realm.
God's "sovereignty," if we can use the term, is limited to giving
the gift of freedom:

> God is the cause of the fact of freedom, and humans
> are the cause of the acts of freedom. God made the agent,

but the agents cause the actions. God gives people power (of free choice), but they exercise it without coercion. Thus God is responsible for bestowing freedom, but humans are responsible for behaving with it. (p. 79)

God's "responsibility" is limited to giving men freedom: nowhere in these discussions do we see any emphasis at all upon *God's freedom*. While it is definitional in Geisler's view that man be free, it does not seemingly follow that when it comes to actions in time, it is definitional that *God be free as well*.

Open Theism

These issues were again addressed in the context of a critique of "open theism" in Dr. Geisler's 1997 Bethany House Publication, *Creating God in the Image of Man?* This is most significant in light of the fact that if anywhere the freedom of God, His sovereign decree, and His *active and free* determination of events in time will be confessed by Dr. Geisler, it would have to be here. Open theism is specifically designed to undercut and deny the sovereignty of God and the idea that He is accomplishing a specific, freely chosen purpose in this world. While Dr. Geisler identifies it as at least a "theistic" system, I would assert open theism is *fundamentally incompatible* with Christian theism, and is hence opposed to Christian truth. It is in the context of defining the Christian position that Dr. Geisler again makes clear his opposition to the Reformed position and Reformed theology:

> In brief, God can know a "must be" through a "may be" but not a "can't be." Therefore, an omniscient being (God) knows all future contingents as necessarily true. This he can do because God knows necessarily that what will be must be. That is, if it will and God knows it, then what God knows about what will be must be true. An omniscient mind cannot be wrong about what it knows. Therefore the statement "Everything known by God must

necessarily be" is true if it refers to the statement of the truth of God's knowledge, but it is false if it refers to the necessity of the contingent events. This view of God's foreknowledge and free will is compatible with both classical Arminianism and moderate Calvinism.[13]

This is consistent with what has come before: there is *passive yet perfect knowing of future contingencies* but the *active determination* of what takes place in time remains within the purview of the *creature*, not the *Creator*. This is confirmed a little later:

> Actually, God knew from eternity who would repent. And God's will includes intermediate causes such as human free choice. So God knows what the intermediate causes will choose to do. And God's will is in accord with his unchangeable knowledge. Therefore, God's will never changes, since he wills what he knows will happen. That is to say, what is willed by conditional necessity does not violate human freedom, since what is willed is conditioned on their freely choosing it. God wills the salvation of men only conditionally. Therefore, God's will to salvation does not violate human free choice; it utilizes it. Both classical Arminians and moderate Calvinists agree. Among evangelicals, only extreme Calvinists demur.[14]

Not only does Dr. Geisler here admit that his view is in harmony with the Arminian view[15] and contradictory to the historic Reformed position, but he in essence undermines his own previous assertion that predetermination and foreknowledge are "one" and indistinguishable by saying that "what is willed is *conditioned on* (my emphasis) their freely choosing it." It is almost frightening to consider that here God's will is said to be "in accord with his unchangeable knowledge," and that his will never changes "since he wills what he knows will happen." It is vital to see this: men act freely, autonomously, while God's will is defined by His knowledge of what takes place in time. Truly this makes man the determiner and God the "perfect knower." Yet, the only positive, free, active will in all of this is man's, not God's. At its root, this in no way differs from the Arminian viewpoint that God elects on the basis of what he foresees.

Chosen But Free

We can now evaluate the presentation in *CBF* in light of the consistent teachings of its author over the preceding two decades. Remembering that Dr. Geisler calls himself a "moderate Calvinist," we immediately note that at the most basic, definitional point of Calvin's theology, that being the absolute freedom and sovereignty of God in decreeing whatsoever comes to pass in time, Geisler is in strong disagreement. His presentation begins with an affirmation of the sovereignty of God:

> Nothing catches God by surprise. All things come to pass as He ordained them from all eternity.[16]

Such language *sounds* very Calvinistic until one remembers that "ordained" is not meant in the sense of the positive, all-encompassing decree of God whereby He accomplishes all of *His* (not man's) holy will. This comes out even when speaking of "sovereignty." Note well the words used:

> Even those who would eventually be saved were known by God (1 Peter 1:2) before the foundation of the world (Eph. 1:4). By His limitless knowledge God is able to predict the exact course of human history (Dan. 2, 7), including the names of persons generations before they were born (cf. Isa. 45:1).[17]

These words are carefully chosen: those who would "eventually" be saved are "known" to God (no mention of God's ordination or sovereign choice), and God does not *decree* the course of human history, but rather *predicts* it (flawlessly). If you *predict* something you do not *control* it. God does not need to *predict* what He has created, for example: if God is the Creator of time and all the events in time, then He knows what will take place *because He decreed it*, not because He *predicts* it. Even when speaking of the term "sovereignty" this element is seen:

> Whatever else may be said, God's sovereignty over the human will includes His initiating, pursuing, persuading, and saving grace without which no one would ever will to be saved. For "there is no one who understands, *no one who seeks God*" (Rom. 3:11).[18]

Again the words are specific: God initiates, God pursues, God persuades, God gives saving grace, but, despite it all, the final decision is man's, "without which no one would ever *will to be saved.*" God wills to save man, but unless man wills to save himself, he will not be saved. This is thorough-going Arminianism.

Dr. Geisler turns to the main issue under the title of "Sovereignty and Responsibility."

> No one has ever demonstrated a contradiction between predestination and free choice. There is no irresolvable conflict between an event being predetermined by an all-knowing God and it also being freely chosen by us.[19]

When one realizes that "predetermined" means simply "perfectly known but not decreed" this position makes sense: one must simply sacrifice the meaning of "predestined" and the rest falls into place. Note again the conjunction of the phrase "all-knowing" with the term "predetermined." This equation of "knowledge results in passive determination" is laid out explicitly as Dr. Geisler presents an example of his theory:

> (2) Whatever God foreknows must come to pass (i.e., is determined).[20]

What God "foreknows" (*not* decrees) must come to pass (since God's knowledge is perfect); this is here explicitly equated with "determination." For Geisler, to say that God "determines" something means that God knows it will happen, *not* that He positively, actively *decrees* that it should take place. This is fully consistent with what we saw in earlier publications. This concept continues:

> (4) Therefore, it *had to come to pass* (i.e., was determined) that Judas would betray Christ.
> The logic is flawless. If God has an infallible knowledge of future free acts, then the future is completely determined. But what *does not* follow from this is that
> (5a) Judas was not free to betray (or not to betray) Christ.
> This is because there is no contradiction in claiming that God *knew for sure* (i.e., predetermined) that Judas would *freely* (i.e., with free choice) betray Christ.[21]

What then, ultimately, is the force that determines such events as this? Is it God's *active and sovereign will*, or the *free action of man* known perfectly, yet *passively* by God in His "foreknowledge"? The answer is clear: in this system, man determines the shape and form of actions in time, and God passively "determines" that it should be so.

> Therefore, if God has infallible foreknowledge of the future, including our free acts, then everything that will happen in the future is predetermined, even our free acts. This does not mean these actions are not free; it simply means that God knew how we were going to use our freedom—and that He knew it *for sure*.[22]

Therefore, to be "determined" means *only* to be "known certainly," so that the ultimate "free will" in the events of man is man, not God. Man acts freely, God knows those actions perfectly, and hence "determines" them. No decree, no active sovereignty, no "free will" of God accomplishing *His* desire. That is why Geisler can say there is no contradiction in saying Jesus' death on the cross was "predetermined from God's standpoint and free from Jesus' perspective. It is determined in *the one sense* that God foresaw it. Yet it is also true in *another sense* that Jesus freely chose it."[23]

The majority of the specific argumentation regarding Geisler's unique view of God "determinately knowing" is found in his definition of the view of "moderate Calvinism" on pages 52-54. Most of this material appeared in the previous publications we have already examined. By now, however, we should be able to understand exactly what *CBF* is communicating here:

> Hence, both foreknowledge and predetermination are one in God. Whatever God knows, He determines. And whatever He determines, He knows.
>
> More properly, we should speak of God as *knowingly determining* and *determinately knowing* from all eternity everything that happens, including all free acts. For if God is an eternal and simple Being, then His thoughts must be eternally coordinate and unified.
>
> According to the moderate Calvinist's view, whatever God forechooses cannot be based on what He foreknows. Nor can what He foreknows be based on what He forechose. Both must be simultaneous, eternal, and coordinate acts of God. Thus, our actions are truly free, and God determined that they would be such. God is totally sovereign in the sense of actually determining what occurs, and yet man is completely free and responsible for what he chooses.[24]

God's sovereignty is here limited to the "sense" in which He "determines" (passively, as we have seen) what takes place: the only reference to a freely acting agent is to man.

> Likewise, the extreme view of God predetermining things in spite of (or without regard to) His foreknowledge is not plausible. For God's foreknowledge and his foredetermination cannot be separated. God is one simple (indivisible) Being. In Him knowledge and foredetermination are identical. Hence, He had to pre-

determine in accordance with His foreknowledge. And
He must have foreknown in accordance with His predetermination.[25]

We saw this assertion in Dr. Geisler's 1985 work, and have
already noted that this assertion is without basis and is in error. Knowledge and foredetermination are *not* identical, and,
we submit, if they are, and we cannot discuss the logical relationship between what God *decrees* and what God *knows*, then
it follows that God is truly enslaved to the free choices of men,
and the creature, in fact, becomes the *determiner* of the course
of all things in human history.

While the preceding citations are certainly enough to establish the position, we should avail ourselves of another source
in *CBF* to confirm our conclusions, that being Geisler's attack
upon the view of what he calls "extreme Calvinism" (i.e., the
Reformed position). You often say more about your own position when you criticize someone else's, and that is the case
here. In responding to "extreme Calvinism," Geisler defines
the position in these words:

> According to this view, God's predetermination is done
> *in spite of* His foreknowledge of human free acts. God
> operates with such unapproachable sovereignty that His
> choices are made with total disregard for the choices of
> mortal men.[26]

There are two problems here: first, it assumes the *philosophical* meaning of "foreknowledge" rather than the *biblical* meaning.[27] And while using this meaning it is said that God's "predetermination" (we assume here that this would be the "normal" meaning in everyday language of the term "predetermination," since this is speaking now of Reformed theology) is
done *in spite of* this foreknowledge. To be accurate, however,
the proper description would be "independent of" merely knowing future events, or, even better, independent of *anything* other
than His own sovereign and perfect will and purpose. God acts

with complete freedom in all things. His is the only truly "free will" in the universe, since He is the Creator. God does not act "in spite of" knowledge He has of the universe: the knowledge He has of the universe is due to the fact that He *created it*. Secondly, God does not act with "total disregard" of the choices of His creatures: His actions *determine* the *free* choices of His creatures. Dr. Geisler denies that an *actively* determined action can be "free," but in reality, Reformed theologians insist that for one to be free as a *creature* then one must have first and foremost a sovereign *Creator*. God is the free and sovereign *Creator* and acts freely in that realm that is His: we are mere creatures, never sovereign, never autonomous (i.e., without law, without a superior authority), but *responsible within the realm of our createdness*. Despite all this, there is one truth presented here: the Reformed position plainly asserts that God "does according to His will in the host of heaven and *among* the inhabitants of earth" (Daniel 4:35) and He does so *solely on the basis of His own desire and decree*, never on the basis of anything outside of Himself. As the 1689 Baptist Confession states,

> God hath decreed in himself, from all eternity, by the most wise and holy counsel of his own will, freely and unchangeably, all things, whatsoever comes to pass" (Chapter 3, "Of God's Decree").

CBF then provides this interesting insight:

> There is an important corollary to this view. If free choices were not considered at all when God made the list of the elect, then irresistible grace on the unwilling follows. That is, man would have no say in his own salvation. Accordingly, the fact that all men do not choose to love, worship, and serve God will make no difference whatsoever to God. He will simply "doublewhammy" those He chooses with His irresistible power and force them into His kingdom against their will.[28]

The first thing that strikes the reader is that this criticism begins with a fundamental denial of the assertion that God's "foreknowledge" and "predetermination" are "one." There is a plain priority in *CBF*'s presentation to the "free choices" of men which then influences (indeed, determines) the making of the "list of the elect." Obviously, this indicates a priority of the free choices of men: the "list of the elect" seemingly is made up of those who vote for themselves. Again, God is not presented as the free and sovereign *elector*, but the one who *responds* to the "free choices" of men, even in the making of the "list of the elect"!

Next, *CBF* constantly insists the Reformed position teaches "irresistible grace on the unwilling." As we will note later, this is straw-man argumentation, for it ignores the fact that Reformed theologians believe fallen man to be dead in sin, an enemy of God, in need of spiritual resurrection and a new heart (Ezekiel 36:26). Briefly, there is no more "force" exercised in God's wondrous act of regeneration than was exhibited when the Lord Jesus cried out, "Lazarus, come forth!" (John 11:43). Resurrection is not an action of force against will: it is the bringing of new life to the dead. And that is what Reformed people believe. To call that wondrous act a "doublewhammy" that "forces" people into the kingdom "against their will" is to simply miss the point—completely. R.C. Sproul has rightly pointed out that the Reformed view is simply the Augustinian view, and that this view is often badly misrepresented:

> Augustine's view is frequently said to be that God saves people who are unwilling to be saved, or that his grace operates against their wills, forcing them to choose and bringing them into the kingdom "kicking and screaming against their will." This is a gross distortion of Augustine's view. The grace of God operates on the heart in such a way as to make the formerly unwilling sinner willing. The redeemed person chooses Christ because he wants to choose Christ. The person now wills Christ because God has created a new spirit within the person.

God makes the will righteous by removing the hardness of the heart and converting an opposing will. "...if God were not able to remove from the human heart even its obstinacy and hardness," Augustine writes, "He would not say, through the prophet, 'I will take from them their heart of stone, and will give them a heart of flesh' " [Ezek. 11:19].[29]

Finally, one more quotation from *CBF* should conclude the examination. In defending his concept of man acting in such a way as to be "self-determining," Dr. Geisler writes:

> The answer lies in the fact that God knows—for sure—(infallibly) precisely how everyone will use his freedom. So, from the vantage point of His omniscience, the act is totally determined. Yet from the standpoint of our freedom it is not determined. God knows *for sure* what we will *freely do.* ...This is not to deny that God uses *persuasive* means to convince us to choose in the way that He desires. It is only to deny that God ever uses *coercive* means to do so.[30]

Persuasion versus *coercion*. Gently wooing the free creature, or forcing the free creature against its will. No middle ground is offered, though, of course, such a middle ground exists in Reformed theology, a middle ground that is based not upon the freedom of creatures, but the freedom of the Creator.

A Flawed Foundation

CBF operates on the assertion that God's knowledge and God's predetermination (taken passively) are identical, and that in reality there is no positive, active, sovereign decree of God that gives form and shape to time and history. This viewpoint plays upon the term "determination" and the possibility of taking the word actively or passively. God's "determination" of events becomes passive, yet, despite this, the author connects this passive determination of events in time with the term "sovereignty" which truly admits of no such "passive" concept. The result is a tremendously confusing presentation that *seems* to promote *both* the idea that God is absolutely sovereign *and* man is absolutely free. But in reality, the position presents a God who is limited to having a perfect knowledge of free events; the extent of His sovereign actions is in granting freedom: He does not control what His creatures do with that freedom, but only knows the results *perfectly*. This system is driven primarily by philosophical concerns, *not* by biblical exegesis, as we shall see when we examine the biblical argumentation presented in *CBF*. Charles Hodge expressed it well:

> Who would wish to see the reins of universal empire fall from the hands of infinite wisdom and love, to be seized by chance or fate? Who would not rather be governed by a Father than by a tornado? If God cannot effectually control the acts of free agents there can be no prophecy, no prayer, no thanksgiving, no promises, no security of salvation, no certainty whether in the end God or Satan is to be triumphant, whether heaven or hell is to be the consummation. Give us certainty—the secure conviction that a sparrow cannot fall, or a sinner move a finger, but as God permits and ordains. We must have either God or Satan to rule. And if God has a providence He must be able to render the free acts of his creatures certain; and therefore certainty must be consistent with liberty.[31]

This is the view that then logically gives rise to a rejection of every element of the Reformed faith.[32] It should be noted that this is *not* a Calvinistic view of God's absolute freedom and sovereignty. This is *not* a view that could be called moderately Calvinistic, weakly Calvinistic, or even remotely Calvinistic. And if one rejects the Reformed view at its root, it should not be surprising that the rest of the system likewise suffers at Dr. Geisler's hands. One is not a Potter who has no role in determining the shape, function, and destiny of the pots.

Notes

1   We do not here speak of foreknowledge in the sense of the verbal concept "to foreknow," which in the Bible is not a matter of merely knowing future facts, but of personally entering into relationship with someone. See the discussion in chapter nine.

2   Geisler laid out his view most fully in Basinger & Basinger, 61-88; major elements of this essay appear in various parts of *CBF*.

3   Conspicuously absent is the emphasis upon the absolute freedom of God.

4   Donald Campbell, ed., *Walvoord: A Tribute* (Moody Press, 1982).

5   Ibid., p. 102.

6   Ibid., pp. 102-103.

7   Basinger & Basinger, p. 70.

8   Ibid., p. 86.

9   Ibid., p. 88.

10 This is a particularly troubling statement, for if God's knowledge of future events is not based upon his sovereign decree, then the events that take place in time find their origin and source in something other than God's infinitely wise will.

11 Ibid., pp. 70-71.

12 Ibid., p. 73.

13 Norman Geisler, *Creating God in the Image of Man?* (Bethany House Publishers, 1997), p. 38.

14 Ibid., p. 43.

15 See the discussion of his use of "moderate Calvinist" in the Introduction and throughout this work. Note as well the direct assertion that God's election is conditional: a direct denial of the Reformed belief in unconditional election. Geisler will, in *CBF*, attempt to present a new definition of "unconditional election" so that his denial of it can adopt the same name.

16 Geisler, *Chosen But Free*, p. 15.

17 Ibid., p. 13.

18 Ibid., p. 18.

19 Ibid. p. 42.

20 Ibid., p. 43

21 Ibid.

22 Ibid., p. 45.

23 Ibid., p. 46.

24 Ibid., pp. 52-53.

25 Ibid., p. 54.

26 Ibid, pp. 46-47.
27 That is, the Greek term πρόγνωσις is used in Scripture regarding God's gracious choice to enter into relationship with His people. See the discussion in chapter 9 and in *God's Sovereign Grace*, pp. 117-122.
28 Ibid., p. 47
29 R.C. Sproul, *Willing to Believe*, 1997, pp. 65-66.
30 *CBF*, p. 178.
31 Charles Hodge, *Systematic Theology*, II:301-302.
32 The sole exception being the perseverance of the saints, though, even here, the *basis* of that perseverance is substantially different.

Chapter 3

The Inabilities of Man

Charles Haddon Spurgeon once said, "As the salt flavors every drop in the Atlantic, so does sin affect every atom of our nature. It is so sadly there, so abundantly there, that if you cannot detect it, you are deceived."[1] The great works of Christians down through the centuries are filled with the same testimony: man is the slave of sin, utterly undone outside of Christ. Even those whose theology did not measure up to the biblical standard could not help, in their prayers, to confess what they knew to be true: the fallen sons of Adam are dead in sin, incapable of even the first move toward God. Even more, they are filled with the effect of depravity and alienation from God: enmity and hatred toward His holy standards. This was a common element of Spurgeon's preaching:

> Now, the calling of the Holy Spirit is without any regard to any merit in us. If this day the Holy Spirit shall call out of this congregation a hundred men, and bring them out of their estate of sin into a state of righteousness, you shall bring these hundred men, and let them march in review, and if you could read their hearts, you would be compelled to say, "I see no reason why the Spirit of God should have operated upon these. I see nothing whatever that could have merited such grace as this— nothing that could have caused the operations and motions of the Spirit to work in these men." For, look ye

here. By nature, men are said to be dead in sin. If the Holy Spirit quickens, it cannot be because of any power in the dead men, or any merit in them, for they are dead, corrupt and rotten in the grave of their sin. If then, the Holy Spirit says, "Come forth and live," it is not because of anything in the dry bones, it must be for some reason in His own mind, but not in us. Therefore, know ye this, men and brethren, that we all stand upon a level. We have none of us anything that can recommend us to God; and if the Spirit shall choose to operate in our hearts unto salvation, He must be moved to do it by His own supreme love, for He cannot be moved to do it by any good will, good desire, or good deed, that dwells in us by nature.[2]

The "flip-side" of divine freedom is the fact that man, the great image-bearer of God, is a *fallen creature,* a slave to sin, spiritually dead, incapable of doing what is pleasing to God. Just as the great freedom of the Potter offends rebellious pots, so too does the Bible's teaching on the *inabilities* of man due to sin. The fallen sons and daughters of Adam are most adept at finding ways to promote *creaturely* freedom at the cost of God's freedom, while at the same time promoting the *servitude* of God to the whims and will of man. It would be humorous if it were not so serious: the pots gathering together and assuring each other that the Potter either doesn't exist, or, at worst, will sit idly by while they take control and "run the show" themselves. Yet this is the impact of sin upon the thinking of man. Man suppresses the truth of his createdness and invariably attempts to find a means to "control" God. One wisely put it this way:

Again, it is certain that man never achieves a clear knowledge of himself unless he has first looked upon God's face, and then descends from contemplating him to scrutinize himself....So it happens in estimating our spiritual goods. As long as we do not look beyond the earth, being quite content with our own righteousness, wisdom, and virtue, we flatter ourselves most sweetly, and fancy ourselves all but demigods. Suppose we but once begin to raise our thoughts to God, and to ponder his nature, and how completely perfect are his righteousness, wisdom, and power—the straightedge to which we must be shaped. Then, what masquerading earlier as righteousness was pleasing in us will soon grow filthy in its consummate wickedness. What wonderfully impressed us under the name of wisdom will stink in its very foolishness. What wore the face of power will prove itself the most miserable weakness. That is, what in us seems perfection itself corresponds ill to the purity of God.[3]

Truly recognizing one's spiritual state is a gift of grace. Outside of God opening the eyes of the heart man thinks himself wonderfully pure, or at least acceptable in God's sight. That is why the unregenerate person cannot understand the urgency of the gospel message: until they see the depth of their sin and the holiness of God, they find no reason to seek remedy for their condition.

Man's religions consistently promote the myth of man's autonomy: his absolute freedom to act outside of any eternal decree of God. "Man is the master of his destiny" seems to be the watchword of the religions of men, and even of many in Christendom today. How many times have you heard a preacher say, "In the matter of election, God has cast his vote for you, Satan has cast his against you, and now the final vote is up to you"? Such an assertion not only makes man's choice equal with God's, but it likewise places the final decision for what takes place in time squarely in the hands of man, not of God.

A Definition

What do Reformed Christians believe concerning the will of man? The reader of *CBF* would have to conclude that true Calvinists believe man's will is "destroyed" and done away with, resulting in nothing more than an automaton, a robot. But this is not the case at all. Chapter 9 of the *London Baptist Confession* (1689)[4] is succinct and clear:

1   In the natural order God has endued man's will with liberty and the power to act upon choice, so that it is neither forced from without, nor by any necessity arising from within itself, compelled to do good or evil.

2   In his state of innocency man had freedom and power to will and to do what was good and acceptable to God. Yet, being unstable, it was possible for him to fall from his uprightness.

3   As the consequence of his fall into a state of sin, man has lost all ability to will the performance of any of those works, spiritually good, that accompany salvation. As a natural (unspiritual) man he is dead in sin and altogether opposed to that which is good. Hence he is not able, by any strength of his own, to turn himself to God, or even to prepare himself to turn to God.

4   When God converts a sinner, and brings him out of sin into the state of grace, He frees him from his natural bondage to sin and, by His grace alone, He enables Him freely to will and to do that which is spiritually good. Nevertheless certain corruptions remain in the sinner, so that his will is never completely and perfectly held in captivity to that which is good, but it also entertains evil.[5]

5   It is not until man enters the state of glory that he is made perfectly and immutably free to will that which is good, and that alone.

The final section especially should be noted: when in heaven the ultimate "freedom" will not be "freedom to choose evil or good as we may desire" but "freedom from the presence of, and inclination toward, evil." Any person who believes that the redeemed in heaven will be forever perfected must likewise believe that they will no longer commit sin. Does this mean that they will somehow be less than human? Or is freedom to perfectly will good a greater freedom than the ability to choose between good and evil?

The Scriptural Witness

The biblical doctrine of total depravity combines the truth of man's createdness (the pot that is formed by the Potter) with the truth of man as *sinner*. The result is a view of man that is pre-eminently biblical and perfectly in line with what we see in mankind all around us.

To say something is a biblical doctrine requires that we demonstrate this from the text. Briefly, here are a few of the more important passages teaching the Reformed doctrine of the total depravity of man and the bondage of man in sin.

From the earliest records of the Bible, we see that man's corruption extends to his very heart:

> Then the LORD saw that the wickedness of man was great on the earth, and that every intent of the thoughts of his heart was only evil continually. (Genesis 6:5)

This corruption is internal and complete: *every* intent of the thoughts of man's heart was *only* evil *continually*. This is radical corruption, not mere "sickness." Such a person is not "spiritually challenged" but is in firm and resolute rebellion against God. The flood took these people away, yet, even after the flood, God says:

> The LORD smelled the soothing aroma; and the LORD said to Himself, "I will never again curse the ground on account of man, for the intent of man's heart is evil from his youth; and I will never again destroy every living thing, as I have done." (Genesis 8:21)

Man's radical corruption has not changed: from his youth man's heart is evil, not just once in a while, but continually. Can good come forth from an evil heart? Men like to think so. Yet, the Bible says otherwise:

> Can the Ethiopian change his skin
> Or the leopard his spots?
> *Then* you also can do good
> Who are accustomed to doing evil.
> (Jeremiah 13:23)

Just as a person cannot change the color of their skin, or the leopard its spots, so the one who practices evil cannot break the bondage of sin and start doing good. The corruption is indelible and can only be removed by a radical change of the heart. Surely this is not the belief of most of mankind: films, books, and the mass media is constantly telling us that there is a "spark of good" in the heart of man that is just *begging* to be fanned into a flame. So pervasive is this belief that many in the Christian faith have drunk deeply at this well of humanism and have allowed society, rather than Scripture, to determine their view of man. But the consistent testimony of the Word is beyond question:

> The heart is more deceitful than all else
> And is desperately sick;
> Who can understand it?
> (Jeremiah 17:9)

> Behold, I was brought forth in iniquity,
> And in sin my mother conceived me.
> (Psalm 51:5)

> The wicked are estranged from the womb;
> These who speak lies go astray from birth.
> (Psalm 58:3)

It is incredible to find Christians saying, "Well, that refers to only some people. See, it says 'these who speak lies go astray from birth.'" Is there any person who truly knows their own heart who does not confess that they lie *regularly*, if not in word, then in their heart, even to God? Who does *not* lie? Someone might say, "But it says 'the wicked are estranged from the womb,' not *everyone.*" But does not every Christian confess that we were once "children of wrath" even as the rest (Ephesians 2:3)? The true believer knows well the corruption from which Christ has rescued us.

The New Testament continues the testimony to the radical depravity of man. In fact, when Paul seeks to present a systematic argument for the gospel to the Romans, he does not begin with "Jesus loves you" or "God has a wonderful plan for your life." Showing that he would fail almost every evangelism class currently offered in seminaries in our land, Paul begins with a dreadfully long discussion of the universal sinfulness of man. Without a single poem, no funny illustrations or multimedia aids, the inspired Apostle drags on about the sinfulness of men, Jew and Gentile alike. It is no wonder this section is so little preached in our day. But might it just be that the *good news* cannot be properly understood unless the *bad news* is fully realized? Such would seem to be the case.

A biblical view of man must find a large portion of its substance in the words of Paul in Romans 1 and 3. Hear again these words penned by the Spirit of God:

> For even though they knew God, they did not honor Him as God or give thanks, but they became futile in their speculations, and their foolish heart was darkened. Professing to be wise, they became fools, and exchanged the glory of the incorruptible God for an image in the form of corruptible man and of birds and four-footed animals and crawling creatures. Therefore God gave them over in the lusts of their hearts to impurity, so that their bodies would be dishonored among them. For they exchanged the truth of God for a lie, and worshiped and served the creature rather than the Creator, who is blessed forever. Amen. (Romans 1:21-25)

Man, the image-bearer of God, *knows* God exists. There is no honest atheist. Man suppresses that knowledge (Romans 1:18) and twists his irrepressible religiosity into the horror that is idolatry. We can find men bowing down and worshiping every single element of the created world, from the most obvious forms of idolatry such as the worship of animals, the sun, moon, and stars, to the more subtle but no less horrific forms where men worship pleasures, possessions, and most often, themselves (humanism). It is the very essence of sin to twist the proper relationship of God as Creator and man as creation. When man usurps *any* of the authority of God he is, in so doing, giving loud testimony to the radical depravity that grips every fallen child of Adam. But Paul goes on to compile a list of testimonies from the ancient Scriptures to seal his case:

> As it is written,
> "There is none righteous, not even one;
> There is none who understands,
> There is none who seeks for god;
> All have turned aside,
> Together they have become useless;
> There is none who does good,
> There is not even one.
> Their throat is an open grave,
> With their tongues they keep deceiving,
> The poison of asps is under their lips;
> Whose mouth is full of cursing and bitterness;
> Their feet are swift to shed blood,
> Destruction and misery are in their paths,
> And the path of peace they have not known.
> There is no fear of god before their eyes."
> (Romans 3:10-18)

This litany of quotations is specifically designed to have one effect: to shatter, destroy, and obliterate any last shred of self-righteousness that might remain after the preceding arguments have been understood. These testimonies are fatal to any kind of "optimistic humanism." Outside of God's grace, man is a corrupted creation, violent, hateful, without understanding, without fear of God. Rather than finding in man "seekers" who simply need a "nudge" in the right direction, Scripture tells us that man does *not* understand and does *not* seek after God. Man is deceitful, even with himself, and is quick to curse God. Total depravity painted in the most vivid colors.

Dead in Sin

Scripture teaches that men are spiritually *dead* and in need of new life. Paul taught that this was the universal condition of mankind, for he said that all Christians, prior to being born anew, were dead in their sins:

> And you were dead in your trespasses and sins, in which you formerly walked according to the course of this world, according to the prince of the power of the air, of the spirit that is now working in the sons of disobedience. (Ephesians 2:1-2)

> When you were dead in your transgressions and the uncircumcision of your flesh, He made you alive together with Him, having forgiven us all our transgressions, (Colossians 2:13)

The contrast between *spiritual death* before Christ and *resurrection life* in Him reveals to us the *depth* of the meaning of "dead in sins." The one who is spiritually dead is separated from the only source of true life: the Creator. Spiritual death is the result of the fall of Adam, and one who is spiritually dead cannot pass on to his descendants a life that he himself does not possess. All in Adam then are born in this state of spiritual death, while all who are in Christ share His life.

When the Scriptures say that men are spiritually dead, we are not to understand this to mean that they are spiritually *inactive*. Men are active in their rebellion, active in their suppression of the truth, active in their sin. Instead, spiritual death refers to alienation from God, the destruction of the positive, active desire to do what is right in God's sight, and most importantly, *the ability to do what is good and holy*. It is this last assertion that is so often denied, though the Scriptural testimony is strong and unequivocal:

> For those who are according to the flesh set their minds
> on the things of the flesh, but those who are according
> to the Spirit, the things of the Spirit. For the mind set
> on the flesh is death, but the mind set on the Spirit is
> life and peace, because the mind set on the flesh is hos-
> tile toward God; for it does not subject itself to the law
> of God, for it is not even able *to do so*, and those who are
> in the flesh cannot please God. (Romans 8:6-8)

The fleshly (unregenerate) mind is hostile toward God (never
neutral), for it does not subject itself to the law of God. But it
is the assertion that follows this that causes so many to stumble:
the fleshly mind "is not able." *Subjection to God's law is outside
the capacity of the fallen man.* Since we know that God's law
commands us to repent and believe as well as to perform that
which is righteous in God's sight, we can see the tremendous
extent of the corruption of human nature and the resultant
spiritual inabilities.

We must understand the Scriptural argument at this point.
Those who promote the theory of "free will" normally mean
this in the sense of *creaturely autonomy.* The idea is that man,
even in sin, is in reality at a neutral point where he is still free
to will good or evil, all depending on his own desires and choice.
The idea that man's will is controlled by his nature, and that
man's fallen nature is enslaved to sin because it is corrupted,
is denied. Yet this is *exactly* what Paul teaches in this passage.
It is specifically, biblically set forth that the unregenerate, fleshly
mind is not *capable* of *doing what is right in God's sight.* The
lost man *cannot please God.* Is repentance and faith pleasing to
God? Yes. Is submission to the commands of God pleasing to
Him? Of course. Therefore, regeneration must take place first.

This truth came out in glowing colors when Jesus was faced
with an entire crowd of would-be disciples who refused to accept the centrality of His own person to God's work of salvation. Upon miraculously feeding the five thousand on the previous day, Jesus is followed by an entire group of people very

excited about His supernatural powers and abilities. He purposefully separates Himself from them, rejecting their attempt to make Him a king. The next day they find Him in the synagogue in Capernaum. Christ exposes their true motivations for following Him by refusing to pander to their "felt needs" and instead points them to the only source of life: Himself, the Bread of Life. Unregenerate men are offended when they are told they are helpless and utterly reliant upon another for salvation (as we will see again below in John 8). They begin to grumble, especially when Christ explains their unbelief in terms of God's sovereignty. The Lord Jesus explains their faithlessness in blunt terms:

> Jesus answered and said to them, "Do not grumble among yourselves. No one can come to Me unless the Father who sent Me draws him; and I will raise him up on the last day." (John 6:43-44)

While modern evangelicals normally seek reasons for rejection of Christ in psychology, upbringing, background, or in the failure of the "presentation," Jesus goes beyond the creaturely and touches upon the eternal reality. Again we find man's *inabilities* put in the forefront in contrast with God's *ability*. Why do these stand before the incarnate Lord in disbelief? Because they are not able, in and of themselves, to come to the very Bread of Life. "No one can come to Me" Christ says.

These are not words to be glossed over. Non-Reformed Protestants simply cannot explain Jesus' meaning. The religions of men, Roman Catholicism, and Arminianism, all share one thing in common: the deep desire to maintain the ability of man to control the work of God in salvation and *always* have the "final say." The blunt assertion of Christ refutes this error. The fact is, outside of the divine action of drawing the elect to Christ *none* would come to Him. It is beyond the capacity of the fallen man.

Normally this assertion is "softened" by saying, "Yes, without God first moving toward us, we would never be able to move toward Him." But this is not the teaching of the Lord.

The emphasis is on the *inability* of man to do something outside of the action of the Father. Christ, and His message, is not "naturally attractive" to the unregenerate person. In fact, it is foolishness and those who proclaim it a "smell of death" (2 Corinthians 2:16). Something has to change the person who is naturally the enemy of God into one who desires to follow Christ. That "something" is the "drawing" of the Father.

Many are willing to go this far and say that yes indeed, we must be drawn. But they will then say "but God draws all men." Is this what Jesus says? Such an assertion turns the text on its head. The Lord is explaining the *disbelief* of the crowds. If all are drawn, and that equally, why are these men not being drawn? No, an often missed truth of the passage is this: *all who are drawn are also raised up.* "And I will raise *him* (the one who is drawn by the Father to the Son) up on the last day" is the Lord's promise. So, if every individual is drawn, then every individual is raised up. Universalists adopt just this theology. Evangelicals do not. Dr. Geisler does not address the assertion of inability that is so plainly presented here. We will address his denial that the "drawing" spoken of in John 6:44 is the same as the "irresistible grace" of the Reformed faith in a later chapter.

Another analogy used by the Lord to describe the state of man in sin is that of slavery. In the eighth chapter of John the Lord addresses Jews who "had believed" in Him. John does not use the normal terms he uses for true believers, but instead indicates that the kind of faith these men had was a surface level, one-time faith, not the on-going, saving faith seen throughout the Gospel of John. To these would-be disciples Jesus says,

> So Jesus was saying to those Jews who had believed Him, "If you continue in My word, *then* you are truly disciples of Mine; and you will know the truth, and the truth will make you free." They answered Him, "We are Abraham's descendants and have never yet been enslaved to anyone; how is it that You say, 'You will become free'?" Jesus an-

swered them, "Truly, truly, I say to you, everyone who
commits sin is the slave of sin." (John 8:31-34)

These "disciples" are offended by a truth that every true child
of God knows so well: we were once slaves to sin, but Christ,
our Master and Redeemer, has freed us. These surface-level
seekers after miracles did not understand their desperate need,
their helpless estate. And so they assert their creaturely freedom. Of course, as Jews, they had in fact been under the control of Rome for many decades, so their response was patently
false. But Christ was not speaking of slavery to Rome. He was
speaking of slavery to sin. The person who does not realize the
power of sin is a person who does not yet realize the need for a
Liberator, a Savior.

The one who commits sin is the slave of sin. Slavery is
servitude, not freedom. Christ's words tell us that sin is a task-
master, we the servants. We do not rule over it. It rules those
who are under its power. Slavery is antithetical to "free will."
Man in sin is not free to do what is good.

It is utterly amazing, then, to read the words of Dr. Geisler
who writes, "We are born with a bent to sin, but we still have a
choice whether we will be its slave."[6] How can this be when
the Lord teaches that sin brings slavery? What kind of "choice"
is left to the slave concerning his servitude?

The testimony of Scripture is clear: the fallen sons and
daughters of Adam are in need of a Savior to free them from
the bonds of sin and raise them to spiritual life. The radical
corruption of the heart of man is explicitly asserted and implicitly proven throughout Scripture. To conclude our survey
let us hear again the words of Spurgeon:

> What a vain pretense it is to profess to honor God by a
> doctrine that makes salvation depend on the will of man!
> If it were true, you might say to God, "We thank thee, O
> Lord, for what thou hast done; thou hast given us a great
> many things, and we offer thee thy meed of praise, which
> is justly due to thy name; but we think we deserve more,
> for the deciding point was in our free will." Beloved, do

not any of you swerve from the free grace of God, for the babblings about man's free agency are neither more nor less than lies, right contrary to the truth of Christ, and the teachings of the Spirit.

How certain, then, is the salvation of every elect soul! It does not depend on the will of man; he is "made willing" in the day of God's power. He shall be called at the set time, and his heart shall be effectually changed, that he may become a trophy of the Redeemer's power. That he was unwilling before, is no hindrance; for God giveth him the will, so that he is then of a willing mind. Thus, every heir of heaven must be saved, because the Spirit is put within him, and thereby his disposition and affections are molded according to the will of God.[7]

But, man—even religious man—does not wish to be reminded of his true condition. And so we now respond to the attempts to promote the myth of man's free will and creaturely autonomy.

Notes

1 Metropolitan Tabernacle Pulpit 21:365.
2 "Free Grace," a sermon preached January 9, 1859.
3 Calvin, Institutes I:2:2, pp. 37-38.
4 Citation is from A *Faith to Confess: The Baptist Confession of Faith of 1689, Rewritten in Modern English* (Carey Publications, 1986).
5 Despite the fact that this is a common element of Reformed writing on the subject of the will, Dr. Geisler can ask, "Fifth, if what is evil can't will good, and if what is good can't will evil, then why do Christians who have been given good natures still choose to sin?" (pp. 28-29).
6 Norman Geisler, *Chosen But Free*, p. 65.
7 "The Holy Spirit in the Covenant," a sermon preached in 1856, *The Charles H. Spurgeon Collection* (Ages Digital Library, 1998).

Chapter 4

The Will of Man

The single most important quotation in all of *Chosen But Free* is found on pages 233-234:

> God's grace works synergistically on free will. That is, it must be received to be effective. There are no conditions for giving grace, but there is one condition for receiving it—faith. Put in other terms, God's justifying grace works cooperatively, not operatively. Faith is a precondition for receiving God's gift of salvation....Faith is logically prior to regeneration, since we are saved "through faith" (Eph. 2:8-9) and "justified by faith" (Rom. 5:1 NASB).

Synergism versus monergism. Grace dependent upon man's volition versus the powerful, all-sufficient grace preached by the Reformation. Faith, the ability of the unregenerate man, versus saving faith as a divine ability given to the elect. These are all issues that defined the Reformation, yet, here Dr. Geisler summarizes his soteriology by promoting the very position the Reformers rejected long ago. Saying that God's grace "works synergistically on free will" is not a Reformed view. It is not a Calvinistic view. At the most fundamental level it is a belief that is opposed to the Reformation,[1] and I believe opposed to biblical teaching regarding God, man, and grace. Rome likewise teaches this kind of synergism, making grace an aid that is, in the final analysis, dependent upon man's choice for its effectiveness. In fact, one need only read the following sections of the Catechism of the Catholic Church (1994) to see the striking similarity, even to the level of phraseology, between the assertions made by Arminians, and by Dr. Geisler above, and the official position of the Roman Catholic Church even to this day:

> In faith, the human intellect and will cooperate with divine grace: "Believing is an act of the intellect assenting to the divine truth by command of the will moved by God through grace." (155)

We should note that the quotation in paragraph 155 is from Thomas Aquinas: a source used by Dr. Geisler with great regularity. Later the Catechism says,

> The merit of man before God in the Christian life arises from the fact that God has freely chosen to associate man with the work of his grace. The fatherly action of God is first on his own initiative, and then follows man's free acting through his collaboration, so that the merit of good works is to be attributed in the first place to the grace of God, then to the faithful. Man's merit, moreover, itself is due to God, for his good actions proceed in Christ, from the predispositions and assistance given by the Holy Spirit. (2008)

Synergism is the hallmark of man's religions: monergism the mark of the biblical gospel. So indelibly written on the theology of Norman Geisler is the concept of man's complete freedom and a synergistic view of grace that he is able to assert:

> In short, it is God's ultimate and sovereign will that we have free will to resist His will that all be saved.[2]

It seems that at least on one issue God's sovereign will is accomplished perfectly: the institution, perpetuation, and maintenance of human free will. While God *tries* to save as many people as possible (limited, however, by human free will), one thing He manages to do without hindrance is to sovereignly will the freedom of man to resist His salvific will.

The concept of human free will is taken as a philosophical presupposition by *CBF*. The person seeking a biblical presentation of "free will" will be sorely disappointed, however, in the presentation of the text. For example, Dr. Geisler begins:

> One of the things God gave His good creatures was a good power called free will. Mankind intrinsically recognizes freedom as being good; only those who usurp and abuse power deny it, and yet even these value and seek it for themselves.[3]

Unfortunately, *CBF* not only misrepresents the Reformed understanding of the will, but it makes no attempt to establish its own view through the use of meaningful exegesis. The careful student will note that the book *begins* with the assertion of the necessity of "free will" and "human freedom," and only after establishing these necessities via philosophical argument do we encounter any biblical discussion. This is exactly backwards from the proper methodology: we begin with God's revelation concerning the nature of man and then move *from* revelation *to* reason. *CBF* barely makes it three pages into its critique of the "extreme" viewpoint before the conclusion of the entire book is reached, and it is said it must be "rejected."[4] No biblical examination has taken place to this point: the position is rejected on the basis of philosophical assumptions, not exegesis of the biblical text.

Geisler begins by arguing that men must be free or else 1) God is to be blamed for the origin of evil and 2) men cannot be held responsible otherwise. The fact that the Bible addresses both of these issues clearly (as we have seen above) is not addressed *before* Geisler comes to his conclusion that the Reformed viewpoint *cannot* be the right one. The lengthy discussions in answer to these very objections, found in Reformed works from Calvin,[5] Turretin,[6] Hodge,[7] Wright,[8] or

Reymond[9] (to name just a few) are completely ignored. This is one of the major reasons why knowledgeable Reformed readers are so troubled by *CBF*'s cavalier attitude toward such vital issues. To conclude that the entire system is bankrupt *by the third page* of the "discussion" shows a lack of concern for meaningful interaction or representation.

Three years before *CBF* was published, InterVarsity Press published R.K. McGregor's *No Place for Sovereignty: What's Wrong with Freewill Theism*, which constitutes a defense of the Reformed position and a critique of the very position espoused by Dr. Geisler in *CBF*. This work is cited a few times elsewhere in *CBF*,[10] but it is not cited in the very section where the majority of its argumentation is focused. This is perhaps due to the fact that Geisler's presentation here is *thoroughly Arminian* and cannot, in any fashion, be described as Calvinistic, moderate or otherwise. The second chapter of *CBF* presents the following reasons why "free will" must be true: 1) Without it, men are not responsible for their actions (p. 25); 2) It is part of the way God created man (p. 22); 3) The Bible teaches free will (p. 32); 4) Denial of free will makes God the author of sin (pp. 20-21). Later in the book he argues that to embrace the Reformed position with its denial of human "free will" leads to "failing to take personal responsibility for our actions."[11] Yet Wright had written:

> Arminians generally argue as follows: 1. *If we have no free will, we are not responsible for our actions....* 2. *It is essential to the image of God....* 3. *The denial of free will undermines both human effort and morality....* 4. *The Bible teaches free will....* 5. *Free will gets God off the hook in the problem of evil.*[12]

Wright managed to outline the second chapter of *CBF* two years before it was written! Yet, there is not a single citation of Wright's *response* to these assertions in *CBF*. Indeed, when one reads the discussion in both books, this example of a conversation between a Calvinist and an Arminian fits the presenta-

tion in *CBF* so closely that one again cannot miss the identification of Dr. Geisler's position as thoroughly Arminian:

> *Arminian*: Well, we must have a free will to be respon-
> sible human beings.
> *Calvinist*: But what do you mean by "responsible"?
> A: Responsibility means we make real choices.
> C: What do you mean by a "real" choice? Isn't a choice
> real if it actually occurs at all?
> A: Responsibility means that we act individually as com-
> plete human beings, in our own integrity.
> C: You seem to assume that free will is a part of our
> humanness.
> A: Well, it is. Free will is part of the image of God, and
> that's what makes us human.
> C: So we have free will because we act in our own
> integrity.
> A: Yes, and because we are responsible for our actions.
> C: But a moment ago you based responsibility on free
> will. Now you are basing free will on responsibility.
> A: Well, it's like a chicken-and-egg situation, and it's
> not too easy to decide which comes first.
> C: But in the case of the chicken we know which came
> first: God created the first chicken.
> A: Well, God created us with free will.
> C: But how do you know that? Is it in the Bible?
> A: But if we don't have free will we can't be held re-
> sponsible for our actions.
> And so forth....[13]

The concept of an Arminian "free will" is central to Dr.
Geisler's "moderate Calvinism." We are told that reason "demands that all moral creatures be morally free, that is, they
have the ability to respond one way or another."[14] Why or how
reason can "demand" this is not clear. Here are the assertions
that are made:

From the beginning to the end the Bible affirms, both

implicitly and explicitly, that human beings have free choice. This is true both prior to and after the Fall of Adam, although free will is definitely affected by sin and severely limited in what it can do.[15]

Exactly how the "free will" is "severely limited" is hard to say. Whatever these limitations involve, one thing they do not do is keep man from being able to savingly believe in Christ. He goes on to assert,

> Both Scripture and good reason inform us that depraved human beings have the power of free choice. The Bible says fallen man is ignorant, depraved, and a slave of sin. But all these conditions involve a choice....Even our en-slavement to sin is a result of a free choice....Even spiritual blindness is a result of the choice not to believe....Fallen beings are free....And the vertical ability to believe is everywhere implied in the Gospel call (cf. Acts 16:31; 17:30). Freedom for God's creatures, as it is for the God in whose image they are made, is described in James 1:18: "*Of his own will* begat he us with the word of truth..." (KJV).[16]

It seems that being ignorant, depraved, and a slave still does not change the assertion that man has a "free choice." It is not explained how one can be a slave to sin and still have a free choice regarding sin, but it is certainly *CBF*'s assertion that the fallen man *is* free to will good, *is* free to will what is pleasing to God. We have already seen Paul taught the exact opposite at Romans 8:5-9. The *inability* to believe is directly presented in John 6:44 and yet this passage is unanswered in *CBF*. The issue of faith as a gift, which comes up so often in connection with man's will, shall be addressed under the topic of the work of God in regeneration (irresistible grace).

Dr. Geisler asserts that "free will" is a part of the image of God,[17] which explains the consistent misrepresentation of the Reformed position throughout *CBF* in the constant assertion that "extreme Calvinists" teach the image of God has been destroyed. In presenting his novel re-definition of the "Five Points of Calvinism," Dr. Geisler claims:

> *T*—Total depravity is amply supported by Scripture in the moderate Calvinist sense. All the Scriptures used by extreme Calvinists are accepted by moderate Calvinists; the only difference is that moderates insist that being "dead" in sin does not mean that unsaved people cannot understand and receive the truth of the gospel as the Spirit of God works on their hearts. That is, it does not in effect *erase* the image of God (but only *effaces* it).[18]

Dr. Geisler knows that true Calvinists do not make the claim that the image of God is erased, for he includes a footnote that says,

> Some extreme Calvinists deny that they believe the image of God is "destroyed" in fallen humans—at least formally. But *logically* this is what their view demands and practically this is what they hold.[19]

We are given no logical reason to accept this claim, and given the many errors found in *CBF*'s understanding of the Reformed position, there is really no reason to extend credulity to such an assertion.[20] Geisler goes so far as to say that the "extreme Calvinist" teaches that the human will is "destroyed"[21] even though, on the same page, he admits this is not the case, for he writes,

> While extreme Calvinists admit that fallen human beings have biological life, they deny they are alive in any sense in which they can respond to God; their natures are so totally corrupt that sin is an unavoidable necessity. And whereas the faculty of will is present, nonetheless, the ability to choose to follow God is destroyed.

Do Calvinists believe man has a will or not? It seems that it is *CBF*'s position that unless the will is "free" it is not "real." An enslaved will is a "destroyed" will, the clear distinctions of Reformed confessions of faith notwithstanding.

There is a further error in *CBF*'s understanding of the Reformed position in this quotation. Dr. Geisler says that "extreme Calvinists" believe unregenerate men cannot "respond to God." This is simply untrue. Unregenerate men who are enemies of God most assuredly respond to God: in a universally negative fashion. They are constantly suppressing the knowledge of God that is within their hearts, so it is simply untrue to assert they do not respond to God. They respond in rebellion and sinfulness, but respond they do!

The idea of "free choice" is so fundamental to the view of *CBF* that even the view of salvation as a gift is seen as teaching the idea:

> Even unsaved people have a free choice as to either receiving or rejecting God's gift of salvation (Rom 6:23). Jesus spoke of those who rejected Him saying, " 'O Jerusalem, Jerusalem...how often I have longed to gather your children together, as a hen gathers her chicks under her wings, but *you were not willing*' " (Matt 23:37).[22]

As we will note in a later chapter, this is a great misuse of Matthew 23:37. But the main point one has to offer to this kind of reasoning is this: Romans 6:23 says the wages of sin is death. There is nothing in the passage that speaks of "free choice" in the context of creaturely autonomy as *CBF* presents it. Salvation is surely the free gift of God's grace, but it is a long leap to assume that the nature of the *gift* indicates the autonomy of the *recipient*. Life was a gift given to Lazarus, but the giving of the gift did not in any way indicate an ability on the part of the one who received it.

It is important to note a common error in the argumentation of Arminians that appears in *CBF*. Dr. Geisler says that we cannot believe that God "violates" the free choice of any human being in order to save that person. We saw earlier that Dr. Geisler calls this a "dehumanizing" of man, "God will not dehumanize in order to save"[23] is his assertion. But what if man is enslaved to sin, spiritually dead, and incapable of freeing himself? Are we to believe that God is unable to free the objects of His love from their bondage to sin and spiritual death without "dehumanizing" them? The Bible is very clear that God in His sovereign mercy frees men from bondage and sin and raises them to spiritual life. He does so not because the sinner does something to *allow* Him to so act, but solely on the basis of His sovereign power. This is not *dehumanizing* man but *freeing* man. Because of this fundamental misunderstanding, *CBF* represents the Reformed view as teaching a "violation" of man's will. Note this quotation written in response to John Gerstner's identification of Geisler as an Arminian:

> If affirming that God will not violate the free choice of any human being in order to save that person is an "Arminian" view, then every major church father from the beginning, including Justin, Irenaeus, Athenagoras, Clement, Tertullian, Origen, Methodius, Cyril, Gregory, Jerome, Chrysostom, the early Augustine, Anselm, and Thomas Aquinas (whom Sproul greatly admires) were Arminians! Further, if Sproul's radical reformation view is correct,[24] then even most Lutherans who follow Melanchthon, not Luther's *Bondage of the Will*, on this point are Arminians![25]

When one looks at the citation quoted by Gerstner[26] (to which Geisler is responding) there is no *other* way of interpreting Geisler's intention. He was not merely saying that God would not "violate" man's freedom: he was explicitly asserting that God "will do everything within His loving power to save all He can." That phrase *"all He can"* is anathema to *any* kind of Reformed belief: it is pure, 100% Arminianism, as Gerstner rightly said. The God of Scripture is able to save perfectly and completely all He desires to save: the fact that not all are saved leads inexorably to the truth of divine election. Therefore, *CBF* denies this divine truth and instead replaces it with the idea of "determinately knowing" already reviewed in chapter two.

Dead In Sin

Reformed authors frequently point to the biblical teaching that man is "dead in sin" as substantiation of their belief that God *must* be absolutely sovereign and salvation *must* be completely of free grace and *not* a synergistic cooperation between God and man since man is not *capable* of "cooperating" anymore than a corpse is able to help in its own resurrection. Because of this, CBF invests a great deal of effort in the attempt to redefine "spiritual death" so that it is no longer incompatible with "free choice" and human autonomy. We have already seen that CBF indicates that God's creation of the "list" of the elect is based, in some way, upon the actions of men. Therefore, CBF must find a way for man to be active even though spiritually dead. Even though dead, man must be able to do "vertical" or spiritual good. Geisler rightly defines the Calvinistic view at one point:

> But they are incapable of any "vertical" or spiritual good and, according to extreme Calvinism, they are totally incapable of initiating, attaining, or ever receiving the gift of salvation without the grace of God.[27]

As a result, CBF sees the result of believing in this "extreme" view of total depravity:

> Extreme Calvinists believe that a totally depraved person is spiritually dead. By "spiritual death" they mean the elimination of all human ability to understand or respond to God, not just a separation from God. Further, the effects of sin are intensive (destroying the ability to receive salvation), not extensive (corrupting the ability to receive salvation).

It must immediately be said that it is *not* the Reformed position that spiritual death means "the elimination of all human ability to understand or respond to God." Unregenerate man is fully capable of understanding the facts of the gospel: he is simply incapable, due to his corruption and enmity, to submit himself to that gospel. And he surely responds to God every day: negatively, in rebellion and self-serving sinfulness. The Reformed assertion is that man cannot understand *and embrace* the gospel nor respond *in faith and repentance* toward Christ without God first freeing him from sin and giving him spiritual life (regeneration).

So how does Dr. Geisler respond to the clear assertion of Scripture that man is, indeed, dead in sin? Here is his response to Ephesians 2:1 and the Reformed interpretation of it:

> This extreme Calvinistic interpretation of what is meant by spiritual "death" is questionable. First of all, spiritual "death" in the Bible is a strong expression meaning that fallen beings are totally separated from God, not completely obliterated by Him. As Isaiah put it, "your iniquities have *separated* you from your God" (Isa. 59:2). In brief, it does not mean a total destruction of all ability to hear and respond to God, but a complete separation of the whole person from God.[28]

Each assertion in this response is flawed. First, Geisler misrepresents the Reformed position by contrasting "total separation from God" with the strange idea of being "completely obliterated by Him." Where do Reformed writers say spiritual death involves "complete obliteration" by God? Being dead in sin does refer to separation from godly life; such is a partial truth. But obviously Paul intends something more than "separation" when he contrasts the horrific state of the "spiritually dead" with the glorious position of the person who is alive in Christ. The very use of the imagery of resurrection shows us this. But no one asserts this means "total obliteration." What is "obliterated" is the ability of man to subject himself to the law of God, not the man himself.

Next, we are not told how the true statement found in Isaiah 59:2 is relevant to the conclusion that follows its presentation. Isaiah 59 is cited by Paul in Romans 3:15f as evidence of the universal sinfulness of man. But how does the single assertion that sin brings separation a basis for saying that this is *all* it brings?

Finally, if a person experiences complete separation from God, does it not follow that one is separated from the only source of goodness, light, and truth? Are we to believe that such a person who is totally separated from God can come up with righteous desires, love for truth, repentance toward God, etc., simply from themselves? Geisler goes on:

> Second, even though they are spiritually "dead," the unsaved persons can perceive the truth of God. In Romans, Paul declares emphatically that God's truth is "clearly seen" by them so that they are "without excuse" (1:20).[29]

Again, no Reformed exegete would say otherwise. But Dr. Geisler confuses the contexts of Romans 1 and Ephesians 2. Romans 1 is referring to the truth of the existence of God that is revealed through creation itself and is known by all men (Romans 1:18-23). Paul is *not* addressing the truth of the gospel message in Romans 1. So while the unsaved man knows the truth of God's existence, this is clearly not the same thing as asserting that he is able to embrace and obey the gospel. The two concepts are completely distinct, and no effort is made by CBF to connect the two. So far, no commentary has been offered by Dr. Geisler *on the actual text of Ephesians 2:1*. But we press on:

> In short, depravity involves the *corruption* of life but not its *destruction*. The image of God in fallen humans is effaced but not erased. Even unsaved people are said to be in God's image (Gen. 9:6). The image is marred by not eradicated by sin (cf. James 3:9).[30]

This is reiteration, not exegesis. This is what Dr. Geisler believes, and even though it again misrepresents the Reformed position (i.e., the assertion that the Calvinist believes the image of God is "eradicated"), it does not provide any kind of positive evidence or discussion of the *meaning* of Ephesians 2 and the phrase "dead in sin." Calvinists often refer to "radical corruption" as a synonym for "total depravity." Surely man is *corrupted* in the fall. But the issue is, what does it mean that he is "dead in sin" as described in Ephesians 2:1? Quite simply, Geisler doesn't deal with the passage. Instead, the misrepresentation of the Reformed position is pressed forward:

> Fourth, if spiritually "dead" amounts to a kind of spiritual annihilation, rather than separation, then the "second death" (Rev. 20:10) would be eternal annihilation, too—a doctrine rejected by extreme Calvinists.[31]

It is difficult to know how to respond to this kind of argumentation, as it is based upon such obvious errors. First, it is *Dr. Geisler's* assertion that Calvinists equate being dead in sin with annihilation: it is *not* the assertion of Calvinists. Hence, the proffered argument has no merit even if one were to buy the idea that the term "dead" must mean exactly the same thing in all contexts (something no sound exegete would affirm anyway). Geisler's attempted response to the passage ends with no exegetical content, but only a repeat of the primary assumptions of his entire system:

> A spiritually dead person, then, is in need of spiritual life from God. But he does exist, and he can know and choose. His faculties that make up the image of God are not absent, they are simply incapable of initiating or attaining their own salvation. Like a drowning person, a fallen person can reach out and accept the lifeline even though he cannot make it to safety on his own.[32]

First, this is surely the Arminian position. The analogy of the drowning person is semi-Pelagian/Arminian. What it surely is not is Calvinistic. But what does it mean to say that a spiritually dead person, while dead, can still "reach out and accept the lifeline"? How can that be? Dead men do not reach out for anything.

Colossians 2:12-13 likewise teaches the truth that man is dead in sin outside of Christ. CBF provides a two sentence response to this passage:

> Finally, in the parallel passage (Col. 2:12-13) Paul speaks of those "dead in your sins and in the uncircumcision of your sinful nature" being able to believe. For he said, "you have been raised with him through *your faith* in the power of God."[33]

This is all that is said. The analogy of baptism that is used in 2:11-12 *precedes* Paul's use of the word "dead," which instead is again connected with "being made alive" by Christ. Seemingly the assertion being made is the person who has faith in the power of God is an unregenerate, spiritually dead person. How this is proven from the text, or why we should believe this in light of Paul's statement in Romans 8:8, is not explained. In short, CBF's theology simply cannot provide a coherent explanation of Ephesians 2:1/Colossians 2:13, and none is offered. Instead, the response offered is nothing but a mixture of straw man arguments against Calvinism with the simple reiteration of the Arminian mantra of free-willism.

Notice the amazing use of the phrase "so dead" in the following citation based upon the presentation of the Puritan writer William Ames:

> What is more, according to Ames, God determines to save whomever He wishes regardless of whether they choose to believe or not. In fact, God gives the faith to believe to whomever He wills. Without this God-given faith they could not and would not believe. In fact, fallen human beings are so dead in sin that God must first

regenerate them before they can even believe. Dead men
do not believe anything; they are dead![34]

Are there degrees of "deadness," so that one can be dead, yet
not *so* dead as to require spiritual life before believing? If men
are dead in sin at all, it follows that they must have spiritual
life restored to them before they can do spiritually good things.
The only error in the above presentation is that Ames does not
say "dead men do not believe anything." Spiritually dead men
believe all sorts of things: just not those things that are pleasing to God.

A Tremendous Inconsistency

Before examining specific Scriptural passages cited in *CBF*
regarding total depravity a tremendous example of inconsistency in the presentation of the work should be noted. Responding to Arminians who say that if you chose to get "into"
salvation you can surely choose to get "out" of it, *CBF* makes
the following amazing statements:

> First of all, this rationale is not *biblically based*; it is
> *speculative* and should be treated as such.

The same can be said for the vast majority of *CBF*'s assertions
about the will of man and any number of other arguments.

> Second, it is not logically necessary to accept this rea-
> soning, even on a purely rational basis. Some decisions
> in life are one-way with no possibility of reversing them:
> suicide, for example. Saying "oops" after jumping off a
> cliff will not reverse the consequences of the decision.

Quite true, but such seems to prove far more than Dr. Geisler
would like: committing a single act of sin makes one a sinner
and places one under the power of death and condemnation.
While Geisler insists that one *chooses* to remain a slave of sin,
and can, at any time, simply choose by the exercise of free

choice to become a believer and cease being a slave, here he argues that once you accept Christ the decision is inalterable and there is no escaping the consequences. Logically his position is inconsistent at best.

> Third, by this same logic the Arminian would have to argue that we can be lost even after we get to heaven. Otherwise, he would have to deny we are free in heaven. But if we are still free in heaven and yet cannot be lost, then why is it logically impossible for us to be free on earth and yet never lose our salvation? In both cases the biblical answer is that God's omnipotent power is able to keep us from falling—in accordance with our free choice.[35]

First, *CBF* does not offer us an explanation of how we can be "free" in heaven and yet not able to fall. Given the very definition of freedom found throughout *CBF* it would have to follow of necessity that the redeemed human being in glory would *have* to be able to commit an act of sin *or else be "dehumanized."* Evidently, the ability to sin is *not* constitutional or definitional of true humanity. So this response fails in all three attempts (showing that Geisler's acceptance of "eternal security" is inconsistent with his emphasis upon human ability and free will). But what is even more troubling to the careful reader is this: the final statement promotes the idea that even the eternal state of the redeemed, while supported by "God's omnipotent power," is *still* a function of that power working "in accordance with our free choice." The centrality—indeed, supremacy—of man's freedom over God's in this viewpoint is an amazing thing to ponder.

Numerous passages of Scripture are cited in the text of *CBF*. We now turn to an examination of the exegesis offered in support of the "moderate Calvinist" position (i.e., Arminianism).

John 12:39-40

> For this reason they could not believe, for Isaiah said again, "HE HAS BLINDED THEIR EYES AND HE HARDENED THEIR

HEART, SO THAT THEY WOULD NOT SEE WITH THEIR EYES AND
PERCEIVE WITH THEIR HEART, AND BE CONVERTED AND I HEAL
THEM."

At the end of Jesus' public ministry a group of Greeks sought
out Jesus. This prompted the Lord to complete His public
teaching and withdraw in preparation for His passion. As John
records these words he provides a theological commentary on
the close of this phase of Jesus' ministry. He draws from passages in Isaiah as prophetic substantiation of the ministry of
Christ. In 12:39-40 John explains *why* the Jews, despite seeing
the very Incarnate Son, did not believe. The first statement
that *must* be explained by Geisler is clear: "For this reason
they could not believe." This is not a mistranslation. The Greek
is plain: διὰ τοῦτο οὐκ ἠδύναντο πιστεύειν, "for this reason
(introducing the quotation that follows) they were *not able* to
believe (common word for "believe" or "have faith"). Surely if
one's entire position is based upon the assertion that *all* are
able to believe, a clear Scriptural passage that speaks of *anyone's*
inability to believe should receive a large amount of in-depth,
contextual response. Dr. Geisler provides three points in response that will be useful in establishing the kind of herme-
neutic used by *CBF*:

> (1) Belief was obviously their responsibility, since God
> held them responsible for not believing. Only two verses
> earlier we read, "Even after Jesus had done all these mi-
> raculous signs in their presence, *they still would not be-
> lieve in him*" (John 12:37).

One could argue that perfect behavior is the responsibility of
all men, but it does not follow that sinful man has the capacity
to do so. One does read of their unwillingness to believe two
verses earlier. However, John then explains that unwillingness
to believe in 12:38, by stating, "This was to fulfill the word of
Isaiah the prophet which he spoke: 'LORD, WHO HAS BELIEVED OUR
REPORT? AND TO WHOM HAS THE ARM OF THE LORD BEEN REVEALED?'"
John's own interpretation of their unbelief was that it was a

fulfillment of prophecy. So the first response does not substantiate Dr. Geisler's free-will theory.

> (2) Jesus was speaking to hardhearted Jews who had seen many indisputable miracles (including the resurrection of Lazarus [John 11]) and who had been called upon many times to believe before this point (cf. John 8:26), which reveals that they were able to do so.

Actually, these words are John's, not Jesus', and these are comments about the unbelief of the Jews in general. Yes, they had been called upon to repent and believe. It does not follow, however, that "they were able to do so" when verse 39 says they were *not* able to do so. Here we have the plain assertion of Scripture being overturned because it *can't* mean what it says. The assumption is that if God commands all men everywhere to repent, then that must mean that all men everywhere are morally neutral creatures with free wills who are not enslaved by sin. But this does not follow. God commands all men everywhere to love Him with all their heart, soul, mind and strength, but sin does not allow any of the fallen sons of Adam to do so. So we turn to the last attempt to answer the passage:

> (3) It was their own stubborn unbelief that brought on their blindness. Jesus said to them, "I told you that you would die in your sins, *if you do not believe* that I am, you will indeed die in your sins." (John 8:24). Thus, it was chosen and avoidable blindness.[36]

It is an assumption that the audience in John 12 is identical with that of John 8.[37] But that issue aside, this final response again fails to deal with the simple statement of the passage concerning the *inability* of these men to believe. Let's say they had indeed engaged in "stubborn unbelief." Are we to believe that this practice eventually robs a man of his free will? The passage explains their unbelief as a fulfillment of prophecy, not the result of anything these men did themselves. If it was stubborn unbelief that brought on their blindness (something the passage does not assert), then their stubborn unbelief was just as much a fulfillment of the prophecy as anything else. None of this, including the citation of a different context (John 8) in any way 1) answers the plain assertion of the passage that belief was *not* within their ability, nor 2) provides any kind of substantiation for the conclusion that it was "chosen and avoidable blindness." If it was avoidable, does that mean the prophecy itself was avoidable? No one argues that these men did not choose to not believe: the issue is was their choice a part of God's sovereign decree or was God limited to their "free choices" and His perfect knowledge of them? The conclusion provided by *CBF* is not derived *from* the text but is forced *onto* the text: a classic example of eisegesis.[38]

I Corinthians 2:14

Paul spoke of the spiritual inabilities of the natural (unregenerate) man when he wrote to the Corinthians:

> But a natural man does not accept the things of the Spirit of God, for they are foolishness to him; and he cannot understand them, because they are spiritually appraised.

Let's briefly note some exegetical points about the passage: it is clearly two parallel statements, which could be put this way:

> But a natural man
>   does not accept the things of the Spirit of God,
>   for they are foolishness to him;
>   and he cannot understand them,
>   because they are spiritually appraised.

The first line identifies the subject. The next two clauses are parallel assertions containing first an inability of the natural man followed by an explanation of why this is so. Therefore, the meaning of "does not accept" and "cannot understand" are parallel to one another and must be interpreted in light of the other. Likewise, the foolishness of the things of the Spirit of God is due to the fact that they are spiritually appraised, and the natural man is not a spiritual man.

CBF presents this passage and asserts that it "is used by extreme Calvinists to support the idea that unregenerate persons cannot even understand the Gospel or any spiritual truths of Scripture."[39] The term "understand" should be taken as it is used in this passage: the natural man cannot *accept and embrace* spiritual things because he himself is not spiritually alive. He may well completely understand the proclamation of the gospel itself: but until spiritual life is given to him, the words are empty. Geisler comments:

> This interpretation, however, fails to take note that the word "receiveth" (Greek: *dekomai*) means "to welcome." It simply affirms that while he does *perceive* the truth (Rom. 1:20), he does not *receive* it. There is no welcome in his heart for what he knows in his head. He has the truth, but he is holding it down or suppressing it (Rom. 1:18). It makes no sense to say that an unsaved person cannot understand the gospel before he is saved. On the contrary, the entire New Testament implies that he cannot be saved unless he understands and believes the gospel.[40]

The Greek term δέχομαι *can* mean "welcome," but as we noted, its meaning here should be paralleled with "spiritual understanding." There is no exegetical or contextual reason to bring in Romans 1:20, for the two contexts are addressing different things. As we have noted, Romans 1 is speaking of general revelation in creation itself, not the "spiritual things" of the gospel that Paul is addressing when speaking to the Corinthians.

Next, we note that CBF's attempted exegesis focuses upon one phrase while ignoring how that line relates to the rest of the sentence. Why no discussion of the things of the Spirit being "foolishness" to the natural man? If the natural man has the ability to embrace these things and believe them, as Geisler asserts, would it not be incumbent upon him to explain how what was once foolishness becomes wisdom *without* regeneration taking place first? Why no discussion of the inability of man to "know" or "understand" them, as the text plainly asserts? Why no response to the fact that the things of the Spirit are "spiritually appraised" by spiritual men but not by the natural man, *who lacks the ability to do so?* Is it because the Arminian position *must* hold to the idea that the unregenerate man *can*, to some extent, know, understand, appreciate, and in fact, accept, spiritual things so that the spiritually dead rebel can then cause his own regeneration by exercising true saving faith that is pleasing to God? Such seems to be the case. Geisler continues:

> Total depravity is to be understood in an *extensive*, rather than an *intensive* manner. That is, sin extends to the whole person, "spirit, soul and body" (1 Thess. 5:23), not just to part of the person. However, if depravity has destroyed man's ability to know good from evil and to choose the good over the evil, then it would have destroyed man's ability to sin. If total depravity were to be true in this intensive (read: extreme Calvinist) sense, it would destroy man's ability to be depraved at all. For a being with no moral faculties and no moral abilities is not a moral being at all; instead, it is amoral, and no moral expectation can be held over it.[41]

We see again the error of *CBF*'s entire understanding of the position it seeks to deny. No one asserts total depravity has destroyed man's ability to know good from evil. This is yet another straw man. There is a world of difference between saying a man is *enslaved to sin* so that it is the constant desire of his or her heart to be in rebellion against God and to serve *self* rather than God, and saying man no longer knows good from evil. Hence, the assertion that this representation of "intensive" depravity is the Reformed viewpoint is simply a basic error of understanding. And once more, we see that this para-

graph has little, if any, connection with the Scriptural passage it
is allegedly responding to (1 Corinthians 2:14).

John 8:34-48

We noted the witness of John 8:31-34 in the previous chapter. These words of the Lord introduce a discussion that includes clear teaching on the sovereignty of God in salvation.
For example:

> "Why do you not understand what I am saying? *It is*
> because you cannot hear My word. You are of *your* father
> the devil, and you want to do the desires of your father"
> (8:43-44), and "He who is of God hears the words of
> God; for this reason you do not hear *them*, because you
> are not of God" (8:48).

Again the Reformed and biblical view of man is presented with
force: Jesus teaches that the Jews *cannot* (there's that word of
inability again) hear His word and do *not* understand what He
is saying. He is not saying they are confused: He is saying they
lack the spiritual ability to appraise spiritual truths. Their nature is fleshly, natural, and in fact, demonic, in that they desire
to do the desires of their father, the devil. Then, a few verses
later, the Lord speaks words that are normally turned completely upside down by Arminian interpreters. Jesus explains
why these men do not "hear" His words. Now obviously, they
could hear Him just fine. He was not speaking too softly to be
heard. But they could not *hear* with understanding nor acceptance. The one who is "of God" hears His words: the one who
is not does not. Jesus specifically says these Jews are not "of
God," or as the NIV puts it, do not "belong to God." While
Arminians would say "If you act upon what you hear you will
become one that belongs to God," Jesus says just the opposite: until one "belongs to God" one will not "hear" the words
of Jesus. As in John 6 we see that something must happen
before a person can "hear" or believe in Christ: and that is the

work of God in regenerating the natural man and bringing him to spiritual life.

CBF completely ignores John 8:48, not mentioning it, or its witness to the Reformed proclamation. But a brief response is offered to John 8:44, though again without accurately representing the Calvinistic position. Here is the assertion:

> From this text extreme Calvinists conclude that fallen humans cannot avoid sinning because they are by nature "the children of the devil" (1 John 3:10) who have "been taken captive by him to do his will" (2 Tim. 2:25-26 NKJV).[42]

Actually, the Calvinistic use of the passage is that man does the desires of his heart, and until a heart is renewed, those desires are not pleasing to God. An unregenerate man can choose not to commit a particular act of sin: what he cannot do is choose to do that which is spiritually pleasing to God. Geisler comments:

> But it does not follow that we have no free choice in the matter. Jesus said, "I tell you the truth, *everyone who sins* is a slave to sin' " (John 8:34). In fact, in the very text cited to support the extreme Calvinist view, note that it says, " 'You *want* [*will*] to carry out your father's [the devil's] desire' " (John 8:44). It is by their choice that they follow the devil.

But surely the text teaches exactly what Dr. Geisler is denying! Of course they *want* to do the will of their father, that's the whole point. They *always* want to do this! That's total depravity and enslavement to sin. What they are *not* able to do is will to do the will of God the Father, that which is holy and just and right (Romans 8:7-8). "Everyone who sins is a slave to sin" means *all* are slaves to sin since *all* sin! It is a continuation of the straw-man argumentation that marks CBF to say that the Reformed do not say that man *chooses* to sin. Man *always* chooses to sin: our assertion is that one cannot choose to do what is holy and righteous before God unless he or she is given a new nature in regeneration.

Romans 3:10-11

In the previous chapter we noted the testimony of Romans 3:10-18 to the utter and universal depravity of man. We noted especially the words of verse 11, where we are told that there is *none* who understands and *none* who seeks for God. These words have to be explained by the Arminian who seeks to promote the theory of free-will. If there is "no God-seeker" (the literal rendering of the passage), the assertion that men seek after God and choose to believe and repent outside of the work of God's sovereign grace is refuted. Does Geisler offer an exegetical response? Let's see:

> The moderate Calvinist (and Arminian) has no problem with such a rendering of these verses. It is God who *initiates* salvation....We seek Him, then, only because He has first sought us. However, as a result of the convicting work of the Holy Spirit on the whole "world" (John 16:8) and "the goodness of God" (Rom. 2:4 NKJV), some people are moved to repent. Likewise, as a result of God's grace some seek Him.[43]

One cannot help but find somewhat humorous the conjunction of the "moderate Calvinist" and Arminian, since, in reality, they hold to the same fundamental beliefs, as we have seen proven repeatedly already. But no one can find the attempted response worthwhile. Yes, God initiates salvation: and that perfectly. God initiates the salvation of His elect. It seems the idea being promoted here is that God's prevenient grace moves some, but not all. We will see the error of this view as we move shortly to the discussion of God's unconditional election of a specific people in Christ.

Romans 8:7-8

The final passage we will examine is the strident claim by Paul that the person who is still in the flesh is *unable* to submit himself to the law of God and *cannot* please God. It is my position that this text is *completely* opposed to the central assertion that is made in *CBF* regarding the "freedom" of the fallen man. Dr. Geisler offers a single paragraph in response. Is the response based upon the text? Is it exegetical in content? Or philosophical and a-contextual? Here it is:

> It is true that we are sinners by nature, but that old nature does not make sin *necessary* any more than a new nature makes good acts necessary. The old nature only makes sin *inevitable*, not unavoidable. Since we are free, sin is *not* necessary. Again, as Augustine said, we are born with the propensity to sin, not the necessity to sin. If sin were necessary, then we would not be responsible for it…, which the Bible declares we are (Rom. 3:19). Furthermore, Paul makes it clear in this section of Romans that our enslavement to sin is our free choice. He wrote, "Don't you know that *when you offer yourselves to someone to obey* him as slaves, you are slaves to the one whom you obey—whether you are slaves to sin, which leads to death, or to obedience, which leads to righteousness?" (Rom. 6:16). We are born with a bent to sin, but we still have a choice whether we will be its slave.[44]

This is the kind of response provided to the vast majority of biblical argumentation in *CBF*: there is no exegesis of the text here. There are philosophical assertions, linguistic distinctions, and citations of foreign contexts, but the text is not touched. The point of the passage is that men cannot will to do what is *pleasing* to God. It seems Dr. Geisler believes in the ability to perform *neutral* actions: actions that are neither good nor bad. But that point aside, does any of this respond to what Paul actually says? In no way. Look again at the text:

"the mind set on the flesh is hostile toward God...."

It does not say "the mind set on the flesh is sometimes hostile, sometimes friendly, sometimes neutral, all depending on its own free choice." If there is constant hostility between the unregenerate human and the holy God (as there of necessity must be as long as the sin issue is unresolved, the very wrath of God *abides* upon the sinner, and that sinner remains in active *rebellion* against God) how can it be that the sinner can "choose" to do what is good and right in God's sight?

"for it does not subject itself to the law of God..."

This is a statement of fact untouched by *CBF* in its attempted response. There is nothing more pleasing to God than submission to His law: but the fleshly mind is in rebellion, not subjection, to God's law. And we note that such things as repentance and faith are surely a part of subjection to God's law: but Paul says the fleshly mind does *not* subject itself to that law.

"for it is not even able *to do so.*"

This is an absolutely crucial statement that is lost in *CBF*'s response. While Geisler takes as a presupposition "we are free," the text speaks of the *inability* of fallen man. The fleshly mind *lacks the ability to subject itself to the holy law of God.* The Greek is not ambiguous or difficult: οὐδὲ γὰρ δύναται is literally translated "for it is not even able," the NASB providing the assumed phrase *to do so.* The issue is not whether a person can choose to commit a heinous sin or a less heinous sin: everyone agrees that no man has been as bad as he *could* be. The issue is plainly stated by the text: is fallen man free to do what is pleasing to God outside of regeneration? The answer is an unequivocal "no." Yet Geisler's entire system is based upon the absolute necessity of affirming the opposite. But Paul nails the coffin closed on free willism:

"and those who are in the flesh cannot please God."

Paul does not say "those who are in the flesh at times do things that are displeasing to God, but at other times do things that are pleasing to Him." He does not teach that "men are free to believe in Christ at any time" for obviously, such an action is well-pleasing to God. How can a person in the flesh do such things as repent, believe, turn from sin, embrace holiness, etc., when they are still in the flesh? Unregenerate man lacks the ability to please God. Something must happen first: he has to be translated from the realm of the flesh to that of the spirit. He must be raised to spiritual life so that he can do what is pleasing to God: repent and believe in Christ.

CBF does make reference to a previous context, Romans 6:16, where Paul is speaking to regenerate men about the struggle that is theirs in this life, and how they must serve Christ in their bodies (rather than sin). But this is manifestly a different topic than that which Paul is addressing in Romans 8:7-8.

Notes

1 Robert Reymond in his *A New Systematic Theology of the Christian Faith* (Thomas Nelson, 1998) writes, "The Reformers of the sixteenth century...rejected the synergistic stance of Roman Catholic soteriology and returned to the earlier best insights of the later Augustine and to the inspired insights of Paul in his letters to the Romans and the Galatians" (p. 469).

2 *CBF*, p. 95.

3 Ibid., p. 22.

4 Ibid., p. 21.

5 *Institutes* I:XV-XVIII.

6 Francis Turretin, *Institutes of Elenctic Theology* (Presbyterian and Reformed, 1992), I:659-682.

7 See especially the discussion found in his *Systematic Theology*, Part II, Ch. IX

8 R.K. McGregor Wright, *No Place For Sovereignty* (InterVarsity Press, 1996), pp. 177-203.

9 Robert L. Reymond, *A New Systematic Theology of the Christian Faith* (Thomas Nelson, 1998), pp. 346-378, 453-458.

10 Specifically, 85, 199.

11 Ibid, p. 132.

12 Wright, pp. 40-41.

13 Wright, p. 46.

14 *CBF*, p. 29.

15 Ibid., p. 32.

16 Ibid., p. 33.

17 Ibid. p. 32.

18 Ibid., p. 116.

19 Ibid.

20 Indeed, the statement quoted above, aside from redefining total depravity, continues the misunderstanding of the Reformed belief, for Calvinists surely *do* believe that unsaved people *can* and *do* understand the truth of the Gospel, and they universally reject it outside of the divine act of regeneration. The difference between the Arminian and the Calvinist is that the Arminian can speak of the Spirit of God working in the heart *but failing to bring about salvation* while the Calvinist has no such concept. If the Spirit of God works in the heart of the elect individual to bring about spiritual life and faith, He will not fail in His work. As we will see later, Dr. Geisler *vehemently* denies that the Spirit of God can infallibly bring spiritual life (i.e., irresistible

grace), and since we have already seen that he asserts that God will save as many *as He can*, it follows without question that his is the Arminian, not the Calvinistic, viewpoint.

21 Ibid. p. 57.

22 Ibid., p. 34.

23 Donald Campbell, ed., *Walvoord: A Tribute* (Moody Press, 1982). p. 103.

24 One cannot help but notice this phrase for it seems to indicate clearly that Dr. Geisler separates himself from the "radical reformation" view espoused by Luther and Calvin. There is likewise a clear categorical error in such an assertion: Arminians may well share the common error of detracting from God's freedom and asserting creaturely autonomy with many previous religious movements, but that does not make everyone else an "Arminian." Semi-Pelagianism might be a better term to use for the view that mixes sovereign grace and human ability, ultimately making grace dependent upon man's will for its efficacious power (something Dr. Geisler plainly states as we have seen). But we can only again express amazement that Geisler would even desire to be called a "moderate Calvinist" when he separates himself so strongly from Calvin and Calvinism as a whole on such fundamental issues.

25 *CBF*, p. 53.

26 Provided in chapter 2 and taken from Geisler's article in the Walvoord tribute, pp. 102-103.

27 *CBF*, p. 56.

28 Ibid., p. 57.

29 Ibid., pp. 57-58.

30 Ibid., p. 58.

31 Ibid.

32 Ibid., p. 58.

33 Ibid.

34 Ibid., p. 47.

35 Ibid., pp. 122-123.

36 Ibid., p. 35.

37 Beyond this, John 8 teaches the same concept of man's inability in 8:43ff.

38 Should anyone be offended at the charge of eisegesis, it should be pointed out that Dr. Geisler often made this assertion (we believe wrongly) in *CBF*. For example, in footnote 15 on page 28 he writes, "It is painful to watch extreme Calvinists go through these exegetical contortions to make a text say what their preconceived theology mandates that it must say." It is the conviction of this writer, and

many others who have reviewed this work, that the "exegetical contortions" are found in the pages of *CBF*, not in the pages of the works of such fine expositors as Owen, Piper, Gerstner or Sproul.

39 Ibid., p. 60.
40 Ibid., pp. 60-61.
41 Ibid., p. 61.
42 Ibid., p. 62.
43 Ibid., p. 66.
44 Ibid., p. 65.

Chapter 5

Unconditional Election a Necessity

Some terms and phrases are self-definitional. They contain within themselves their own meaning. The theological phrase "unconditional election" would *seem* to indicate an election or choice made without conditions. And historically that is how the phrase has been understood. But *CBF* presents an interesting twist on the phrase. Dr. Geisler claims to believe in unconditional election "as held by moderate Calvinists." And what does this involve? "It is unconditional from the standpoint of the Giver, even though there is one condition for the receiver—faith."[1] What does this mean? Earlier in the work Geisler concludes a section "Avoiding Extreme Calvinism's View of Unconditional Election" by stating, "In short, we are chosen *but free*—which is directly contrary to the conclusion of the extreme Calvinists."[2] So whatever else he means, one thing is for certain: he does *not* mean what Reformed writers have meant down through the centuries. So what does he mean? Here's his conclusion:

> In summary, the error of extreme Calvinism regarding "unconditional election" is the failure to adhere to an election that is unconditional from the standpoint of the Giver (God), but has one condition for the receiver—faith. This, in turn, is based on the mistaken notion that

faith is a gift only to the elect, who have no choice in receiving it.[2]

Unconditional election, then, is unconditional only in that God gives salvation without conditions; it is *conditioned upon faith* on the part of the recipient, who, we have already seen, is strongly affirmed by Dr. Geisler to be *free* to believe as he or she wishes. Election then is conditioned upon human faith: God gives it freely to all who will believe. As Geisler said in another work:

> God wills the salvation of men only conditionally. There-fore, God's will to salvation does not violate human free choice; it utilizes it.[3]

We need to remember that *CBF* promotes a most unusual view of God's foreknowledge and man's freedom. In chapter two we laid out the position that leads Geisler to say, "there is no chronological or logical priority of election and foreknowl-edge." Which "comes first" is something he insists cannot (and should not) be answered, since they are "one" in God. We saw that this argument is based upon false premises and is not valid. We likewise saw that it does not work, for it becomes obvious that in Geisler's view man's free choice *does* become determinative. God's "determination" is passive while man's "free choice" is active. In attacking the Reformed position on unconditional election, Geisler reveals his position clearly:

> According to this view, God's predetermination is done *in spite of* His foreknowledge of human free acts. God operates with such unapproachable sovereignty that His choices are made with total disregard for the choices of mortal men.[4]

Remember, *CBF* is here *denying* that this is true. If it is *untrue* that God operates with "total disregard for the choices of mor-tal men," then it follows that it is *true* that He operates *in light of* the choices of mortal men. And this is exactly what is asserted in *CBF*:

> There is an important corollary to this view. If free choices were not considered at all when God made the list of the elect, then irresistible grace on the unwilling follows. That is, man would have no say in his own salvation.[5]

It follows then that Geisler operates on the basis of believing that man's free choices *were* "considered" when "God made the list of the elect." *CBF* is saying man *does* have a say in his own salvation, the work is synergistic, a matter of cooperation. Therefore, there can be no use of the term "unconditional election" in its consistent and historic meaning, for if the term means anything, it means that salvation is totally of God and not of man.

In all fairness it appears that Dr. Geisler lives on both sides of this issue, however, for in a footnote on page 117 he writes,

> This does not mean the sinner does something to become one of the elect. God alone does that on the basis of grace alone ….It means only that the elect must believe in Christ to receive this gift of salvation.

Are there a specific elect people, chosen distinctly from the non-elect, chosen without any reference to their own free choices? It will become painfully obvious as we examine *CBF*'s attempts to present biblical arguments against the Reformed position that the answer to this question is "no." Despite the complications and philosophical distinctions, when one boils it all down to the basic questions, Geisler holds to the Arminian view:

> Few teachings are more evident in the New Testament than that God loves all people, that Christ died for the sins of all human beings, and that God desires all persons to be saved.[6]

Just What Does Unconditional Election Mean?

Given the confusion introduced by Dr. Geisler's use of the phrase "unconditional election" to actually refer to an unconditional decision to offer salvation that is conditioned, with reference to the actual accomplishment of the salvation of any individual, upon the free choices of men, it is necessary to establish the historic meaning of the phrase before we can respond to CBF's unique viewpoint.

A modern language rendition of the London Baptist Confession of Faith (1689) says the following concerning election:

> God's decree is not based upon His foreknowledge that, under certain conditions, certain happenings will take place, but is independent of all such foreknowledge.

> By His decree, and for the manifestation of His glory, God has predestinated (or foreordained) certain men and angels to eternal life through Jesus Christ, thus revealing His grace. Others, whom He has left to perish in their sins, show the terror of His justice.

> The angels and men who are the subjects of God's predestination are clearly and irreversibly designated, and their number is unalterably fixed.

> Before the world was made, God's eternal, immutable purpose, which originated in the secret counsel and good pleasure of His will, moved Him to choose (or to elect), in Christ, certain of mankind to everlasting glory. Out of His mere free grace and love He predestined these chosen ones to life, although there was nothing in them to cause Him to choose them.

> Not only has God appointed the elect to glory in accordance with the eternal and free purpose of His will, but He has also foreordained the means by which His purpose will be effected. Since His elect are children of Adam

and therefore among those ruined by Adam's fall into sin, He willed that they should be redeemed by Christ, and effectually called to faith in Christ. Furthermore, by the working of His Spirit in due season they are justified, adopted, sanctified, and 'kept by His power through faith unto salvation'. None but the elect partake of any of these great benefits.[7]

The Westminster Confession of Faith reads very much the same. The same concepts will be found in many of the great confessions that came out of the Reformation. A few points that should be emphasized:

1   There is a positive, specific decree of God.
2   This decree of God involves specific actions in time, including, but not limited to, the salvation of a specific people.
3   This decree is antecedent to creation itself: not only is it made "before time," but it is made "independent" of all such foreknowledge God has of what will take place in time.[8]
4   The decree of God predestines certain *specific individuals* to eternal life and others it leaves to justice. This is an election *unto salvation* and not merely a choice to provide salvation *without any specificity as to the number or identity of the elect.*
5   This decree of election is *utterly unconditional.* It involves the election of *specific individuals* to eternal life and is based utterly, completely, and totally upon His "eternal, immutable purpose, which originated in the secret counsel and good pleasure of His will."
6   This election is not conditioned upon *anything* in the human, either foreseen faith, actions, dispositions, or desires. It is *without* conditions.

One will find this concept clearly laid out in the great works of systematic theology produced by Reformed writers. James P. Boyce, one of the founding professors of Southern Seminary, a leading light in the Southern Baptist Convention, put it this way in his work, *Abstract of Systematic Theology:*

> The latter theory [i.e., the Calvinistic theory, which Boyce defends and teaches] is that God (who and not man is the one who chooses or elects), of his own purpose (in accordance with his will, and not from any obligation to man, nor because of any will of man), has from Eternity (the period of God's action, not in time in which man acts), determined to save (not has actually saved, but simply determined so to do), [and to save (not confer gospel or church privileges upon),] a definite number of mankind (not the whole race, nor indefinitely merely some of them, nor indefinitely a certain proportionate part; but a definite number), as individuals (not the whole or a part of the race, nor of a nation, nor of a church, or of a class, as of believers or the pious; but individuals), not for or because of any merit or work of theirs, nor of any value to him of them (not for their good works, nor their holiness, nor excellence, nor their faith, not their spiritual sanctification, although the choice is to a salvation attained through faith and sanctification; nor their value to him, though their salvation tends greatly to the manifested glory of his grace); but of his own good pleasure (simply because he was pleased so to choose).
>   This theory, therefore, teaches that election is:
>   1 An act of God, and not the result of the choice of the elect.
>   2 That this choice is one of individuals, and not of classes.
>   3 That it was made without respect to the action of the persons elected.
>   4 By the good pleasure of God.
>   5 According to an eternal purpose.
>   6 That it is an election to salvation and not to outward privileges.[9]

W.J. Seaton defines unconditional election by citing the same

Baptist Confession given above, and then commenting,

> The doctrine of unconditional election follows naturally from the doctrine of total depravity. If man is, indeed, dead and held captive, and blind, etc., then the remedy for all these conditions must lie outside man himself [that is, with God]. We asked in the last chapter: 'Can the dead raise themselves?' and the answer must inevitably be: 'Of course not.' If, however, some men and women *are* raised out of their spiritual death — 'born again' as John's Gospel puts it — and since they are unable to perform this work themselves, then we must conclude that it was God who raised them. On the other hand, as many men and women are not "made alive', we must likewise conclude that that is because God has *not* raised them. If man is unable to save himself on account of the Fall in Adam being a *total* fall, and if God alone can save, and if *all* are not saved, then the conclusion must be that God has not chosen to save all.[10]

Duane Edward Spencer spoke of unconditional election and put it this way:

> As we think of this point we will remember that the Arminian view is that *foreknowledge* is based upon the positive act of man's will as the *condition* or cause that moved God to elect him to salvation. All of the great confessions, in agreement with the Protestant Reformers, declare that election is "unconditional." In other words, the *foreknowledge* of God is based upon His decree, plan, or purpose which expresses His will, and not upon some foreseen act of *positive volition* on the part of man.[11]

A little later he adds, upon citing Romans 9:11,

> Here the apostle declares that the ground of election is God Himself, which is to say in His will and purpose,

and not in an act of faith or some *"condition"* (as Arminians would say) in the children for good or evil. Election is *unconditional*. Man can do nothing to merit it.[12]

Lorraine Boettner touched upon this subject as well:

> The Reformed Faith has held to the existence of an eternal, divine decree which, antecedently to any difference or desert in men themselves separates the human race into two portions and ordains one to everlasting life and the other to everlasting death. So far as this decree relates to men it designates the counsel of God concerning those who had a supremely favorable chance in Adam to earn salvation, but who lost that chance. As a result of the fall they are guilty and corrupted; their motives are wrong and they cannot work out their own salvation. They have forfeited all claim upon God's mercy, and might justly have been left to suffer the penalty of their disobedience as all of the fallen angels were left. But instead the elect members of this race are rescued from this state of guilt and sin and are brought into a state of blessedness and holiness. The non-elect are simply left in their previous state of ruin, and are condemned for their sins. They suffer no unmerited punishment, for God is dealing with them not merely as men but as sinners.[13]

As did Edwin Palmer:

> But, amazing as it may seem, divine election is always an unconditional election. God never bases His choice on what man thinks, says, does, or is. We do not know what God bases His choice on, but it is not on anything that is in man. He does not see something good in a particular man, something that he does that makes God decide to choose him.[14]

C. Samuel Storms summarized the meaning of unconditional election in the same fashion:

It is when the basis or grounds for God's choice is discussed that the Arminian parts company from the Calvinist. As we saw in the previous chapter, the Arminian insists that God elects men and women on the basis of what he, from eternity past, knew that they, in present time, will do when confronted with the gospel. Thus the basis or ground for being chosen *by* God is one's freewill choice *of* God. God's election of us is, in effect, no more than a divine echo of our election of him.

The Calvinist, on the other hand, insists that election is not grounded or based upon any act of man, for good or ill. Election "does not depend on the man who wills or the man who runs, but on *God* who has mercy (Rom. 9:16, italics added). That God should set his electing love upon any individual is not in any way dependent upon that person's will (Rom. 9:16), works (2 Tim. 1:9; Rom. 9:11), holiness (Eph. 1:4), or obedience (1 Peter 1:1-2). Rather, election finds its sole and all-sufficient cause in the sovereign good pleasure and grace of God (Eph. 1:9; Rom. 9:11; 11:5; Matt. 11:25-26; 2 Tim. 1:9). Were election to be based upon what God foreknows that each individual will do with the gospel it would be an empty and altogether futile act. For what does God foresee in us, apart from his grace? He sees only corruption, ill will, and a pervasive depravity of heart and soul that serves only to evoke his displeasure and wrath.

What this means is that Calvinism is *monergistic* when it comes to the doctrine of salvation. This simply means that when a person is saved it is due wholly to the working of one source of power, God. Arminianism is by necessity *synergistic*, in that it conceives of salvation as the joint or mutual effort of both God and man.[15]

The writings of Francis Turretin remain to this day a monument to depth of thought and exhaustiveness of consideration. He represents the period of Protestant orthodoxy that produced the Westminster Confession of Faith and other like documents. Note well his words:

The Arminians (who bring popery and Pelagianism in by the back door) have struck against the same rock. For although they endeavor with great labor to prove that they do not make faith the cause of election (in order to shun the odium of semi-Pelagianism deservedly charged upon them), still they do not deny that it is the cause *sine qua non* or the prerequisite condition necessary in those to be elected. Yea, not obscurely can we gather that they proceed further and attribute a certain causality to faith, so that God is moved by its foresight to choose this rather than that one. Otherwise why would they say so often that election is founded on the foresight of faith unless they meant that the consideration of faith influenced the election of one before another?... Moreover, they make a twofold decree of election: the first general, of saving believers; the second special, of saving individuals by name whom God foresaw would believe. They hold that no other cause of the first can be given than the pure will of God, but as to the second (although it also is founded upon the divine will), they hold it supposes the consideration and regard of faith, so that God is moved by it to elect one rather than another....This, therefore, is the opinion of our churches—that election to glory as well as to grace is entirely gratuitous. Therefore no cause, or condition, or reason existed in man, upon the consideration of which God chose this rather than another one. Rather election depended upon his sole good pleasure (*eudokia*) by which, as he selected from the corrupt mass a certain number of men neither more worthy nor better than others to whom he would destine salvation, so in like manner he decreed to give them faith as the means necessary to obtain salvation.[16]

Finally, John Gill laid it out plainly:

This is to be understood of the choice of certain persons by God, from all eternity, to grace and glory; it is an act by which men are chosen of God's good will and pleasure, before the world was, to holiness and happiness, to salvation by Christ, to partake of His glory, and to enjoy eternal life, as the free gift of God through him, Eph. i. 4, 2 Thess. ii. 13, Acts xiii. 38....Nor is faith the moving cause of election; the one is in time, the other in eternity; whilst men are in a state of unregeneracy, they are in a state of unbelief; they are, as without hope in God, so without faith in Christ; and when they have it, they have it not of themselves, of their own power and free-will; but they have it as the gift of God, and the operation of his Spirit, flowing purely from his grace; and therefore cannot be the cause of electing grace.[17]

What do all of these citations have in common? *They all define unconditional election as being without conditions!* Such is hardly surprising except that we are here dealing with Dr. Geisler's insistence that unconditional election means that the choice to save *someone* is unconditional whereas it is *very* conditional on the part of the "recipient" of salvation (it is conditioned upon the free choice of faith). To call CBF's position "moderate Calvinism" is again to completely redefine the issue. Indeed, let us allow Calvin to speak plainly to the topic:

We shall never be clearly persuaded, as we ought to be, that our salvation flows from the wellspring of God's free mercy until we come to know his eternal election, which illumines God's grace by this contrast: that he does not indiscriminately adopt all into the hope of salvation but gives to some what he denies to others (*Institutes* III:21:1).

It can safely be said that CBF would *never* endorse such a statement.

As Scripture, then, clearly shows, we say that God once established by his eternal and unchangeable plan those whom he long before determined once for all to receive into salvation, and those whom, on the other hand, he would devote to destruction. We assert that, with respect to the elect, this plan was founded upon his freely given mercy, without regard to human worth; but by his just and irreprehensible but incomprehensible judgment he has barred the door of life to those whom he has given over to damnation. Now among the elect we regard the call as a testimony of election. Then we hold justification another sign of its manifestation, until they come into the glory in which the fulfillment of that election lies. But as the Lord seals his elect by call and justification, so, by shutting off the reprobate from knowledge of his name or from the sanctification of his Spirit, he, as it were, reveals by these marks what sort of judgment awaits them (*Institutes* III:21:7).

The Reformed position on election is, first and foremost, a biblical one. Yes, it flows from the sovereignty of God and the deadness of man in sin; however, it is just as clearly and inarguably stated in Scripture. So we turn to the biblical text and *CBF*'s attempts to respond to those passages that teach this divine truth.

Notes

1   *Chosen But Free*, pp. 116-117.
2   Ibid., p. 73.
3   Norman Geisler, *Creating God in the Image of Man?* (Bethany House Publishers, 1997), p. 43.
4   *Chosen But Free*, pp. 46-47.
5   Ibid., p. 47
6   Ibid., p. 77.
7   A *Faith to Confess: The Baptist Confession of Faith of 1689, Rewritten in Modern English* (Carey Publications, Ltd., 1986), 3:2-6.
8   Logically by necessity when one considers the issue: if God's decree determines what takes place in time it cannot be based upon that which it creates by its very existence. This is why Dr. Geisler has to create a new category of theology with his "knowingly predetermining" viewpoint: if there is a positive decree that conditions time itself then the relationship between that decree and the actions of men is beyond dispute. By saying that we cannot determine the logical or temporal relationship between the free actions of man and the decree of God, and by making God's "determination" a passive, perfect knowledge rather than an active, creating decree, Geisler seeks to avoid the historic confession of the necessity of predestination and election.
9   James P. Boyce, *Abstract of Systematic Theology* (1887), pp. 347-348.
10 W.J. Seaton, *The Five Points of Calvinism* (The Banner of Truth Trust, 1970), pp. 11-12.
11 Duane Edward Spencer, *TULIP: The Five Points of Calvinism in the Light of Scripture* (Baker Book House, 1979), pp. 29-30.
12 Ibid., p. 30.
13 Lorraine Boettner, *The Reformed Doctrine of Predestination* (Presbyterian and Reformed, 1932), pp. 83-84.
14 Edwin Palmer, *The Five Points of Calvinism* (Baker Book House, 1986), p. 26.
15 C. Samuel Storms, *Chosen for Life: An Introductory Guide to the Doctrine of Divine Election* (Baker Book House, 1987), pp. 29-30.
16 Francis Turretin, *Institutes of Elenctic Theology* (Presbyterian and Reformed, 1992), I:356-357.
17 John Gill, *A Body of Doctrinal and Practical Divinity* (The Baptist Standard Bearer, 1989), pp. 180, 187.

Chapter 6

CBF's "Big Three" Verses

Throughout his work, Dr. Geisler quotes a set of three verses as evidence that God *wants* to save all men, but is unable to do so outside of their freely willing it to be so. This set of verses appear repeatedly throughout the text of the work. They are:

> Matthew 23:37, "Jerusalem, Jerusalem, who kills the prophets and stones those who are sent to her! How often I wanted to gather your children together, the way a hen gathers her chicks under her wings, and you were unwilling" (cited eleven times).

> 1 Timothy 2:4, "who desires all men to be saved and to come to the knowledge of the truth" (cited ten times).

> 2 Peter 3:9, "The Lord is not slow about His promise, as some count slowness, but is patient toward you, not wishing for any to perish but for all to come to repentance" (cited twenty times).

These passages are often cited together, or in a pair, in the work.[1] When one excludes the sections of the book that do not deal with biblical argumentation, *one of these verses appears on average every three to four pages.* CBF assumes a particular meaning for each passage and then utilizes that interpretation as the *primary* refutation of any and all passages that would disagree with the Arminian view. Over and over again biblical passages will receive no exegesis outside of, "Well, it can't mean this, because we know 2 Peter 3:9 says...." For example, in responding to the clear teaching of John 6:65, *CBF* uses two of these three verses as proof-texts:

> Moderate Calvinists and Arminians agree with this. As Sproul himself admits, the *real* question is, "Does God give the ability to come to Jesus to all men?" The answer is that there is nothing here or anywhere else to say God limits His willingness to provide this ability to only some. Indeed, the Bible is clear that He is patient, "not wanting anyone to perish, but everyone to come to repentance" (2 Peter 3:9), and that He "wants all men to be saved and to come to a knowledge of the truth" (1 Tim. 2:4; see also Ezek. 18:32).[2]

But are the interpretations CBF *assumes* valid? If we find that the Reformed view can provide a more consistent interpretation of these passages, the *entirety* of the presentation in *CBF* is undermined, for if these passages do not teach what the book assumes, its primary foundation is washed away.

Matthew 23:37

CBF offers no in-depth exegesis of this passage. Instead, we are given two sentences that summarize Geisler's interpretation of it:

> Also, Matthew 23:37 affirms emphatically that Jesus desired to bring the Jews who rejected Him into the fold but could not because they would not. He cried, "O Jerusalem, Jerusalem, you who kill the prophets and stone those sent to you, how often I have longed to gather your children together, as a hen gathers her chicks under her

wings, *but you were not willing.*" God's grace is not irresistible on those who are unwilling.[3]

We first note that "irresistible grace" is a reference to God's
sovereign regeneration of His elect: any other use of the phrase
is in error. Hence, it would seem to be that Dr. Geisler is promoting the following ideas regarding this text: 1) that Jesus
wanted to save the Jews to whom (or about whom) He was
speaking in this passage; 2) That though this was Christ's desire He *could not* fulfill His desire; 3) Christ could not bring
these Jews into the fold because they "would not." The conclusion then is, God's grace is dependent upon the will of man.
If a man is willing, God's grace will prevail. But grace cannot
change the will of man.

Of course, these are assertions that are not given with any
interpretational foundation. No exegesis is offered, just conclusions. How Dr. Geisler arrived at these conclusions, we are
not told. Later we are informed that it is the "plain meaning"
of the text, and are asked rhetorically, "What could be more
clear: God wanted all of them, even the unrepentant, to be
saved."[4]

This verse is then used in conjunction with 1 Timothy 2:4
and 2 Peter 3:9 as evidence that it is God's *desire* to save every
single man, woman and child on earth. But is that what this
passage is teaching? Let's provide an exegetical interpretation
of the passage and compare it with the presentation in *CBF.*

The first fact to ascertain in examining any passage of Scripture is its *context.* This passage comes in the midst of the proclamation of judgment upon the leaders of the Jews. Matthew
23 contains the strongest denunciations of the scribes and
Pharisees in all of the Gospels.

Who, then, is "Jerusalem"? It is assumed by Arminian writers that "Jerusalem" represents individual Jews who are, therefore, capable of resisting the work and will of Christ. But upon
what warrant do we leap from "Jerusalem" to "individual Jews"?
The context would not lead us to conclude that this is to be

taken in a universal sense. Jesus is condemning the Jewish leaders, and it is to them that He refers here. This is clearly seen in that:

1 It is to the leaders that God sent prophets;
2 It was the Jewish leaders who killed the prophets and those sent to them;
3 Jesus speaks of "your children," differentiating those to whom He is speaking from those that the Lord desired to gather together.
4 The context refers to the Jewish leaders, scribes and Pharisees.

A vitally important point to make here is that the ones the Lord desired to gather are *not* the ones who "were not willing"! Jesus speaks to the leaders *about* their children that they, the leaders, would not allow Him to "gather." Jesus was not seeking to gather the leaders, but their children. This one consideration alone renders the passage useless for the Arminian seeking to establish freewillism. The "children" of the leaders would be Jews who were *hindered* by the Jewish leaders from hearing Christ. The "you would not" then is referring to the same men indicated by the context: the Jewish leaders who "were unwilling" to allow those under their authority to hear the proclamation of the Christ. This verse, then, is speaking to the same issues raised earlier in Matthew 23:13:

> But woe to you, scribes and Pharisees, hypocrites, because you shut off the kingdom of heaven from people; for you do not enter in yourselves, nor do you allow those who are entering to go in.

John Gill added this insight:

> That the persons whom Christ would have gathered are not represented as being *unwilling* to be gathered; but their rulers were not willing that they should. The oppo-

sition and resistance to the will of Christ, were not made by the people, but by their governors. The common people seemed inclined to attend the ministry of Christ, as appears from the vast crowds which, at different times and places, followed him; but the chief priests and rulers did all they could to hinder the collection of them to him; and their belief in him as the Messiah, by traducing his character, miracles, and doctrines, and by passing an act that whosoever confessed him should be put out of the synagogue; so that the obvious meaning of the text is the same with that of verse 13...and consequently is no proof of men's resisting the operations of the Spirit and grace of God, but of obstructions and discouragements thrown in the way of attendance on the external ministry of the word.[5]

So we can now plainly see that *CBF* has absolutely no basis for its assertion that it is the "plain meaning" of the text that God wanted "all of them, even the unrepentant, to be saved." One of the three primary passages used in *CBF* is seen, then, to have no connection with the application made of it over and over again in the text. We turn now to the second.

1 Timothy 2:4

The key to this passage, again, is the context:

First of all, then, I urge that entreaties *and* prayers, petitions *and* thanksgivings, be made on behalf of all men, for kings and all who are in authority, so that we may lead a tranquil and quiet life in all godliness and dignity. This is good and acceptable in the sight of God our Savior, who desires all men to be saved and to come to the knowledge of the truth. For there is one God, *and* one mediator also between God and men, *the* man Christ Jesus, who gave Himself as a ransom for all, the testimony *given* at the proper time.

The first appearance of the phrase "all men" comes at the end of verse 1, and its meaning is unambiguous. Paul is not instructing Timothy to initiate never-ending prayer meetings where the Ephesian phone book would be opened and every single person listed therein would become the object of prayer. The very next phrase of the sentence explains Paul's meaning: "for kings and all who are in authority." Why would Paul have to give such instructions?

We must remember that the early Christians were a persecuted people, and normally the persecution came from those in positions of power and authority. It is easy to understand why there would have to be apostolic commandments given to pray for the very ones who were using their power and authority to *persecute* these Christians.

Who are kings and all who are in authority? They are kinds of men, classes of men. Paul often spoke of "all men" in this fashion. For example, in Titus chapter 2, when Paul speaks of the grace of God which brings salvation appearing to "all men" (Titus 2:11), he clearly means all *kinds* of men, for the context, both before and after, speaks of *kinds* of men. In the previous verses Paul addresses such groups as older men (v. 2), older women (v. 3), younger women (v. 4), young men (v. 6), bondslaves (v. 9-10), and rulers and authorities (3:1). No one would suggest that in fact Paul is speaking of every single older man, older woman, etc.; he speaks of kinds of people within a particular group, that being the fellowship of the Church. Likewise, "rulers" and "authorities" are obviously generic classifications that everyone would understand needs to be applied to specific locations in specific times.

The same kind of usage (all *kinds* of men being in view) is found elsewhere in Paul, such as Titus 3:2:

> to malign no one, to be peaceable, gentle, showing every consideration for all men.

This should be connected to the fact that in the very commissioning of Paul, this phrase is used in a way that cannot be made universal in scope:

> For you will be a witness for Him to all men of what you have seen and heard (Acts 22:15).

Of course, Paul would not think that these words meant that he would witness of Christ to every single individual human being on the planet. Instead, he would have surely understood this to mean all *kinds* and *races* of men. Likewise, the allegation against Paul was that he preached "to all men everywhere" against the Jews and the Law and the Temple (Acts 21:28). Paul speaks of *kinds* of people in other places as well:

> A renewal in which there is no distinction between Greek and Jew, circumcised and uncircumcised, barbarian, Scythian, slave and freeman, but Christ is all, and in all (Colossians 3:11).

> There is neither Jew nor Greek, there is neither slave nor free man, there is neither male nor female; for you are all one in Christ Jesus (Galatians 3:28).

So it is perfectly consistent with the immediate and broader context of Paul's writings to recognize this use of "all men" in a generic fashion.

Returning to 1 Timothy 2, Paul then states that such prayers for all kinds of men is good and acceptable "in the sight of God our Savior, who desires all men to be saved and to come to the knowledge of the truth." If we are consistent with the preceding context we will see "all men" here in the same manner as "all men" of the preceding verses: all kinds of men, whether rulers or kings (yes, God even saves people who used to persecute Christians, a fact Paul knew all too well). But there is much more reason to understand Paul's statement in this way.

Almost invariably, proponents of Arminianism isolate this

passage from the two verses that follow. This must happen of necessity for the questions that can be asked of the non-Reformed position based upon verses 5 and 6 are weighty indeed. Verse 5 begins with the word "for," indicating the connection between the statement made in 3-4 and the explanation in 5-6. Why should Christians pray that all men, including kings and rulers, be saved and come to a knowledge of the truth? Because there is only one way of salvation, and without a knowledge of that truth, no man can be saved. Paul says, "there is one God, and one mediator between God and men, the man Christ Jesus, who gave Himself a ransom for all." This immediately takes us into the meat of the discussion of the atonement, but for now just a few points should be made.

First, *if* one takes "all men" in verse 4 to mean "all men individually," does it not follow that Christ of necessity must be mediator for *all men* as well? If one says, "Yes, Christ mediates for every single human being," does it not follow that Christ *fails* as mediator every time a person negates His work by their all-powerful act of free will? One could hope that no biblical scholar would ever promote such an idea, for anyone familiar with the relationship between atonement, mediation and intercession in the book of Hebrews knows well that to make such an assertion puts the entire argument of Hebrews 7-10 on its head. For the moment, we simply point out that it is far more consistent with biblical theology to recognize that Christ mediates in behalf of the elect and perfectly saves them than it is to assert that Christ mediates for all (but fails to save all).

The second point is closely related to the first: the ransom that Christ gives in His self-sacrifice is either a *saving* ransom or a *non-saving* one. If it is actual and really made in behalf of all men, then inevitably all men would be saved. But we again see that it is far more consistent to recognize that the same meaning for "all men" and "all" flows through the entire passage, and when we look at the inarguably clear statements of Scripture regarding the actual *intention* and *result* of Christ's cross-work, we will see that there is no other consistent means of interpreting these words in 1 Timothy.

It is tremendously disappointing, then, to turn to the pages of *CBF* and examine the assertions made about this passage. Dr. Geisler is fully aware of the Reformed exegesis of both 1 Timothy 2:4 and 2 Peter 3:9 (seen below). It would be incumbent then upon him to provide as meaningful and thorough a discussion of the passage as has been provided by Reformed writers in the past. Instead, we find him providing responses based upon types of argumentation that are simply below a scholar of his experience.

The first form of argumentation is found in the repetition of the phrase "the plain meaning." Rather than providing contextual, grammatical, exegetical responses to the arguments set forth above, *CBF* chooses to simply mock the Reformed position and quote Charles Spurgeon (who did not take the Reformed view of the passage). We are told,

> From the time of the later Augustine this text has been manhandled by extreme Calvinists.[6]

This is Geisler's way of admitting that Augustine held the same view as we have presented above. But to accuse someone of "manhandling" a text requires more than brute assertion. And what evidence is given? A quotation of a sermon by Spurgeon. No response is provided to the contextual arguments, the parallel uses elsewhere, the consistency of the passage. Even Spurgeon's argumentation is uncharacteristically shallow.

Some attempt is made to deal with 1 Timothy 2:6 and its reference to a ransom for "all men." Geisler writes,

> Of this and like passages John Owen offers the dubious view that "all" does not mean "all" here. His tactic is to divert the issue to other passages where "all" does not mean the whole human race.[7]

When Dr. Geisler refers to other passages that are not at all related to the context, does he see this as a "tactic" in his own writing? Owen was establishing the fact that "all" is often used in senses that are *not* universalistic, and that in fact, it is the Arminian who must provide a solid ground upon which to argue that it should be taken that way in any given context. Geisler is the one diverting the weight of Owen's exegesis when he writes, "But here the category and context is the whole human race, for the use of 'all' as an object of God's love and redemption is used generically, not geographically." To which we simply respond, "Why do you say this?" This is an unfounded assertion, not an argument of fact. If *CBF* were to attempt to offer *some* kind of meaningful response to the extensive argumentation found in Owen's work at this point (the single chapter to which Geisler refers in Owen's book comprises thirteen pages of small type containing numerous references to the original languages) we might have some basis upon which to accept these assertions. But we are left with none. Instead, we read the following:

> First, he could have used the word "some," if he had chosen to do so, but he did not. Second, his reference to "men" in verse 5 is clearly generic—meaning all men, since it is used as the other pole from God that the Mediator, Christ, brings together. But generic usages of "all" in a redemptive context are usually, if not always, of the entire human race. Third, the desire for "all men" to be saved is parallel with that same desire expressed in other passages (2 Peter 3:9). Finally, the Bible tells us elsewhere that what hinders His desire from being fulfilled is not the universal scope of His love (John 3:16) but the willing rejection of some creatures—*"you were not willing"* (Matt. 23:37).[8]

In reply: first, the argument "he could have used such and such a term" is the weakest that can be offered. Jehovah's Witnesses often say "John could have said 'The Word *eternally* existed in the beginning' if that is what he wanted to communicate." The issue is not what a writer *might* have written, but, what does it mean *in the context as written*? Second, we have already seen that the consistent meaning of "all men" is "all *kinds* of men" from the context. We are given no citations, quotations, or references to substantiate the assertion that "generic usages of 'all' in a redemptive context are usually, if not always, of the entire human race." Third, as we will see immediately below, 2 Peter 3:9 is misused by Dr. Geisler with regularity. And finally, as we saw above, Matthew 23:37 does not support CBF's use of it here (or anywhere else). We are again left with the assertion that God's grace, God's purpose, and God's love is set at naught by the almighty will of the fallen creature.

2 Peter 3:9

This is surely the most popular passage cited (almost never with any reference to the context) to "prove" that God could not possibly desire to save a *specific* people but instead desires to save *every single individual person*, thereby denying election and predestination. The text seems inarguably clear. But it is always good to see a text in its own context:

> Know this first of all, that in the last days mockers will come with *their* mocking, following after their own lusts, and saying, "Where is the promise of His coming? For *ever* since the fathers fell asleep, all continues just as it was from the beginning of creation." For when they maintain this, it escapes their notice that by the word of God *the* heavens existed long ago and *the* earth was formed out of water and by water, through which the world at that time was destroyed, being flooded with water. But by His word the present heavens and earth are being reserved for fire, kept for the day of judgment and destruction of ungodly men. But do not let this one *fact* escape your notice, beloved, that with the Lord one day is like a thousand years, and a thousand years like one day. The Lord is not slow about His promise, as some count slowness, but is patient toward you, not wishing for any to perish but for all to come to repentance. But

the day of the Lord will come like a thief, in which the heavens will pass away with a roar and the elements will be destroyed with intense heat, and the earth and its works will be burned up. Since all these things are to be destroyed in this way, what sort of people ought you to be in holy conduct and godliness, looking for and hastening the coming of the day of God, because of which the heavens will be destroyed by burning, and the elements will melt with intense heat! But according to His promise we are looking for new heavens and a new earth, in which righteousness dwells.

Immediately one sees that unlike such passages as Ephesians 1, Romans 8-9, or John 6, this passage is not speaking about salvation as its topic. The reference to "coming to repentance" in 3:9 is made in passing. The topic is the coming of Christ. In the last days mockers will question the validity of His promise. Peter is explaining the reason why the coming of Christ has been delayed as long as it has. The day of the Lord, he says, will come like a thief, and it will come at God's own time.

But the next thing that stands out upon the reading of the passage is the clear identification of the audience to which Peter is speaking. When speaking of the mockers he refers to them in the third person, as "them." But everywhere else he speaks directly to his audience as the "beloved" and "you." He speaks of how his audience should behave "in holy conduct and godliness," and says that they look for the day of the Lord. He includes himself in this group in verse 13, where "we are looking for a new heavens and a new earth." This is vitally important, for the assumption made by the Arminian is that when verse 9 says the Lord is "patient toward you" that this "you" refers to *everyone*. Likewise, then, when it says "not wishing for *any* to perish" but "*all* to come to repentance," it is *assumed* that the "any" and "all" refers to *anyone at all of the human race*. Yet, the context indicates that the audience is quite specific. In any other passage of Scripture the interpreter would realize that we must decide who the "you" refers to and use this to limit the "any" and "all" of verse 9. For some reason, that simple and fundamental necessity is overlooked when this passage is cited.

2 Peter 1:1-3 tells us the specific identity of the audience to which Peter is writing:

> Simon Peter, a bond-servant and apostle of Jesus Christ, to those who have received a faith of the same kind as ours, by the righteousness of our God and Savior, Jesus Christ: Grace and peace be multiplied to you in the knowledge of God and of Jesus our Lord; seeing that His divine power has granted to us everything pertaining to life and godliness, through the true knowledge of Him who called us by His own glory and excellence.

Peter writes to a specific group, not to all of mankind. "To those who have received a faith of the same kind as ours." This not only refers to faith as a gift, as we will see in a later chapter, but it surely limits the context to the saved, for they have received this faith "by the righteousness of *our* God and Savior, Jesus Christ" (emphasis added). There is nothing in chapter three that indicates a change in audience, and much to tell us the audience remains exactly the same.

Since this is so, it becomes quite clear that the Arminian is badly misusing this passage by ignoring what Peter is really saying. The patience of the Lord is displayed toward His elect people (the "you" of verse 9). Therefore, the "not wishing any to perish" must be limited to the same group already in view: the elect. In the same way, the "all to come to repentance" must be the very same group. In essence Peter is saying the coming of the Lord has been delayed so that all the elect of God can be gathered in. Any modern Christian lives and knows Christ solely because God's purpose has been to gather in His elect down through the ages to this present day. There is no reason to expand the context of the passage into a universal proclamation of a desire on God's part that every single person come to repentance. Instead, it is clearly His plan and His will that *all the elect* come to repentance, and they most assuredly will do so.

Dr. Geisler is well aware of this interpretation. But he uses the same kinds of erroneous forms of argumentation in response to this exegesis of the text so as to avoid its force that we saw with reference to 1 Timothy 2:4. Again the assertion is made that *CBF*'s interpretation is the "plain meaning" of the text. He writes,

> And contrary to the unreasonable view of the extreme Calvinists, this does not mean "all classes of men," namely, the elect from all nations. Words have limits to their meaning by context. And when "any," "all men," and the "whole world" (1 John 2:2) are taken to mean only "some" (unless used as figures of speech), then language has lost its meaning.[9]

We are not told how it is "unreasonable" to recognize the contextual clues we noted above. Words do have limits to their meaning by context, and we have demonstrated that the context *clearly* tells us who the "you" and "any" and "all" of 2 Peter 3:9 is.

But most disturbing is the response offered by Geisler to the exegesis we offered above. Here are his words:

> Others offer an even less plausible suggestion: that "God does not will that any of us (the elect) perish." As a firm believer in inerrancy, R.C. Sproul is aware of how dangerous it is to change the Word of God. God the Holy Spirit was surely capable of using the word "some" instead of "all." But He did not. Furthermore, the "any" and "all" are called to repent. Also, the "all" who need to repent cannot mean the "beloved," (vv. 1, 8), since they were already saved and in no need of repenting. In addition, this would mean that God is not calling on the non-elect to repent, which is clearly opposed to other

> Scriptures where "he commands *all people everywhere* to repent" (Acts 17:30). "All people everywhere" does not mean "some people everywhere" or "some people somewhere." The text speaks for itself.[10]

Amazingly, the argument begins with the accusation that recognizing the use of "all" in the sense of "all kinds" is an implicit denial of inerrancy and runs the danger of changing the Word of God! Such an accusation is simply without merit. Saying, "Well, God could have said 'some' if that is what he meant" is a tremendously weak argument, normally reserved for use when no exegetical argument can be presented. The fact is that *CBF* does not even attempt to offer a response to the arguments drawn from the text itself. There is no discussion of the grammar, pronouns, or anything else relevant to the passage, in *CBF*. Just assertions. Peter limited his use of "all" and "any" to a specific audience, "you." This is a fact of the text utterly ignored by *CBF*.

Next, it is asserted that the "any" and "all" are "called to repent." Actually, the text says that God wills (βουλόμενός) for the "all" to come to repentance, and of course, this is quite true. And since God *grants* repentance (2 Tim. 2:24-25), God's purpose *will* be accomplished, and *is* accomplished in the elect. They all, as a group, *do* repent. Why anyone would wish to say "It is God's will that every single individual repent, but, alas, His will is constantly thwarted and refuted by the will of the creature" is hard to say.[11] *CBF* misses the point when it asserts that this cannot be the "beloved" because they have already repented. The point of the passage is that God will bring the elect to repentance throughout the time period prior to the parousia, the coming of Christ. At the point of Peter's writing, the repentance of every single individual reading this book was yet future.

Next Dr. Geisler confuses the prescriptive will of God found in His law, which commands all men everywhere to repent, with the gift of repentance given to the elect in regeneration. It does not follow that if it is God's will to bring the elect to repentance that the law does not command repentance of *everyone*. This is a common error in Arminian argumentation.

Dr. Geisler is right about one thing: the text speaks for itself. But when we actually *exegete* the text, what it says is the opposite of what the Arminian *assumes* it says.

The person inclined to accept the thesis of *CBF* should consider this issue well: it is an understatement to say that Dr. Geisler relies upon Matthew 23:37, 1 Timothy 2:4, and 2 Peter 3:9 as his *key* Scriptural passages. If, in fact, one can present an interpretation of *each* that is *at least* as valid, if not much more so, than his own, does it not follow that the vast majority of the biblical response provided in *CBF* becomes suspect?

Notes

1   For example, pp. 79, 95, 199-200, 233.
2   *Chosen But Free*, p. 60.
3   Ibid., p. 95.
4   Ibid., p. 200.
5   John Gill, *The Cause of God and Truth* (The Baptist Standard Bearer, 1992), p. 29.
6   *Chosen But Free*, p. 201.
7   Ibid., p. 202.
8   Ibid., pp. 202-203.
9   Ibid., p. 199.
10 Ibid., pp. 199-200.
11 We do not here refer to the revealed will of God found in His law which commands all men everywhere to repent: we speak of His saving will that all the elect come to repentance, and His ability to perform that will.

Chapter 7

Jesus Teaches "Extreme Calvinism"

If believing that man is "so dead"[1] in sin that he is incapable of coming to Christ on his own is "extreme Calvinism," then the Lord Jesus beat Calvin to the punch by 1500 years with His preaching in the synagogue in Capernaum recorded in John 6. Here we have the Lord teaching almost everything Norman Geisler identifies as "extreme Calvinism." Jesus teaches that God is sovereign and acts independently of the "free choices" of men. He likewise teaches that man is incapable of saving faith outside of the enablement of the Father. He then limits this drawing to the same individuals given by the Father to the Son. He then teaches irresistible grace *on the elect* (not on the "willing") when He affirms that *all* those who are given to Him *will* come to Him. John 6:37-45 is the clearest exposition of what *CBF* calls "extreme Calvinism" in the Bible. And yet, *CBF* ignores the vast majority of the passage, offers one response to verse 44 that is simply incomprehensible, and offers one sentence in response to verse 45. We have already seen that John 6:37 is cited a few times, but no interpretation of it is offered.

There is a good reason why *CBF* stumbles at this point: there is no meaningful non-Reformed exegesis of the passage available. As numerous as the attempts of Arminian exegetes to find *some way* around the testimony of these verses has been, not even a plausible solution has been offered that does not require the complete dismantling of the text, redefinition of words, or the insertion of utterly foreign concepts. One thing is absolutely certain: Jesus taught the complete sovereignty of grace to the people who gathered in the synagogue in Capernaum nearly two millennia ago. If we wish to honor His truth, we can do no less.

Let us listen to Jesus teach "extreme Calvinism" almost 1500 years before Calvin was born in the words of the gospel of John.

John 6:37-40

> All that the Father gives Me will come to Me, and the one who comes to Me I will certainly not cast out. For I have come down from heaven, not to do My own will, but the will of Him who sent Me. This is the will of Him who sent Me, that of all that He has given Me I lose nothing, but raise it up on the last day. For this is the will of My Father, that everyone who beholds the Son and believes in Him will have eternal life, and I Myself will raise him up on the last day. (John 6:37-40)

Despite the richness of this passage, an honest effort will be made to be brief in providing commentary.[2] The setting is important: Jesus speaks to the crowds gathered in the synagogue at Capernaum. They have followed Him there after the feeding of the five thousand the day before. They are seeking more miracles, and more food. Jesus does not pander to their "felt needs," but goes directly to the real issue: who He is and how He is central to God's work of redemption. He identifies Himself as the "Bread of life" (v. 35), the source of all spiritual nourishment. In our modern setting we might not feel the force of His words as they must have felt them that morning. "Who is this man to speak this way of Himself?" they must have thought. Not even the greatest prophets of Israel had directed people to faith in *themselves!* Not even an Abraham or an Isaiah would claim to have come down from heaven, nor would they ever say "the one coming to Me will never hunger and the one believing in Me will never thirst." We must attempt to feel the sharp impact of these words just as they were spoken.

The blessed Lord was quite blunt with His audience. He knew they did not possess real faith. "But I said to you that you have seen Me, and yet do not believe" (v. 36). They had seen Him with their eyes, but unless physical sight is joined with spiritual enlightenment, it profits nothing. Often the importance of this statement is overlooked. Verse 36 is a turning point in the chapter. Jesus now explains their unbelief. How is it that these men could stand before the very Son of God, the Word made flesh, and *not* believe? Anyone who does not take seriously the deadness of man in sin should contemplate this scene. The very Creator in human form stands before men who are schooled in the Scriptures and points to their unbelief. He then explains the *why*, and yet so few today will listen and believe.

"All that the Father gives Me will come to Me." These are the first words to come from the Lord in explanation of man's unbelief. We dare not engage in hopscotch across this text and ignore the very order of teaching He provides. The first assertion is one of complete divine sovereignty. Every word speaks volumes.

"All that the Father gives Me." The Father gives someone to Christ. The elect are viewed as a single whole,[3] given by the Father to the Son.[4] The Father has the right to give a people to the Son. He is the sovereign King, and this is a divine transaction.

All that are given by the Father to the Son come to the Son. Not some, not most, but all.

All those given by the Father to the Son *will come* to the Son. It is *vital* to see the truth that is communicated by this phrase: *the giving by the Father to the Son precedes and determines the coming of the person to Christ.* The action of giving by the Father *comes before* the action of coming to Christ by the individual. And since *all* of those so given *infallibly come,* we have here both unconditional election as well as irresistible grace, and that in the space of nine words! It becomes an obvious exercise in eisegesis to say, "Well, what the Lord really means is that all that the Father has seen will believe in Christ will come to Christ." That is a meaningless statement. Since the action of *coming* is dependent upon the action of *giving*, we can see that it is simply not exegetically possible to say that we cannot determine the relationship between the two actions. God's giving results in man's coming. Salvation is of the Lord.

But note as well that it is *to the Son* that they come. They do not come to a religious system. They are *coming* to Christ. This is a personal relationship, personal faith, and, given that the ones who come are described throughout the passage by the present tense participle, it is not just a coming that happens once. This is an on-going faith, an on-going looking to Christ as the source of spiritual life. The men to whom the Lord was speaking had "come" to Him for a season: they would soon walk away and follow Him no more. The true believer *is* *coming* to Christ, always. This is the nature of saving faith.

"And the one who comes to Me I will never cast out." The true believer, the one "coming" to the Son, has this promise of the Lord: using the strongest form of denial possible,[5] Jesus affirms the eternal security of the believer. Jesus is the one who gives life and raises His own up at the last day. He promises that there is no possibility whatsoever that any one who *is* *coming* to Him in true faith could ever find Him unwilling to save. But this tremendous promise *is the second half of a sentence*. It is based upon the truth that was first proclaimed. This promise is to those who are given by the Father to the Son *and to no one else*. Of course, we will see in verse 44 that no one but those who are so given will be coming to Christ in faith anyway: but there are surely those who, like many in that audience in Capernaum, are willing to follow *for a while*, willing to believe *for a season*. This promise is *not* theirs.

The promise to the elect, however, could not be more precious. Since Christ is able to save perfectly (He is not dependent upon man's will, man's cooperation), His promise means the elect cannot ever be lost. Since He will not cast out, and there is no power greater than His own, the one who comes to Christ will find Him an all-sufficient and perfect Savior. This is the *only* basis of "eternal security" or the perseverance of the saints: they look to a perfect Savior who is able to save. It is *Christ's* ability to save that means the redeemed cannot be lost. If it were, in fact, a synergistic relationship, there could never be any ground for absolute confidence and security.

Many stop at verse 37 and miss the tremendous revelation we are privileged to receive in the following verses. Why will Christ never cast out those who come to Him? Verse 38 begins with a connective that indicates a continuation of the thought: verses 38 and 39 explain verse 37. Christ keeps all those who come to Him for He is fulfilling the will of the Father. "I have come down from heaven, not to do My own will, but the will of Him who sent Me." The divine Messiah always does the will of the Father. The preceding chapter in John's Gospel had made this very clear. There is perfect harmony between the work of the Father and the Son.

And what is the will of the Father for the Son? In simple terms, it is the Father's will that the Son *save perfectly.* "This is the will of Him who sent Me, that of all that He has given Me I lose nothing, but raise it up on the last day." It is vital to remember that this *continues* the explanation of why He does not cast out the one coming to Him. We must see this for some might be tempted to say that the Father has entrusted all things into the hands of the Son, and that this passage is saying nothing more than the Son will act properly in regards to what the Father has given Him. But the context is clear: v. 37 speaks of the Father "giving" the elect to the Son, and v. 39 continues the same thought. Those who are given infallibly come to the Son in v. 37, and it is these same ones, the elect,[6] who are raised up at the last day. Resurrection is the work of Christ, and in this passage, is paralleled with the giving of eternal life (see v. 40). Christ gives eternal life to all those who are given to Him and who, as a result, come to Him.

We must ask the Arminian who promotes the idea that a truly saved person can be lost: does this not mean that Christ can fail to do the will of the Father? If the will of the Father for the Son is that He lose *none* of those that are given to Him, does it not follow inexorably that Christ is *able* to accomplish the Father's will? And does this not force us to believe that the Son is able to save *without introducing the will of man as the final authority in the matter?* Can any synergist (one who teaches, as Dr. Geisler does, that God's grace works "synergistically" and that man's free will is a vitally important part of the salvation process, and that no man is saved unless that man wills it) believe these words? Can one who says that God *tries* to save as many as "possible" but *cannot* save any man without that man's cooperation fully believe what this verse teaches? It is not the Father's will that Christ *try* to save but that He save *a particular people perfectly.* He is to lose *nothing* of all that He is given. How can this be if, in fact, the final decision lies with man, not with God? It is the Father's will that results in the resurrection to life of *any individual.* This is election in the strongest terms, and it is taught with clarity in the reddest letters in Scripture.

Verse 39 begins with "This is the will of Him who sent Me," and verse 40 does the same, "For this is the will of My Father." But in verse 39 we have the will of the Father for the Son. Now we have the will of the Father for the elect. "That everyone who beholds the Son and believes in Him will have eternal life, and I Myself will raise him up on the last day." Amazingly, many wrench this verse out of its context, misunderstand the reference to "every one who beholds...every one who believes in Him," and say, "See, no divine election here! Any one can do this." But it is obvious, when the text is allowed to stand as a whole, that this is not the intention of the passage. Who is the one "beholding" the Son and "believing" in Him? Both these terms are present participles, referring to on-going action, just as we saw in "the one coming" to Christ in verse 37. Jesus raises up on the last day *all* those who are given to Him (v. 39) and *all* those who are looking and believing in Him (v. 40). Are we to believe these are different groups? Of course not. Jesus only raises one group to eternal life. But since this is so, does it not follow that all those given to Him will look to Him and believe in Him? Most assuredly. Saving faith, then, is exercised by all of those given to the Son by the Father (one of the reasons why, as we will see, the Bible affirms clearly that saving faith is a gift of God).

John 6:41-45

> Therefore the Jews were grumbling about Him, because He said, "I am the bread that came down out of heaven." They were saying, "Is not this Jesus, the son of Joseph, whose father and mother we know? How does He now say, 'I have come down out of heaven'?" Jesus answered and said to them, "Do not grumble among yourselves. No one can come to Me unless the Father who sent Me draws him; and I will raise him up on the last day. It is written in the prophets, 'AND THEY SHALL ALL BE TAUGHT OF GOD.' Everyone who has heard and learned from the Father, comes to Me.

The Jews were grumbling by this point in the dissertation. They rejected His claim to divine origin, assuming instead that He was but a mere man, the son of Joseph. Jesus is not turned from His presentation by their meandering thoughts and confusion. He instructs them to stop grumbling (v. 43) and then explains their persistent unbelief.

"No one can come to Me." Literally Jesus says, "No man is able to come to Me." These are words of *incapacity* and they are placed in a universal context. All men share this in common: they lack the ability to come to Christ in and of themselves. Shared inability due to a shared fallen nature. This is Paul's "dead in sin" (Eph. 2:1) and "unable to please God" (Rom. 8:8). It is the Reformed doctrine of total depravity: man's inability taught by the Lord who knows the hearts of all men. If the text ended here there would be no hope, no good news. But it doesn't stop there.

"No one can come to Me unless the Father who sent Me draws him." The good news is that there is an "unless" in John 6:44, just as there is a "But God" in Ephesians 2:4. In both instances it is not the free will of man that comes to the rescue, but the free will of God. All men would be left in the hopeless position of "unable to come" *unless* God acts, and He does by drawing men unto Christ. Outside of this divine enablement (cf. 6:65) no man can come to Christ. No man can "will" to come to Christ outside of this divine drawing.

Of course, the immediate response of many is, "Yes indeed, God must provide some kind of prevenient grace, some kind of drawing, before any man can choose to believe." But is this what the text is saying? Remember that these words come immediately after the assertion that *all* that the Father *gives* the Son *will come* to the Son (v. 37). Reformed scholars assert that the ones who are drawn are the ones who are given by the Father to the Son: i.e., the elect. They point to the immediate context which identifies those who come to Christ as the elect. But the rest of verse 44 explains why it *must* be so: "and I will raise him up on the last day." Who does Jesus raise up on the last day? Verse 39 says He raises *all* those given to Him by the Father; verse 40 says He raises *all* who are looking and believing in Him; verse 44 says He raises *all* those who are *drawn by the Father.* The identity of those raised on the last day to eternal life *is absolutely co-extensive* with the identity of those who are drawn! If a person is drawn, he will also be raised up to eternal life. Obviously, then, it cannot be asserted that Christ, in this context, is saying that the Father is drawing *every single individual human being*, for 1) the context limits this to those given by the Father to the Son, 2) this passage is still explaining the *unbelief* of the Jews, which would make no sense if in fact the Father were drawing these unbelievers to Jesus, and 3) if that were so, universalism would be the result, for *all* who are drawn are likewise *raised up* at the last day.

John Calvin is admitted, even by his foes, to have been a tremendous exegete of Scripture. Fair and insightful, Calvin's commentaries continue to this day to have great usefulness and benefit to the student of Scripture. Here are his comments on John 6:44:

> To come to Christ being here used metaphorically for believing, the Evangelist, in order to carry out the metaphor in the apposite clause, says that those persons are drawn whose understandings God enlightens, and whose hearts he bends and forms to the obedience of Christ. The statement amounts to this, that we ought not to wonder if many refuse to embrace the Gospel; because no man will ever of himself be able to come to Christ, but God must first approach him by his Spirit; and hence it follows that all are not drawn, but that God bestows this grace on those whom he has elected. True, indeed, as to the kind of drawing, it is not violent, so as to compel men by external force; but still it is a powerful impulse of the Holy Spirit, which makes men willing who formerly were unwilling and reluctant. It is a false and profane assertion, therefore, that none are drawn but those who are willing to be drawn, as if man made himself obedient to God by his own efforts; for the willingness with which men follow God is what they already have from himself, who has formed their hearts to obey him.[7]

Jesus continues this thought in verse 45, drawing from a prophecy of Isaiah, and says, "Everyone who has heard and learned from the Father, comes to Me." To hear and learn from the Father is paralleled with being drawn in verse 44. Jesus would later use the same kind of terminology when He taught that only those who "belong to God" can hear His words (John 8:47).

In sum, then, Jesus surely taught the absolute sovereignty of God, the inabilities of man, the unconditional election of a people unto salvation, the efficient grace of God that *infallibly* brings salvation to the elect, and the final perseverance of those elect into eternal life. It is one of the *key* texts supportive of the Reformed position identified as "extreme Calvinism" in *CBF.*

CBF's Response

As with all the other key passages (Romans 8, 9, Ephesians 1, and John 6), *CBF* offers no contextually-based, careful exegesis of the passage. We saw in the introduction that John 6:37, while cited, is never discussed. Nothing is said about its witness to unconditional election or irresistible grace. It is, simply, ignored. The book's cover claims to present a definitive study of the issue of divine sovereignty and free will. Such would require extensive work on these key passages. None is offered, and what is offered is not exegetical in nature.

Only three arguments are provided in the book in response to John 6:44, and one to John 6:45. Given that the relationship to the rest of the passage is not even noted, it is not surprising that the passages are not exegeted contextually. In fact, little is said about the actual words of the texts. Instead, the plain meaning is explained away by reference to other passages. We begin with John 6:44:

> Second, John 12:32 makes it plain that the word "draw" cannot mean "irresistible grace" on the elect for one simple reason: Jesus said, " 'But I, when I am lifted up from the earth, will draw *all men* to myself' " (John 12:32). No true Calvinist believes that all men will be saved.[8]

This is the most common response: rather than following the course of the sermon delivered by Jesus, Arminians immediately abandon John 6 and cite John 12:32. The meaning of "draw," fully discernable from the text of John 6, is read back from an assumed meaning in John 12. This is a faulty method of exegesis on many fronts. But even here, the Arminian's attempt fails, for John 12:32 does not teach universalism anymore than John 6:44 does. Note the context of the passage:

> Now there were some Greeks among those who were going up to worship at the feast; these then came to Philip, who was from Bethsaida of Galilee, and *began to* ask him, saying, "Sir, we wish to see Jesus." Philip came and told Andrew; Andrew and Philip came and told Jesus. (John 12:20-22)

John 12 narrates the final events of Jesus' public ministry. After this particular incident the Lord will go into a period of private ministry to His disciples right before He goes to the cross. The final words of the Lord's public teaching are prompted by the arrival of Greeks who are seeking Jesus. This important turn of events prompts the teaching that follows. Jesus is now being sought by non-Jews, Gentiles. It is when Jesus is informed of this that He says, "The hour has come for the Son of Man to be glorified."

This then is the context that leads us to Jesus' words in verse 32:

> "Now My soul has become troubled; and what shall I say, 'Father, save Me from this hour'? But for this purpose I came to this hour. Father, glorify Your name." Then a voice came out of heaven: "I have both glorified it, and will glorify it again." So the crowd *of people* who stood by and heard it were saying that it had thundered; others were saying, "An angel has spoken to Him." Jesus answered and said, "This voice has not come for My sake, but for your sakes. Now judgment is upon this world; now the ruler of this world will be cast out. And I, if I am lifted up from the earth, will draw all men to Myself." But He was saying this to indicate the kind of death by which He was to die. (John 12:27-33)

There are two keys to understanding why the Arminian understanding of this passage is utterly untenable: the first we have seen in the fact that what prompted these words was the coming of Gentiles seeking after Jesus. Reformed exegetes believe that "all men" refers to Jews and Gentiles, not to every individual person, and the context points this direction. But even more devastating to the Arminian understanding is a simple question: does the cross draw every single individual man? Is that what the Bible really teaches about the cross? Surely not! The cross is foolishness to Gentiles and a stumbling block to Jews, as Paul taught:

> For indeed Jews ask for signs and Greeks search for wisdom; but we preach Christ crucified, to Jews a stumbling block and to Gentiles foolishness, but to those who are the called, both Jews and Greeks, Christ the power of God and the wisdom of God. (1 Corinthians 1:22-24)

Paul knew this truth just as Jesus taught it: *"to those who are the called, both Jews and Greeks...."* To whom is Christ the power and wisdom of God? To "the called." What is the preaching of the cross to those who are not called? Something that draws them, or repels them? The answer is obvious. The cross of Christ is foolishness to the world. These considerations, along with the immediate context of the Gentiles seeking Christ, make it clear that Jesus was saying that if He is lifted up in crucifixion, He will draw all men, Jews and Gentiles, to Himself. This is the same as saying that He has sheep not of this fold (John 10:16), the Gentiles, who become one body in Christ (Ephesians 2:13-16).

Finally, if we read this errant interpretation of John 12:32 back into John 6:44 (and to do so would require some kind of demonstration that the simple word "draw" *must* have the exact same meaning *and objects* in both contexts, something *CBF* does not even *attempt* to prove) we do exactly as Geisler asserts: create universalism, but not because the Reformed view is in error. We have already seen that *all* who are drawn are *also* raised up. Rather than using this argument to overthrow the plain meaning of 6:44, *CBF* should see that the *group* that is being drawn is not every single individual but the elect (as indicated by the context), and that the result *is* indeed the Reformed view of irresistible grace!

> Third, the word "all" cannot mean only *some* men in John 12:32. Earlier (John 2:24-25) when Jesus said He knew "all" men sin, it was clear that He was not just speaking of the elect. Why then should "all" mean "some" in John 12:32? If He meant "some," He could easily have said so.[9]

Again, this kind of argumentation is completely fallacious. First, John says Jesus "knew all men," not that "all men sin." This is a simple misreading of the text. Secondly, *CBF* makes no attempt to prove that the phrase "all men" in John 2:24 is to be understood as synonymous with the use in John 12:32. Jesus, as God, would "know all *men*" but it does not follow that this means the Father must draw all men to Christ nor that Christ must draw all men to Himself by His death. To *know* and to *draw* are obviously *completely* different actions. Jesus knew as a function of deity: the Father chooses to draw as a function of His freedom. To connect John 2 with John 12 so as to interpret John 6 *should* immediately cause any careful student of the Bible to recognize that we here encounter a glowing example of eisegesis that comes from an unwillingness to accept what the text itself teaches. Further, asking why Jesus said "all" begs the question: if the Reformed exegete is right and Jesus means "all kinds of men" as in Jews and Gentiles, and expected to be understood in that context, why would he then say "some kinds of men"? That would mean Jesus is excluding some kinds of men, which He does not. As the heavenly song rightly says of the Lamb,

> And they sang a new song, saying, "Worthy are You to take the book and to break its seals; for You were slain, and purchased for God with Your blood *men* from every tribe and tongue and people and nation. You have made

> them *to be* a kingdom and priests to our God; and they will
> reign upon the earth." (Revelation 5:9-10)

Christ redeems by His death men from *every* tribe, tongue, people, and nation, not *some* tribes, tongues, peoples and nations. Hence, the argument has no merit when urged against the Reformed position.

Thus far then we have seen only an attempt to insert a foreign meaning into the text on the basis of unsubstantiated connections with two foreign contexts (John 2 and John 12). This should be sufficient to warn us that John 6:44 is not being handled properly. But one last comment is left to be examined on John 6:44:

> Finally, their being drawn by God was conditioned on their faith. The context of their being "drawn" (6:37) was "he who believes" (6:35) or "everyone who believes in Him" (6:40). Those who believe are enabled by God to be drawn to Him. Jesus adds, "This is why I told you that no one can come to me unless the Father has enabled him' " (John 6:65). A little later He says, " 'If anyone *chooses* to do God's will, he will find out whether my teaching comes from God or whether I speak on my own'" (John 7:17). From this it is evident that their understanding of Jesus' teaching and being drawn to the Father resulted from their own *free choice*.

As we will see with Romans 9:16, it is simply amazing that a passage that is so directly contradictory to the Arminian theory of free will can be turned into an affirmation of "free choice." Of all the statements in *CBF* we admit that this one is the most difficult to understand, for it has the least connection to the subject it is allegedly addressing. Remember that this verse begins with the phrase, "No man is able to come to Me," and yet the first line of response is, "Finally, their being drawn by God was conditioned on their faith." This unfounded assertion has no connection to the text whatsoever, and the attempt to prove it only compounds the eisegetical error. Given that this is such a vital passage and the response so indicative of the inability of Arminian writers to handle it, we will point out each error as it is presented:

> The context of their being "drawn" (6:37) was "he who believes" (6:35) or "everyone who believes in Him" (6:40).

Actually, the word "drawn" does not appear in 6:37; instead, that verse (which received no response in CBF) says the Father gives a people to the Son, and as a result, those people infallibly, without fail, come to the Son. This verse definitely provides an important element of the context: one ignored by CBF. Next we are told that this context is "he who believes" (6:35) or "everyone who believes in Him" (6:40). We have seen that those who believe do so, in this text, because the Father gives them to the Son. We also have seen that Jesus is explaining why these men *do not* believe (6:36) These contextual elements are ignored by CBF. Instead, the over-riding assumption of human free will is inserted into the passage without the first attempt to provide a foundation for so doing. But this is followed with the most amazing statement in all of CBF:

> Those who believe are enabled by God to be drawn to Him.

To be honest, this sentence makes no sense. It sounds like it is saying that being "drawn" to God is not salvific: that is, it is more like "drawing nearer to God" in devotion or some such thing. In any case, the meaning surely has nothing whatsoever to do with the text: obviously, coming to Christ *is* believing in Him: they are synonymous in John. So, this passage is not saying that God "draws" believers into a closer relationship with Christ. Instead, it is saying that no man is able to come to Christ in faith unless drawn by the Father, and that *all* who are drawn are raised up, for all that the Father gives the Son *will come* to the Son in saving faith. This coming is *obviously* the act of saving faith, for Jesus says that the one who comes to Him He will not cast out.

Further, it must be pointed out that there is nothing in the passage about faith coming before the drawing: the drawing results in faith. There is nothing in the text about God enabling men *to be drawn*. God draws, period. We cannot help but point out how completely *backwards* this interpretation is from the actual text. But we go on:

> Jesus adds, "This is why I told you that no one can come
> to me unless the Father has enabled him' " (John 6:65).

This is actually a restatement of 6:44 with the change of "enabled" (NASB: "granted him") for "drawn." In both cases the exact same truth is being presented. What is missing in the citation is the fact that Jesus "was saying" this, using the imperfect tense, indicating that He was repeating this. The disciples are walking away, and Jesus explains the mass defection and unbelief in the same way as before: no one can come to me unless the Father grants it to him. And we have already seen the Father grants this to the elect of God *alone*.

> A little later He says, " 'If anyone *chooses* to do God's
> will, he will find out whether my teaching comes from
> God or whether I speak on my own'" (John 7:17).

The context of John 7 is completely different, and no attempt is made to explain why the two verses are relevant to each other. But this aside, it is evident that the idea is that sinners can freely "choose" to do God's will. And just who will choose to do this? Those who are given by the Father to the Son. Those who are not of the elect do not even *hear* His words, let alone seek to do God's will (John 8:47). Finally,

> From this it is evident that their understanding of Jesus'
> teaching and being drawn to the Father resulted from
> their own *free choice*.

We have no idea how this statement can be logically connected, even through the most tortuous line of reasoning, with the text that is being examined. How one goes from "no man is able" to "resulted from their own *free choice*" we honestly cannot say. We cannot even figure out who is being referred to by the phrase "their understanding." Is this in reference to John 6 or John 7? "Understanding teaching" and "being drawn" are two completely different things from two completely different contexts, yet they are thrown together in a confusing conclusion that screams the word "eisegesis."

CBF fails completely to provide an answer to this glorious passage that teaches sovereign grace with grand simplicity. And given the misuse of other passages already cited (Matthew 23:37, 1 Timothy 2:4, 2 Peter 3:9), it can truly be said that CBF has no exegetical basis upon which to stand.

Notes

1   *Chosen But Free*, p. 47.
2   The reader is directed to my brief work, *Drawn by the Father* (Crowne Publications, 1991) for a fuller exegesis of this tremendous passage.
3   The neuter form πᾶν is used when the entire group is in view; when each individual person comes into view with reference to their response of faith the masculine participle ἐρχόμενος is used, showing the personal element of faith.
4   Two tenses are used by the Lord in this passage: here the present tense is used, "all the Father *gives* (δίδωσιν) Me…." In verse 39, however, the perfect tense is used, "all that He *has given* (δέδωκεν) Me…."
5   Here the aorist subjunctive of strong denial, οὐ μὴ ἐκβάλω ἔξω, "I will *never* cast out." The idea is the emphatic denial of the possibility of a future event.
6   Jesus uses the neuter πᾶν again to refer to the elect as an entire group, though the fact that this group is made up of *individuals* is seen in their being raised to life and in their individually coming to Him.
7   John Calvin, *Commentary on the Gospel of John, The Comprehensive John Calvin Collection* (Ages Digital Library, 1998)
8   *Chosen But Free*, p. 93.
9   Ibid.

Chapter 8

Unconditional Election

We have already lamented the fact that *CBF* is long on assertions, but very short on exegesis. Nowhere is this more true
than with reference to one of the *key* passages that is *central* to
this debate: Ephesians 1. While Reformed works present volumes of in-depth work on this section of Scripture, *CBF* offers
almost *nothing* in response to this tremendous passage. The
section is referred to eleven times in the work, but in none of
these is any meaningful exegesis offered of the text. A grand
total of *eight sentences* are offered in response to this grand
passage. There are two main references to this section of Scripture and its witness to personal, specific election of a people
unto salvation. The first is a passing, but important, remark.

While attempting to respond to the assertion of Romans
9:16, we read, "All forms of Calvinism and Arminianism believe that God is the one who initiated salvation, even before
the world began (Eph. 1:4)." Is this indicating that the specific
act of choosing people before the foundation of the world is to
be understood as merely "initiating" salvation? It is hard to
know, though, the context seems to suggest this. As we will see
later, *CBF* can even find in the words of Paul in Romans 9:16
("So then it does not depend on the man who wills or the man
who runs, but on God who has mercy.") the assertion "this
means it is a *free act* of our will in receiving it," so anything is

possible. But this seems to come out most clearly in the specific section where *CBF* provides an "evaluation of verses used to support the extreme Calvinists' view of unconditional election." Here is what is said:

> Moderate Calvinists agree that there are no strings attached to the gift of salvation—it is unconditional. When election occurred—before the foundation of the world (Eph. 1:4)—the elect were not even created yet. God elected on His own, without any conditions that needed to be performed on the part of the elect.
>
> However, the question is not whether there are any conditions for God *giving* salvation; the question is whether there are any conditions for man *receiving* salvation. And here the Bible seems to be very emphatic that faith is the condition for receiving God's gift of salvation. We are "justified by faith" (Rom. 5:1 NASB). We must *"believe* on the Lord Jesus Christ" in order to be saved (Acts 16:31 NKJV). "Without faith it is impossible to please God, because anyone who comes to him *must believe* that he exists and that he rewards those who earnestly seek him" (Heb. 11:6).[1]

We can hardly be charged with exaggeration when we say that a work that seeks to provide reasons to "avoid" the historic Reformed position would *have* to provide some kind of meaningful interaction with such a *central* passage as this. To dismiss this passage of Scripture with the argument, "Well sure God chose to save freely, but man still has to believe to be saved" is to completely miss the heart and soul of the position being attacked. Immediately after this comment Romans 8:28 is cited, and the response is the same: "That these and like texts show the unconditional nature of election from God's point of view is not challenged. But the question is not whether election is unconditional from the vantage point of the *Giver* but whether there are any conditions for the *receiver.*" Keeping in mind Dr. Geisler's definition of God's "predetermination" as a passive thing (perfect foreknowledge), we can understand what is being said in light of a comment made shortly thereafter in response to Romans 8:29, "If so, then God's foreknowledge would not have any reference to foreknowing how the elect would respond. But this is not the case, as our response shows."[2] This is followed by:

> And if God does foreknow infallibly, then He would still foreknow what people would freely believe, and He would still have to decide whether He would have to force them to believe in Him or else elect those He knew could be persuaded to freely accept His grace.[3]

No matter how strongly Dr. Geisler denies it, there is no logical way he can escape one simple fact: his view differs from the Arminian "election based on knowledge of future events" viewpoint solely in terminology, not in substance. *CBF* attempts to avoid saying it, but it's there nonetheless:

> But the question is not whether election is unconditional from the vantage point of the *Giver* but whether there are any conditions for the *receiver*....Election is not *based on* or dependent on foreknowledge. Rather, it is merely *in accord with* it.[4]

There is no real difference between saying God elects *on the basis* of foreknowledge or *in accordance* with it if, in the final analysis, it is the free choice of man, not the free choice of God, that determines who the elect are! *CBF* clearly says that God elects based upon His knowledge that those so elected "could be persuaded to freely accept His grace." The *final, ultimate deciding factor in election is the free acceptance of the human being.* This is glaringly obvious. And, it is fully Arminian.

Another corollary that inevitably flows from this is that if the decree of "election" is not specific and based solely upon the will of God, it must become a decree *to save* based upon what man does in time, nothing else. That is, it becomes *impersonal.* It becomes a decree to save those who fulfill certain conditions (no matter how many *or how few* those conditions might be), not a decree to save *anyone in particular.* This comes out in Geisler's work:

> Why, then, does one person go to heaven and another not? Because God willed that all who receive His grace will be saved and that all who reject it will be lost. And since God knew infallibly just who this would be, both the elect and non-elect were determined from all eternity. And this determination was not based on anything in man, including their free choice. Rather, it was determined on God's choice to save all who would accept His unconditional grace.[5]

It is *vital* to understand what is said here, for the wording is very careful and yet very confusing. Nowhere in this quote, or in *CBF*, will you find the *elect as individuals* being chosen by God solely upon the basis of His will. Look closely at what is said: God wills to do what? Save those who receive His grace and reject all who do not. The will of God in this matter is impersonal: no particular individual is chosen in this fashion to be saved. Instead, *a plan of salvation* is willed. Then, we see again the centrality of the idea of God "knowing infallibly" who would, by a free choice, accept or reject Him so that the elect and non-elect were "determined from all eternity." But we must insist that such language does not differ *in substance* from the Arminian assertion that God elects on the basis of foreknowledge, for the denial that there is any logical relationship between God's knowledge and God's determination has already been seen to be in error. As we have noted, this "determination" is passive: it involves God perfectly knowing the free acts of men *not decreeing them.* When we keep this in mind we can understand the meaning of the rest of the statement: the choice *to save in general* is not based upon what the elect do, *but their particular participation in that plan is not a part of the decree.* God wills to save those who believe, and who believes is *not* the result of the decree but of the "free choices" of men. Again, this is pure Arminianism.

These facts established, it would be most edifying to contrast the "explanation" of Ephesians 1 offered by *CBF* with a brief exegesis of the actual text itself. Let's allow the Word to speak for itself.

> Blessed be the God and Father of our Lord Jesus Christ, who has blessed us with every spiritual blessing in the heavenly places in Christ, [4] just as He chose us in Him before the foundation of the world, that we would be holy and blameless before Him. In love [5] He predestined us to adoption as sons through Jesus Christ to Himself, according to the kind intention of His will, [6] to the praise of the glory of His grace, which He freely bestowed on us in the Beloved. [7] In Him we have redemption through His blood, the forgiveness of our trespasses, according to the riches of His grace [8] which He lavished on us. In all wisdom and insight [9] He made known to us the mystery of His will, according to His kind intention which He purposed in Him [10] with a view to an administration suitable to the fullness of the times, that is, the summing up of all things in Christ, things in the heavens and things on the earth. In Him [11] also we have obtained an inheritance, having been predestined according to His purpose who works all things after the counsel of His will,

Paul begins with a benediction of God the Father, a pronouncement of blessing upon Him. Why? The rest of the passage explains why God is so worthy of our blessing. He is worthy of blessing because He has blessed *us* with "every spiritual blessing in the heavenlies." From the very beginning the emphasis is upon God and God's actions. He acts (blessing) and believers are the recipient of the action. All spiritual blessings flow from God but they do so *only in Christ*. Throughout this passage we will see the phrase "in Christ" or "in Him" repeated over and over again, all to emphasize the uniqueness of the

Christian gospel, where God saves men *in Christ* and in no other way.

Thus: "just as He chose us in Him before the foundation of the world" (v. 4). God here acts. His act is that of election. The Greek term ἐξελέξατο means to "choose or select." God is the subject of the verb. This is God's choice. The rest of the phrase gives us three vital pieces of information: the *object* of the choice, the *sphere* of the choice, and the *time frame* of the choice.

The direct object of the verb "choose" is "us," the first person plural pronoun. If certain theories were correct we might expect something like σῷζειν, "to save," so that the passage would simply be "God chose to save, or make salvation possible, before the foundation of the world." But instead Paul provides a personal direct object, making the choice personal and distinct. He chose "us," not a nameless, faceless class or group, but "us." This truth will be repeated later in the text.

This choice, by necessity, must take place *in Christ*. Christ is not the one here chosen, but those who are chosen are chosen *in Christ*. There is no election *outside* of union with Christ. God saves no one impersonally. All who are elected will *know Christ* for they will of necessity be *in Him*. All who are elected are chosen *in Him*. Christianity is not pluralistic nor syncretistic: it says salvation comes in only one way, in the Son of God incarnate, in Christ.

But this choice is timeless. It is made "before the foundation of the world," before creation itself. The choice is wholly divine and wholly based upon the will of God for at the time of the election of *us* in Christ *nothing else but God existed.* Election is wholly of Him.

We then see that this election is surely to salvation, for the Apostle continues, "that we would be holy and blameless before Him." God's electing grace is *purposeful.* God saves no one outside of holiness and righteousness. It is His purpose that the elect would be perfected by their Savior, the one who is able to save "to the uttermost" those who come unto God by Him (Hebrews 7:25).

"In love He predestined us to adoption as sons through Jesus Christ to Himself." Again we find God is the subject of the action in this verse. We are told *what* God has done, *how* He has done it, *to whom* He has done it, to *what end* it is done, and the *means* used. Specifically, God has predestined. Some are actually shocked to find the word in the text of Scripture, but there it is. The word is used six times in Scripture, and twice in this passage (here and in verse eleven). It refers to deciding or setting apart "beforehand." The object fills out its meaning: "us." Christians were predestined. Again the action is personal, paralleling the "election" of verse 4.

But to what were Christians predestined? "Adoption as sons through Jesus Christ to Himself." God predestined not simply a plan but an *end*, just as we saw in verse 4. Those who are chosen in eternity are predestined *to adoption as sons through Jesus Christ to Himself.* They will experience full and complete salvation and entrance into the very family of God! Paul is saying that it has been God's eternal purpose to *adopt* a people unto Himself through Jesus Christ. And since adoption is always *personal* (God does not adopt plans nor nameless, faceless masses of humans, but *persons*), this is saying exactly what the Baptist Confession of Faith asserted in the previous chapter: personal, specific election of the people of God.

It should be noted that at this point all of the verbs in the passage have had God as their subject. Men have not added an iota to the discussion outside of being adopted into the family of God (i.e., saved, and that perfectly). God is the one who is free in eternity past. He is not controlled by the whims and will of creatures He has yet to bring into existence.

The next phrase answers many a question of mankind: why has God chosen to save a particular people? Why is one man raised to eternal life and another left to eternal destruction? The Scriptures offer an answer that is satisfying to the believer, but insufficient for the person unwilling to trust in God's goodness. What is the basis of God's act of predestination? It is "according to the kind intention of His will." Each word is important. It is *His* will, not *our* will. And remember, this is speaking not of some general plan to "save" so that it is God who "initiates" but man who actuates. This is the specific pre-destination of individuals to sonship. The basis of this specific decree is God's will. No mention is found of man's will.

We need to remember that first and foremost God's action of saving man is an act of grace. His will is not some dark and foreboding thing. The emphasis in Scripture is always on the wonder that God would save *at all*, never upon the idea that God chooses not to save a particular individual, leaving them to perfect justice. It is the "kind intention" of His will that lies at the base of His action of choosing a people in Christ.

Why has God created and redeemed? It is "to the praise of the glory of His grace." The redeemed heart naturally speaks of desiring to glorify God. We sing of living so as to bring glory to God. We know, naturally, that we are to have God's glory as our highest goal, our highest priority. So it should not be at all surprising that the most profound answer Scripture gives to the question of "what's it all about" is that it is about God's glory. *All* of salvation results in the praise of the glory of *His* grace. All honor, glory, and power belong to *Him*. Such is surely the heart-felt sentiment of every believer, yet, our prayers and hymns are often better than our stated theology. For salvation to resound solely to the praise of the glory of *His* grace there can be not an iota of praise to the *creature*. Yet, if we base the success or failure of the *entire work of the Triune God* upon the "free choice" of the sinner (rather than the free choice of the Savior, John 6:37-39, Philippians 2:6-7) then how can we say that *all* glory and praise goes to God's grace alone? If salvation is in *any way synergistic* in its ultimate accomplishment (which is surely the position of Rome, the Arminians, and all the reli-gions of men), then God's glorious grace must *share glory* with the "free will decisions" of men! And is it not an empty thing to say, "Oh yes, God's grace gets all the praise since without His grace, no one could be saved!" Is God's grace to be praised because we *can be* saved or because we *are* saved?

The essential character of grace comes out in the next phrase: "which He freely bestowed on us in the Beloved."

Grace, to be grace, must be *free*. The ideas of grace and merit are mutually exclusive. His glorious grace was *bestowed* upon us. We did not earn it, "accept it" or merit it. There is a play on words here that is lost in English translations: the term translated "bestowed" (ἐχαρίτωσεν) is directly related to the noun "grace." In essence, Paul says, "the glory of God's grace which was graced upon us...." And as with all of this, this grace is only *in Christ*, here called "the Beloved." This transaction took place in eternity past, as the context of this verse indicates, and as is clearly stated by Paul in 2 Timothy 1:9. Why is this important? Because this grace is *specific, efficacious grace:* grace that actually saves (if it isn't, there's no reason to praise God for it). If the elect received this grace in Christ before eternity, then the Arminian position that God's grace is given to all equally and its final effectiveness is left to the time-bound "free choices" of men is impossible. Is someone going to seriously suggest that this grace was given, in eternity past, to those who will abide under the wrath of God in hell for eternity, and that "in Christ"? Is this not to turn the text on its head?

"In Him we have redemption through His blood, the forgiveness of our trespasses, according to the riches of His grace which He lavished on us." In Christ we (those chosen from before the foundation of the world) have redemption through His blood (an assertion supportive of the truth of particular redemption). This is not a hypothetical redemption that we somehow "validated" or "consummated" by the addition of our faith to the work of the cross. When Christ entered the holy place in heaven He had *obtained* eternal redemption (Hebrews 9:12). He had not merely made it a theoretical possibility, dependent for its efficaciousness upon the "free will" of the creature.

The extent of the forgiveness is unlimited in that its measure is the very grace that He has lavished upon His elect. But, if forgiveness of sins is connected with the election and predestination of God, obviously it cannot be said that it is God's intention to simply elect "to save" and leave the results in the hands of men. Forgiveness of sins (redemption) is an intensely personal thing. Christ has forgiven "our trespasses." These are *specific* acts of disobedience, not a general "amnesty for sin." The riches of His grace that brings this forgiveness of sins is "lavished" upon the elect. Are we to believe that this grace is made "to abound" to every single individual, but, despite its power and glory, fails to save so many sinners? Or are we to say that God's grace is "lavished" only after we "enable" it by our free-will choice? Quite simply, the Arminian view finds not even a toe-hold in this granite rock of sovereign election and efficacious grace.

"In all wisdom and insight He made known to us the mystery of His will, according to His kind intention which he purposed in Him with a view to an administration suitable to the fullness of times, *that is,* the summing up of all things in Christ, things in the heavens and things on the earth." God has revealed to His people the centrality of Christ, and His revelation is marked by wisdom and insight. It takes a spiritual mind to apprehend the revelation God has made of His will, and obviously, that revelation has been made to *His people* in particular. It is the Christian community that longs to see the summing up of all things in Christ, and prays toward that end. The centrality of Christ in God's salvific work, seen in the repetition of the phrase "in Him" throughout the passage, is now applied to "all things." The Savior of believers is the central figure not only in all of history, but in all of the universe itself. This truth provides a stark backdrop to the personal application of verse 11.

"In Him also we have obtained an inheritance, having been predestined according to His purpose who works all things after the council of His will." The NIV renders the first phrase "In him we were also chosen." While this is a possible rendering (and would then parallel the same chosen/predestined connection in verses 4-5), many translations see the verb referring to the gaining of an inheritance as the result of the act of predestination according to the will of God. This seems to be the best idea. That which any Christian receives from God in salvation is not due to anything he or she has done or will do: the inheritance we receive is due to the predestinating work of God.[6] But if we translate it this way, we also need to see that here Paul begins to narrow down his scope to his immediate audience, as he does with finality in verse 12, referring to the Christians of his generation and day

And upon what basis did God predestine? Again, the idea that anything in man can function as the basis of God's predestination is thoroughly refuted. Predestination is based upon the divine purpose, nothing else. That purpose flows from the Sovereign of the universe who "works all things after the counsel of His will." This is the Christian confession: God is sovereign over *all things*. Nothing is excepted, and most importantly, in this context, it is beyond dispute that *the matter of human salvation is firmly within the realm of the "all things" that God's will determines*. Nothing in the text tells us man's will is supreme over God's, nor that God's purpose is "after the counsel of the will of man." God works all things after the counsel of His will, including His predestining of men and women to salvation. The result in verse 12 is the repetition of a vital truth: salvation is all to the praise of His glory. Any teaching that detracts in the slightest from the glory of God is not a biblical teaching.

It is clear, then, why Reformed believers understand the Bible to teach God's eternal decree of unconditional election. The few comments above are but a small portion of the discussion that has been presented by writers and interpreters who have wrestled long and hard with this passage. If it is Dr. Geisler's intention to lead people to "avoid extreme Calvinism," that is, avoid the Reformed faith, then he must do more than offer eight short sentences in response to such passages as this.

Responding to Particular Biblical Passages in CBF

As we did when dealing with the assertion of the Arminian position of "free will," we now turn to specific biblical arguments and passages found in *CBF*.

John 1:12-13

> But as many as received Him, to them He gave the right
> to become children of God, *even* to those who believe in
> His name, who were born, not of blood nor of the will of
> the flesh nor of the will of man, but of God.

In the midst of introducing the Word at the beginning of his
Gospel, John cannot help but speak of the work of the Word in
redemption. He speaks of the rejection of some (1:11) and
contrasts this with the acceptance of others. It is to these, and
these alone, that the right to become children of God is given.
Specifically, those who believe in His name. Then John makes
a statement about the identity and nature of those who believe. He speaks of the "birth" of believers and specifically denies certain assertions about their birth. They were not born of
blood nor of the will of the flesh nor of the will of man. How
are we to understand these statements? First, to say they were
not born of blood means that the birth spoken of (the new
birth as we see in John 3) is not limited to a certain people or
race (a necessary statement in light of some of John's day who
saw salvation as race-dependent). Next, "nor of the will of the
flesh nor the will of man" probably refer to the same thing,
encompassing fully by double reference the idea of human
will. Divine birth can have only one origin: God. It is *not* a
matter of human will, human decision. As Calvin commented
on the passage:

> The will of the flesh and the will of man appear to me
> to mean the same thing; for I see no reason why flesh
> should be supposed to signify woman, as Augustine and
> many others explain it. On the contrary, the Evangelist
> repeats the same thing in a variety of words, in order to
> explain it more fully, and impress it more deeply on the
> minds of men. Though he refers directly to the Jews,
> who gloried in the flesh, yet from this passage a general
> doctrine may be obtained: that our being reckoned the
> sons of God does not belong to our nature, and does not

proceed from us, but because God begat us WILLINGLY (James 1:18), that is, from undeserved love. Hence it follows, first, that faith does not proceed from ourselves, but is the fruit of spiritual regeneration; for the Evangelist affirms that no man can believe, unless he be begotten of God; and therefore faith is a heavenly gift. It follows, secondly, that faith is not bare or cold knowledge, since no man can believe who has not been renewed by the Spirit of God.[7]

Spurgeon, as only he could, put the passage in a context that speaks volumes:

Now what is your grace in your heart? Did it spring from the strength of nature? If so, it is but Ishmael, it will be rejected, it is but the bondwoman's child, and will be cast out; but if your piety is the pure gift of God, an Isaac born when human nature was incapable of anything that was good, and when your depravity could produce nothing that was acceptable in the sight of God; if it has been granted to you according to the power of the Holy Ghost, then is it such as shall surely bring you to heaven. The children of God, then, are heirs of promise, not heirs by merit, not heirs by their own will, not heirs by human power. Just in this manner does John describe believers as "born, not of blood, nor of the will of the flesh, nor of the will of man, but of God." John 1:13. Here are sharp distinctions. My soul, canst thou bear them? While listening to them, dost thou feel no rebellion, but rather feel a humble desire to sit down at Jesus' feet and hopefully say, "I trust I also am a child of the promise"? Ah! then is it well with thee.[8]

Dr. Geisler properly understands, and rejects, the Reformed view of the passage:

According to the extreme Calvinist's interpretation of this passage, the new birth does not result from any human decision or free choice—it is from God.[9]

Here is the attempted response:

> There are at least two serious mistakes in such an inter-
> pretation of this text. First, verse 12 makes it plain that
> the means by which this new birth is obtained is by "all
> who *receive* him [Christ]." This involves an act of free
> will. Second, this passage is simply denying that there is
> any other source of the new birth other than God Him-
> self. It is not "of" (Greek: *ek*, out of), human sources,
> whether parents, husband, or ourselves. No one can save
> us but God. God is the *source* by which the new birth is
> given (v. 13), but free will is the *means* by which it is
> "received" (v. 12). It is "by" grace but "through" (Greek:
> *dia*) faith that we are saved (Eph. 2:8).

Let's examine these two "serious mistakes."

First, Dr. Geisler, throughout the book, fails to recognize
that Reformed Christians believe that men believe and choose.
It is the order of events that is in dispute. Every Christian has
chosen Christ, *believed* in Christ, *embraced* Christ, and even more,
continues to do so. The question is not "must a person believe,"
but *can* a person believe while a slave to sin? Further, whose
decision comes first: the decision of God to free the enslaved,
dead sinner and give him *the ability* to believe, or the free-
choice decision of the sinner that then makes him or her one
of the elect?

Dr. Geisler claims, but does not substantiate, that it is the
act of belief that *brings* spiritual life. As we will see when we
examine regeneration and the gift of faith, this is nothing more
than an assertion that is contradictory to biblical teaching (especially to John's writings). If *CBF* is correct, where is the connection drawn between the will of man in belief in verse 12
and the spiritual birth of verse 13? Is not birth logically prior to
action? Even though the passage itself says "not of the will of
man," Geisler can say, "this involves an act of free will." Belief
is a free-will act, but being born again is not?

But the objection does raise an interesting issue: does the
text itself indicate a relationship between believing and the

new birth? There are certainly some points that Dr. Geisler would have to consider to make his assertions carry weight:

1) John, as is his custom, refers to Christians as "the believing ones" (τοῖς πιστεύουσιν). English translations normally miss this important element of John's gospel (the contrast between true, saving faith, which is almost always expressed through the use of the present tense indicating an on-going, living faith, versus false faith which is almost always placed in the aorist tense, making no statement about its consistency or vitality). It is literally, "even to those who are believing in His name" or "the believing ones (who believe) in His name." The term "believing" is a present participle.

2) The verb "born" (ἐγεννήθησαν) is in the aorist passive form. In its context it is plainly said to be an act of God. All human agency is denied.

3) It follows, then, that verse 13 is a description of "the believing ones" of verse 12. Nothing is said in the text that the new birth is "received" by an "act of free will." In fact, *the exact opposite is stated clearly*, "the ones born *not* of the will of man...." It is an amazing example of how preconceived notions can be read into a text that *CBF* can say the text makes the new birth dependent upon an act of "free will" when the text says the opposite.

The second "error" alleged by Dr. Geisler in the Reformed interpretation of John 1:12-13 is his assertion that this passage is "simply denying" that there is any other *source* of the new birth other than God. He then asserts that "God is the *source* by which the new birth is given (v. 13), but free will is the *means* by which it is "received" (v. 12)." The same objection applies here that was stated above: if a person can have saving faith without the new birth, then *what does the new birth accomplish?* Evidently one does not need the new birth to obey God's commands or have saving faith. We certainly agree with Dr. Geisler that this passage denies, in the strongest terms, that man is born again through any human means whatsoever. But there are two problems with Geisler's assertion: first, it is not the new birth that is "received" in 1:12, as he says: it is

Christ that is received. If he wishes to say the two are the same thing, we need more than the mere assertion of the idea. Second, the idea that the use of the preposition "ek" somehow limits this to saying God is the "source," but we are the agent, is in error. The Greek term "ek" *often* refers to direct agency, and surely this is the meaning here. We are caused to be born *by* God. The text nowhere even remotely suggests that John is here speaking of "sources" and not the actual action itself. The fact that he speaks of the "will of a man" makes it *very* clear that he is going far beyond merely saying "God is the source of the new birth" to saying *God is the one who causes the new birth in contrast to any action of the will of man.*

Hence we see that *CBF* fails to substantiate its charge of error against the Reformed interpretation, and instead ends up making the text say the opposite of its actual intention. We will see this happen again in the next chapter when we examine Romans 9:16.

Acts 13:46-48

> Paul and Barnabas spoke out boldly and said, "It was necessary that the word of God be spoken to you first; since you repudiate it and judge yourselves unworthy of eternal life, behold, we are turning to the Gentiles. For so the Lord has commanded us, 'I HAVE PLACED YOU AS A LIGHT FOR THE GENTILES, THAT YOU MAY BRING SALVATION TO THE END OF THE EARTH.'" When the Gentiles heard this, they *began* rejoicing and glorifying the word of the Lord; and as many as had been appointed to eternal life believed.

This passage is not cited in *CBF* as one that is used by "extreme Calvinists" and hence requires a response. Instead, it is listed as a passage that allegedly shows "Salvation: both ordained to it and persuaded into it." This idea is based upon citing Acts 13:48 and then noting that just a few verses later (Acts 14:1) the disciples spoke "in such a manner" that large people believed. We would hope that it is not being suggested that the *quality* of the apostles' speech is being credited with the faith of the multitude: men are not converted by words of wisdom or the persuasive abilities of any man. Men are converted when God changes their hearts and draws them unto Christ.

But Dr. Geisler then adds the following paragraph:

> Some moderate Calvinists, like J. O. Buswell, deny this is a reference to predestination. He wrote, "Actually the words of Acts 13:48-49 do not necessarily have any reference whatever to the doctrine of God's eternal decree of election." The passive participle *tetagmenoi* may simply mean 'ready,' and we might well read, 'as many as were prepared for eternal life, believed.' " He adds, "Commenting on this word, Alford says, 'The meaning of this word must be determined by the context. The Jews had *judged themselves unworthy of eternal life* (v. 46); the Gentiles, "as many as were disposed to eternal life," believed....To find in this text preordination to life asserted, is to force both the word and the context to a meaning which they do not contain.' " [10]

We commend Dr. Geisler for his very conditional presentation of this argument. It is clear that he is well aware that this viewpoint has a *mountain* of argumentation going against it. First and foremost is the fact that the passage is not translated as "made ready" or "were disposed to" in any of the major modern Bible translations:

> and as many as were ordained to eternal life believed. (KJV, 1611)

> and as many as were ordained to eternal life believed. (ASV, 1901).

> And as many as had been appointed to eternal life believed. (NKJV, 1982)

> and all who were appointed for eternal life believed. (NIV, 1984)

> and as many as had been destined for eternal life became believers. (NRSV, 1989)

> and as many as had been appointed to eternal life believed. (NASB Update, 1995)

> and all who were appointed to eternal life became believers. (NLT, 1996)

> and all who had been appointed for eternal life believed. (NET, 1998)

Some have gone so far as to suggest that the participle τεταγμένοι be translated in the middle voice, "considered themselves worthy," and the above assertions seem to parallel that thought, at least in the results.

But what motivates such interpretation? Surely there is nothing in the text to do so. Luke uses this verb, in the passive, to clearly mean "appoint" elsewhere. For example:

> "And I said, 'What shall I do, Lord?' And the Lord said to me, 'Get up and go on into Damascus, and there you will be told of all that has been appointed (τέτακται) for you to do.' (Acts 22:10)

No one would suggest that we should understand this to mean "you will be told of all that you have appointed yourself to do" or "all you have judged yourself worthy of doing." The same is true in Acts 28:23, where they "set a day" for Paul's hearing, again using the passive form of the same verb. Paul was not "disposed toward" a date, he was *appointed* a date.[11]

But there is a grammatical reason why the normal translation and understanding of this passage should be accepted (along with the resultant meaning). The term "appointed" here is found in what is called a *periphrastic construction*. A periphrastic construction involves the use of a participle with a form of the Greek verb of being, εἰμί. By combining different tenses of both elements, a particular result is achieved. In this case, Luke uses the imperfect form of *eimi* together with the perfect passive participle. The result is that the phrase must be translated as a "pluperfect."[12]

A pluperfect sense speaks of a completed action in the past, but unlike the perfect tense, the pluperfect does not contain the idea of a continuation of the past action into the present time. Therefore, the meaning of "appointed" refers to a past action. How can this be if, in fact, we are to understand this as an attitude in the Gentiles who have just heard that the gospel is coming to them? Obviously, to take it in the sense suggested by Buswell or Alford is to understand this action as something that takes place at the very point where the Apostles quote from Isaiah and proclaim that the Gentiles can receive the blessings of the gospel. Luke writes, "When the Gentiles heard this, they *began* rejoicing and glorifying the word of the Lord." How can we think that prior to this they had somehow judged themselves worthy of eternal life? Instead, the most natural way to take the text is to see this as Luke's explanation of why *some* who heard believed while others did not: the difference was not that some were better or more "disposed" toward the gospel than others (the very idea of someone being disposed toward the gospel is utterly contrary to Paul's teaching in Romans 8:7-8): the difference is that some were appointed to eternal life as part of the eternal decree of God, and others were not.

The same is true today. The person who proclaims the gospel with purity and power can trust that God will save His elect. Likewise, we know that others will laugh and mock no matter how clearly or forcefully we present the truth.

In reality the only reason people suggest that the term be taken in such an unusual manner is because they do not wish to accept the teaching of the passage, for it makes it very clear that it is not our presentation, not our skills, not our preaching that brings men to repentance (all can be used by God, but all can likewise come to naught): as many as were appointed by the Lord believed, for faith is, as we will prove later in this work, the divine gift of God given to His elect people.

Matthew 11:25-27

> At that time Jesus said, "I praise You, Father, Lord of heaven and earth, that You have hidden these things from *the* wise and intelligent and have revealed them to infants. Yes, Father, for this way was well-pleasing in Your sight. All things have been handed over to Me by My Father; and no one knows the Son except the Father; nor does anyone know the Father except the Son, and anyone to whom the Son wills to reveal *Him*."

This section of Scripture comes right after an announcement of judgment upon the cities in which Jesus had worked mighty miracles and yet there was no repentance. In what must strike the Arminian ear in a most unusual way, Jesus responds to this wholesale rejection by thousands of individuals He allegedly was doing all He could to save by praising His Father that He (the Father) had in fact *hidden* these things from the wise and prudent and revealed them to babes! He affirms that this is God's plan and it is pleasing in God's sight. This provides the preceding context for the key verse, 11:27.

Jesus affirms His own deity in this passage of Scripture and His unique role as the *only* revealer of the Father (John 1:18). Not only have all things been entrusted to the Son (no mere creature could be given "all things"), but the Person of the Son is so great, so magnificent that *only* the infinite Person of the Father can know Him truly. There is a reciprocal truth: to perfectly reveal the Father requires a perfect, infinite Person: the Son. Jesus is the revealer of the Father. He is the *only* one capable of so doing. And, He does so not because He *must* do so but because He *chooses* to do so.

Who then can know the Father? Every single person who chooses to do so by an act of free will, as *CBF* suggests? No, this revelation is specific for it is by Christ and in Christ alone. It is to the elect, chosen in Him before time began, that Christ makes the wonderful revelation of the Father. Christ *chooses* to make this revelation. He is the one who is free.

The verses that follow are often used to attempt to overthrow the specificity of Christ's revelation of the Father. "Come to Me, all who are weary and heavy laden, and I will give you rest" the Lord says. "See," the Arminian says, "this is a general call to all people, not just the elect." A general call it is, but who is it that knows they are weary and heavy laden? Is the unregenerate man, who is at enmity with God, dead in sin, going to be seeking rest by coming to Christ? While the lost seek their rest in the world's pleasures or religions, the elect seek it in the only place it can be found: in Christ.

CBF seeks to explain Matthew 11:27 as follows:

> God chooses only to reveal Himself personally to the *willing*. Jesus said, " 'If anyone *chooses to do God's will*, he will find out whether my teaching comes from God or whether I speak on my own' " (John 7:17). It is noteworthy also that it does *not* say that Jesus wishes only to reveal the Father to some. Indeed, God desires all to be saved (Matt. 23:37, 2 Peter 3:9).[13]

We have already seen that Dr. Geisler's use of Matthew 23:37 and 2 Peter 3:9 is in error. Further, we should note that elsewhere in his book Dr. Geisler criticizes Reformed exegetes for citing passages "from another book, in another context,"[14] yet, this is exactly what he does here. Next, is it Geisler's position that it is the Son's desire to reveal the Father to every single individual on earth? Then does it not follow that Christ has failed in this task, if, indeed, this is a salvific revelation of the Father?

Very little in *CBF*'s response actually addresses the passage. The assertion that God chooses only to reveal Himself to the willing is based upon the errant interpretation of Matthew 23:37. John 7:17 is a completely different context and has nothing to do with Matthew 11. That passage does not posit a free will in man, but simply states that anyone who *is* willing will know the truth of Christ's teaching. And who knows this but the redeemed? Does not every Christian desire to know of the truthfulness of Christ's teaching? This is descriptive of the believer, not prescriptive of how one *becomes* a believer.

John 5:21

> For just as the Father raises the dead and gives them life, even so the Son also gives life to whom He wishes.

This passage is very similar to Matthew 11:27. The deity of Christ is plainly implied in grand terms, for only God is able to give life, and this ability is the Son's as well. He is able to "give life to whom He wishes." Literally the text says, "He enlivens whom He wishes." The verb (ζωοποιεῖ) is active. This is something the Son does, and the objects of the active verb are human beings raised to spiritual life. It is a free act of the will of the Son that brings life. The Arminian would have to limit this to saying that Christ freely wills *to save* based upon the action of faith in man. Again the object of God's choice would be a plan, not a person. But this is not what the text says. Christ gives life to whom He *wills* (θέλει), not to those who first *will it* thus allowing Him to save.

Commentators recognize that this passage speaks of God as the source of both physical life as well as spiritual life. The words spoken are true both of the raising to physical life in the resurrection as well as the giving of spiritual life in regeneration. This may be indicated by the use of two verbs in 5:21, "to raise up" (the normal term for raising the dead) and "to make alive." A diverse body of exegetes confirm this dual application of the words of Jesus in 5:21, such as Leon Morris,[15] B.F. Westcott,[16] William Hendrikson,[17] J.H. Bernard,[18] Henry Alford,[19] not to mention the great body of older Puritan and Reformed exegetes (Spurgeon included), going back to Calvin's assertion. That there is spiritual life in view is Calvin's position. He wrote, "Again, he does not speak of this life as bestowed indiscriminately on all; for he says that *he giveth life to whom he will*; by which he means that he especially confers this grace on none but certain men, that is, on the elect."[20] We can go all the way back to Augustine in A.D. 415 who commented on this passage,

> Our Lord, for instance, raised Lazarus; He unquestionably was able to do so. But inasmuch as He did not raise up Judas, must we therefore contend that He was unable to do so? He certainly was able, but He would not. For if He had been willing, He could have effected this too. For the Son quickeneth whomsoever He will.[21]

So how does *CBF* handle this passage? Interestingly, it does so in the context of denying particular redemption, not unconditional election. As we will see when we discuss the atoning work of Christ, *the vast majority of Arminian objections to particular redemption are actually confused objections to unconditional election.* The same is true here. *CBF* notes that this passage is sometimes used by Reformed writers "in an attempt to prove limited atonement whereby Christ gives spiritual life only to the elect."[22] But this is clearly an objection against the sovereignty of God in saving only the elect, not to the belief that it was Christ's intention to save the elect perfectly in His death. We note the reasoning provided by *CBF*:

> First of all, if this interpretation were true it would contradict the clear teaching of other texts in John (John 3:16) and elsewhere (1 John 2:2, 2 Peter 2:1).

We are left to assume *CBF*'s interpretation of these passages. In essence, it is being said "it can't be saying Christ gives life only to the elect since we already believe these other verses teach differently."

John 3:16 is cited by *CBF* over and over again as indication that there is no particularity to God's work of salvation. The idea that the term "world" could possibly mean anything other than every single individual (despite the fact that all serious exegetes recognize a *wide* variety of uses of this term in the New Testament and especially in John's writings, for example, John 17:9 and 1 John 2:15) is simply dismissed by *CBF* on numerous occasions. Furthermore, the common misconception that John 3:16 uses an indefinite phrase, "whosoever," is presented as evidence against the particularity of God's work of redemption. However, anyone familiar with the text as it was written knows that the literal rendering of the passage is "in order that every one believing in him should not perish but have eternal life." The verse teaches that the giving of the Son guarantees the salvation of all the believing ones. Sound exegetical practice requires us to then ask, "Does Jesus speak to who will, and who will not, believe?" The answer is yes, He does, in such passages as John 6:37-45.

We will look at the other passages under the topic of the atonement. Geisler continues:

> Second, the use of "just as" in this text indicates the Son is doing the same thing as the Father, and the Father "raises the dead." So it is not a reference to salvation but to resurrection of the dead. Finally, the resurrection in this very chapter of John refers to "all who are in the graves" (5:28), both saved and unsaved (v. 29). Hence, the resurrection life given is not limited to the elect: both saved and unsaved are resurrected.

The attempt to limit this passage to merely the resurrection of the dead leads to a tremendous problem for *CBF*. Are we to believe, then, that John 5:24 does *not* refer to salvation? This passage is closer in context than verses 28-29, cited by Geisler:

> Truly, truly, I say to you, he who hears My word, and believes Him who sent Me, has eternal life, and does not come into judgment, but has passed out of death into life.

Is it not the common view of Protestant exegetes in general that the use of the present tense "has eternal life" in 5:24 means we have this life *now* as a present possession? While 5:24 is not referenced in *CBF*, Dr. Geisler sees it as a reference to salvation (not just resurrection) in his *Baker Encyclopedia of Christian Apologetics*,[23] so if he is consistent, surely the attempt to say that Christ refers here only to physical resurrection must be rejected in light of the proximity of verse 24.

But more importantly, *CBF*'s assertion empties the passage of any meaning. What does it mean that Christ "gives life to whom He wishes" when this simply means that Christ engages in the work of resurrection? Will not all be resurrected, some to a resurrection of life and others to a resurrection of judgment? How is the freedom of Christ to be expressed here? But it is just this divine freedom, so clearly stated in John 5:21, that is denied by *CBF*. To safeguard the freedom of man, the freedom of Christ must be limited so that He does not give spiritual life to those whom He wills, but instead is limited to engaging in the resurrection of the dead prior to judgment *only*. This is obviously an artificial and erroneous view of the passage.

Romans 8:28-30

> And we know that God causes all things to work together for good to those who love God, to those who are called according to His purpose. For those whom He foreknew, He also predestined to become conformed to the image of His Son, so that He would be the firstborn among many brethren; and these whom He predestined, He also called; and these whom He called, He also justified; and these whom He justified, He also glorified.

Few texts of Scripture are so clear, so forceful, in asserting the absolute freedom of God in saving His elect people than these. Every attempt to undermine their testimony truly rings hollow. Simple fairness drives the mind to recognize that these verses speak of *God's* work, not man's. God saves, from beginning to end.

Providing an exegesis of this text would be superfluous, as so many fine examples exist. The reader is directed to the work of John Murray, *The Epistle to the Romans*[24] for an example of the ease with which the Reformed exegete can work with this text by simply allowing it to speak for itself. We are truly on "home court" in Romans 8 and 9.

How does *CBF* attempt to defuse this keystone of the Reformed faith? One should not be surprised that a slight variant of the classic Arminian approach is utilized. In essence, the effort (which, outside of Romans 9, receives the longest block of text in the book, almost a full three pages) provides not a scintilla of exegetical comment on verse 28. The attempted response to verse 29 focuses upon denying that "foreknown" carries the concept of "fore-loved" or "chosen." But the entire effort is summarized in these words:

> For the question still remains as to whether God ordained an act of free choice as a means of receiving His unconditional grace.[25]

We have now seen this tactic repeated many times: did God ordain *people* to salvation or a *plan*? We have seen over and over that the direct object of the words used to describe God's work is *personal*. *People* are predestined, *people* are chosen before the world begins, not acts, not plans, not possibilities. This remains the central error of *CBF*'s argumentation: the unbiblical replacement of the *personal element* of the electing grace of God with a philosophically derived, eisegetically inserted idea of God's ordination of a plan that is dependent upon the actions of man for fruition and success.

In verse 28 Paul identifies those who love God as those who "are called according to *His* purpose." The word "His" is provided for clarity, for it is literally, "called according to purpose." We have seen the call and purpose of God extolled in Ephesians 1. Throughout the passage God is active, calling, predestining, justifying, glorifying. Man is the object of redemption (praise God!), but man in no way rules over it, determines its success, adds to its work, or intrudes on God's glory.

If a man or woman truly loves God (not a god of their own making or their own image, but the true God of the Bible, including all those truths of His being and character that are the most reprehensible to the natural man), that person has been called by God in accordance with His purpose. Indeed, true love for the true God is one of the surest signs of regeneration and redemption.

CBF does not interact with the text of Romans 8:28. Instead, it immediately devolves into the assertion that election and predestination are "in accordance with" foreknowledge. We have already seen what this means and the fact that Geisler's position, while denying election *based on* foreknowledge presents election *in accordance with* foreknowledge. But to substantiate this position he must believe that "to foreknow" in 8:29 has the same meaning as the philosophical use of the term. If we find that in this passage foreknowledge does *not* refer to God's perfect knowledge of the events of the future, including the free acts of human beings, then it can be said that *CBF* offers *no* response to this passage at all. Geisler realizes this, for he accurately describes the Reformed understanding:

> Many extreme Calvinists take "foreknown" to refer to the fact that God foreloved. In this case, to foreknow and to choose or elect would be the same thing. They cite other passages in attempts to support this (e.g., Deut. 7:7-8; Jer. 1:5; Amos 3:2; Matt. 7:22-23). If so, then God's foreknowledge would not have any reference to foreknowing how the elect would respond.[26]

The key is found in the final phrase: for *CBF*'s position to hold it must be proven that "foreknown" in this passage cannot, and does not, mean anything that would conflict with the idea of God knowing the free acts of men.

Without repeating work that has been done elsewhere,[27] let us summarize the position of Reformed exegetes on the meaning of "foreknow."

1   The primary passages that should inform our understanding of the term are those that have God as the subject of the verbal form, as here. Obviously, passages that have humans as the subject would differ, substantially, in their meaning, for God's knowledge is vastly different than man's.

2   The verb προγινώσκω is used three times in the New Testament with God as the subject: Romans 8:29, Romans 11:2, and 1 Peter 1:20.

3   The key issue (normally unaddressed by Arminian writers) lies in the *objects* of God's action of "foreknowing." What, or *who*, is "foreknown" by God? In Romans 8:29 the direct object of the verb is a pronoun that refers back to the elect of verse 28. In Romans 11:2 the object is "His people." And in 1 Peter 1:20 the object is Christ.

4   Every time God is portrayed as "foreknowing" the object of the verb is *personal*.

5   Therefore, to say that God foreknows *acts, faith, behavior, choices, etc.* is to assume something about the term *that is not witnessed in the biblical text*. God foreknows *persons* not *things*.

6   This New Testament usage then decides for us which elements of the Old Testament stream most informs these passages. That is, the Hebrew term *yada* (יָדַע) is used in many different ways. Is there a discernable usage in the Old Testament that comes through to the New Testament that would see this as an *action* that has only *persons* as its object? The answer is a definite yes. Here are some of the key passages where the very same element of personal choice and knowledge is a part of God's "knowing" in the Old Testament:

Before I formed you in the womb I knew you,

> And before you were born I consecrated you;
> I have appointed you a prophet to the nations.
> (Jeremiah 1:5)

Here God's knowledge of Jeremiah is clearly personal. It is paralleled with the term "consecrated" and "appointed," pointing us toward the element of "choice." This knowledge of Jeremiah is not limited to time. In some manner, God "knew" Jeremiah before Jeremiah came into existence.

> The LORD said to Moses, "I will also do this thing of which you have spoken; for you have found favor in My sight and I have known you by name." (Exodus 33:17)

This tremendous passage (which Paul draws upon in Romans 9) reveals the very personal aspect of God's "knowing" of an individual. Obviously the Lord is not revealing to Moses, "I know your name!" This "knowing" is intimate, personal, and is connected with the fact that Moses "found favor" in the sight of God. This is a gracious knowing, a gracious *choosing* of Moses to receive the benefits of God's mercy.

> You only have I chosen among all the families of the earth;
> Therefore I will punish you for all your iniquities."
> (Amos 3:2)

Here the NASB actually translates *yada* as "chosen," so strongly is this element found in the context of this passage. Literally it says, "You (speaking of Israel) only have I *known*...." Obviously God is not denying knowledge of the mere existence of other nations and peoples. There is a special element to this "knowing," an element of gracious choice. Indeed, so personal and intimate can be the use of *yada* that it is said in Genesis 4:1 that when Adam "knew" his wife, the result was a child.

Therefore, the *use* of the verbal concept of "foreknowing" in the New Testament, together with these testimonies from the Old Testament, are more than sufficient basis for asserting that when Paul says "and those whom He foreknew" Paul is speaking about an *action* on God's part that is just as solitary, just as God-centered, and just as *personal* as every other action in the string: God foreknows (chooses to enter into relationship with); God predestines; God calls; God justifies; God glorifies. From first to last it is God who is active, God who accomplishes *all* these things. It is the burden of the Arminian to break this "golden chain of redemption," prove to us that God's foreknowing is a mere passive gathering of infallible knowledge of the future actions of free creatures, and establish that this passage is *not* telling us that all of salvation, from initiation *to accomplishment*, is the work of God for His own glory.

CBF attempts to maintain its Arminian viewpoint by stating:

> First, even if this is true, it is irrelevant, since extreme Calvinists believe in God's infallible foreknowledge (cf., Isa. 46:10) regardless of what these verses teach. And if God does foreknow infallibly, then He would still foreknow what people would freely believe, and He would still have to decide whether He would have to force them to believe in Him or else elect those He knew could be persuaded to freely accept His grace.

We have seen this quotation before, and it again establishes the non-Reformed character of *CBF*. The passage is filled with errors. It does not use "foreknow" in the sense we have just established. It speaks of God deciding to "force" people to believe (rather than the Reformed position that speaks of God's gracious deliverance of them from sin, the renewing of their heart, the granting of spiritual life, the giving of the gifts of faith and repentance). And it again shows its fully Arminian view of salvation by making God's act of predestination dependent upon the pliability of men, those who "could be persuaded to freely accept His grace." Rather than a grace that changes dead sinners, we have a grace that requires the free will of man for its effectiveness.

Then Dr. Geisler attempts to dissuade his readers from understanding "foreknow" as we have presented it above. But his argumentation is seriously deficient. In fact, he engages in the very activity he (errantly) accuses Reformed writers of doing when they seek to establish that such words as "all" and "world" can have specific meanings in specific contexts. He establishes that "to know" can be used with no personal element (i.e., to know simple facts). No one disputes the assertion. No one has said "The Greek word *ginosko* always has this one meaning." The assertion is that when it is used of God in particular contexts in the Old Testament it carries this meaning, and that in *every* usage in the New Testament it does so. Next, he establishes that *ginosko* "usually" does not mean "choose." Again, this is a point not in dispute (though an entire paragraph is dedicated to the demonstration). Finally he proves that even the specific verb, *proginosko,* is used "in reference to advanced knowledge of events." Unfortunately he errs and gives only references that have *men* as the subject of the verb, not the ones that have *God* as the subject. Yet, after all these irrelevant or errant efforts, *CBF* concludes, "Thus, the extreme Calvinist's equating of foreknowing and foreloving does not follow." This is then followed by even more argumentation that is again irrelevant to the actual issue:

> Finally, the word "chosen" by God is used of persons who are not the elect. Judas, for example, was "chosen" by Christ but not one of the elect: "Jesus replied, 'Have I not chosen you, the Twelve? Yet one of you is a devil!' " (John 6:70). Israel was chosen as a nation, but not every individual in Israel will be saved.[28]

Of course the word "chosen" is used in more than one way. No one is arguing that "chosen" always has the same meaning. Instead, the issue is, does "chosen" mean elect in the context of the passages that we have examined? And the answer to that has already been seen: it does.

There remains one key passage that, due to its importance and the length of the attempted response by *CBF*, deserves its own chapter. That is Paul's teaching found in Romans chapter 9.

Notes

1   *Chosen But Free*, pp. 67-68.

2   Ibid., p. 69.

3   Ibid., p. 70.

4   Ibid., p. 68.

5   Ibid., p. 179.

6   As with all else we have seen, we must insist that it is not the mere opportunity of being saved, or receiving an inheritance if we will do certain things (whether those be "good works in a state of grace" or the mere free choice act of faith) that is in view here. There is all the difference in the world between an *actual* work that brings glory to God and a *potential* work that can be set at naught by the supreme will of the creature.

7   John Calvin, *Commentary on the Gospel According to John* (Baker Book House, 1984), p. 43.

8   "A Strong Consolation" preached 9/26/1869, *The Charles H. Spurgeon Library CD ROM* (Ages Digital Library, 1998).

9   *Chosen But Free*, p. 58

10 Ibid., p. 41.

11 See also Romans 13:1 where the same kind of term is used to clearly mean "appointed."

12 For a summary of periphrastic translations, see William Mounce, *Basics of Biblical Greek* (Zondervan, 1993), pp. 276-277 and Daniel Wallace, *Greek Grammar Beyond the Basics* (Zondervan, 1996), pp. 647-649.

13 *Chosen But Free*, p. 72.

14 Ibid., p. 193.

15 Leon Morris, *The Gospel According to John* (Eerdmans, 1971), pp. 314-315. Morris actually asserts that the primary application of Jesus' words in 5:21 is in reference to the giving of life in the current time period, with the later resurrection being only in the background.

16 Brooke Foss Westcott, *The Gospel According to John* (Baker Book House, 1980), p. 191.

17 William Hendriksen, *New Testament Commentary: Exposition of the Gospel According to John* (Baker Book House, 1953), p. 199.

18 J.H. Bernard, *A Critical and Exegetical Commentary on the Gospel According to St. John* (T&T Clark, 1985), p. 241.

19 Henry Alford, *The New Testament for English Readers* Vol. II (Baker Book House, 1983), p. 507. It should be noted that Alford denies that the "whom He wills" involves any particularity, though Alford provides no sound reasoning as to why this is.

20 John Calvin, *Commentary on the Gospel of John*, (Baker Book House, 1984), p. 200.

21 Augustine, *On Nature and Grace*, 2:8.

22 *Chosen But Free*, p. 78.

23 Norman Geisler, *Baker Encyclopedia of Christian Apologetics* (Baker Book House, 1999), pp. 361, 491.

24 John Murray, *The Epistle to the Romans* (Eerdmans, 1997), pp. 314-321.

25 *Chosen But Free*, p. 71.

26 Ibid., p. 69.

27 I have addressed the meaning of προγινώσκω elsewhere. See *God's Sovereign Grace: A Biblical Examination of Calvinism* (Crowne, 1990), pp. 117-122. For the truly brave at heart who wish exhaustive discussions, few are better than Francis Turretin, *Institutes of Elenctic Theology* (Presbyterian and Reformed, 1992), Volume I, p. 355 and following.

28 Ibid., pp. 70-71.

Chapter 9

Responding to CBF on Romans 9

This tremendous passage of Scripture is so clear, so strong, that it truly does speak for itself. The student of Scripture that wishes a full discussion of the passage is directed to John Piper's *The Justification of God*. Before examining Dr. Geisler's comments, a brief exegesis of the passage will be offered.

This portion of Paul's reasoned, organized argument regarding the nature of salvation comes after the announcement of the tremendous blessings of eternal salvation found in chapter 8. Immediately the Apostle must face a crucial issue: what of the Jews? Surely Paul had heard this many times in his public ministry: "If this gospel message you proclaim, Paul, is so wonderful, why is it that only a small number of Jews embrace it, while the majority of the covenant people reject it? Are not your main opponents the Jews, to whom the promises were made? Are you not just a renegade Jew who has left the faith?" Such accusations must have been common place in the public disputations with the Jews. And upon speaking of God's work of predestining, calling, justifying, and glorifying, one can just hear these objections growing in volume. "Oh come now, Paul, if God is so sovereign and powerful, then why do His very people, the Jews, by and large reject Christ?" It is to this issue that Paul now turns.

In Romans 9:1-5, Paul lays out his heart's desire along with the true privileges granted to physical Israel:

> I am telling the truth in Christ, I am not lying, my conscience testifies with me in the Holy Spirit, that I have great sorrow and unceasing grief in my heart. For I could wish that I myself were accursed, *separated* from Christ for the sake of my brethren, my kinsmen according to the flesh, who are Israelites, to whom belongs the adoption as sons, and the glory and the covenants and the giving of the Law and the *temple* service and the promises, whose are the fathers, and from whom is the Christ according to the flesh, who is over all, God blessed forever. Amen.

Paul has not forgotten the Jews. Strong emotion fills his words as he swears that he has sorrow and unceasing grief in his heart over the hard-heartedness of the Jewish people. He even goes so far as to say that he would be willing to be cut off from Christ if this would only bring his brethren to salvation. It should be noted that this immediately raises an important point: *Paul is speaking of individual salvation.* It makes no sense to say "I could wish myself were accursed for the sake of the nation of Israel so that it might be returned to a position of receiving national privileges and favor."

The next verse is vitally important and provides the key to one of the great controversies in interpretation of the rest of the chapter:

> But *it is* not as though the word of God has failed. For they are not all Israel who are *descended* from Israel. (Romans 9:6)

We can surely understand Paul's concern: his ministry had often been charged with teaching a doctrine that made it appear as if the word of God (found in the promises to Israel) had failed due to the rejection of Christ by the Jews. But Paul is quick to reject this errant assertion. His response *must* be understood. "For they are not all Israel who are *descended* from Israel." Why has the word of God *not* failed? Because the accusation is based upon a false premise. Just because a person is a physical descendant of Israel does not mean this person is truly an Israelite. The rejection of those who are only *physically* Jews but not *spiritually* so is not a valid basis upon which to say the promises have been made void. Paul expands upon this point:

> Nor are they all children because they are Abraham's descendants, but: "THROUGH ISAAC YOUR DESCENDANTS WILL BE NAMED." That is, it is not the children of the flesh who are children of God, but the children of the promise are regarded as descendants. For this is the word of promise: "AT THIS TIME I WILL COME, AND SARAH WILL HAVE A SON." (Romans 9:7-9)

The promises remain valid since they were only the possession of the "children of promise" from the beginning. Two truths immediately come to our attention: first, God determined who was, and who was not, a child of promise. This is all God's work. Secondly, *Paul is speaking of the salvation of individuals.* When he says that not all who are descended from Israel are truly children of promise, who is he referring to? Is he not speaking of *persons* within the body of the nation of Israel? Who are these children of promise if not *people*? Remember the accusation to which he responds: "Look, Paul! Your gospel teaches that these Jewish opponents of yours who oppose Christ and His gospel will be accursed! You nullify the word of God!" But Paul's response is, "No, I do not, for simply being a physical descendant of Israel does not make you a true Israelite. God has *always* had an elect people that *He* chooses and it is *not* an external matter, based upon race or nationality." And it is this last point that Paul takes up beginning in verse 9. But the key is this: Paul is *not* talking about nations and he *is* talking about God's sovereign election in salvation, for it was God's right and freedom to limit His promises to the *children of promise*, and not to anyone else.

God has always worked this way, Paul teaches. Salvation

has *always* been under His control. God has *never* been forced to act upon the dictates of human choice or decision. He demonstrates this from Israel's own history:

> And not only this, but there was Rebekah also, when she had conceived *twins* by one man, our father Isaac; for though *the twins* were not yet born and had not done anything good or bad, so that God's purpose according to *His* choice would stand, not because of works but because of Him who calls, it was said to her, "THE OLDER WILL SERVE THE YOUNGER." Just as it is written, "JACOB I LOVED, BUT ESAU I HATED." (Romans 9:10-13)

The declaration of "God's purpose according to *His* choice" (or "election") is the keystone of this section. Everything points to this one assertion. The pronouncement by God that the older would serve the younger was made on the basis of a *choice* by God (dare we say a "free choice"?) that was made *before* their birth and *before* they could "do" anything good or bad. Paul's emphasis is upon the *independence* and *freedom* of God's choice. There was nothing in the twins that determined the choice (which is the point of stating that the pronouncement was made *before* the twins had done "anything good or bad"). Just so that this would not be missed, Paul clarifies and emphasizes his concern: "*not* because of works but because of Him who calls." Literally the text reads "from works....from the One calling," again making the same point: the ground of choice, the source of election, is *solely in God*, not in man. John Piper gave excellent insight into this passage when he wrote,

> First, with the use of the preposition ἐξ Paul makes explicit that God's decision to treat Esau and Jacob differently is not merely *prior* to their good or evil deeds but is also completely *independent* of them. God's electing purpose (Rom 9:11c) and his concrete prediction (9:12c) are in no way *based on* the distinctives Esau and

Jacob have by birth or by action. This rules out the notion of the early Greek and Latin commentators that election is based on God's foreknowledge of men's good works. Second, Rom 9:12b enlarges on 9:11b by going beyond the *negation* of human *distinctives* as the ground for God's predestining of Esau and Jacob. It makes the *positive affirmation* that the true ground of this election is God himself, "the one who calls." The intended force of the phrase "not from works but from the one who calls" is felt most strongly when one *contrasts* it with the similar Pauline phrase "not from works but from faith." In Paul's thinking the latter phrase describes the event of *justification* (Rom 9:32; Gal 2:16), never the event of election or predestination. Paul never grounds the "electing purpose of God" in man's faith. The counterpart to works in conjunction with election (as opposed to justification) is always God's own call (Rom 9:12b) or his own grace (Rom 11:6). The predestination and call of God precede justification (Rom 8:29f) and have no ground in any human act, not even faith. This is why Paul explicitly says in Rom 9:16 that God's bestowal of mercy on whomever he wills is based neither on human *willing* (which would include faith) nor on human running (which would include all activity).[1]

This is likewise the implication of verse 13, where God speaks of His choice of Jacob over Esau. Much is made of the terms "loved" and "hated" here, and we will see how these terms are to be applied when responding to *CBF*'s commentary.

The immediate response that is offered to the assertion of the Potter's freedom to do with His creation as He sees fit is, "But, doesn't that make God unjust?" Paul had "heard it all before" and was ready with a response:

> What shall we say then? There is no injustice with God, is there? May it never be! For He says to Moses, "I WILL HAVE MERCY ON WHOM I HAVE MERCY, AND I WILL HAVE COMPASSION ON WHOM I HAVE COMPASSION." So then it *does* not

depend on the man who wills or the man who runs, but on God who has mercy. (Romans 9:14-16)

Paul is ready with an Old Testament example to buttress his arguments: Exodus 33. This tremendous passage contains themes that find their full expression only in the New Testament's full revelation of the doctrines of God's free and sovereign grace. God showed mercy and compassion to Moses, choosing to reveal His glory as an act of grace. We *must* understand, in light of the prevailing attitude of the world around us, that God's mercy, if it is to be mercy at all, *must be free.* Literally the text speaks of "mercying" and "compassioning," again *verbs of action* that find their subject in God and their object in those chosen by *His* decision. It does not say, "I will have mercy on those who fulfill the conditions I have laid down as the prerequisite of my plan of salvation." Both the "source" of compassion and mercy *and the individual application* find their ultimate ground only in the free choice of *God,* not of man.

This divine truth, so offensive to the natural man, could not find a clearer proclamation than Romans 9:16. We truly must ask, if this passage does not deny to the will of man the all-powerful position of final say in whether the entire work of the Triune God in salvation will succeed or fail, what passage possibly could? What stronger terms could be employed? The verse begins, "so then," drawing from the assertion of God that mercy and compassion are His to freely give. Next comes the negative particle, "not," which negates everything that follows in the clause. Two human activities are listed: willing and literally "running," or striving. Human choice and human action. Paul puts it bluntly: it is *not* "of the one willing" nor is it "of the one running." Paul uses two singular present active participles. The fact that they are singular shows us again the *personal nature* of the passage. The interpretation that attempts to limit Romans 9 to "nations" cannot begin to explain how nations "will" or "run." In contrast to these Paul uses a present active participle to describe God's act of "mercying," showing mercy. Man may strive through his will and his endeavors, but God must show mercy.

Lest someone think, "Well, yes, God shows mercy and *initiates* salvation, and only then does the will of man freely embrace it," as is argued constantly in *CBF*, Paul closes the door by giving as his own interpretation of his argument the example of Pharaoh:

> For the Scripture says to Pharaoh, "FOR THIS VERY PURPOSE I RAISED YOU UP, TO DEMONSTRATE MY POWER IN YOU, AND THAT MY NAME MIGHT BE PROCLAIMED THROUGHOUT THE WHOLE EARTH." So then He has mercy on whom He desires, and He hardens whom He desires. (Romans 9:17-18)

The example of Pharaoh was well known to any person familiar with the Old Testament. God destroyed the Egyptian nation by plagues so as to demonstrate His might and power in the earth, and key to this demonstration was the hardening of Pharaoh's heart. Before Moses had met with Pharaoh the first time God told him:

> When you go back to Egypt see that you perform before Pharaoh all the wonders which I have put in your power; but I will harden his heart so that he will not let the people go. (Exodus 4:21)

It was God's *intention* to bring His wrath upon the Egyptians. God's actions were not "forced" by the stubborn will of the Egyptian leader. God said He would harden Pharaoh's heart, and He did. Listen to the impudent response of this pagan idolater to the command of Moses:

> And afterward Moses and Aaron came and said to Pharaoh, "Thus says the LORD, the God of Israel, 'Let My people go that they may celebrate a feast to Me in the wilderness.'" But Pharaoh said, "Who is the LORD that I

> should obey His voice to let Israel go? I do not know the LORD, and besides, I will not let Israel go." (Exodus 5:1-2)

Is this not what God said He would do? Will someone suggest that Pharaoh's heart is "soft" here? No indeed, and Moses well knew that God was behind this for when the Pharaoh then increased the work load of the Israelites, Moses complained to God in Exodus 5:22. Why complain to God if, in fact, God had nothing to do with it and it was all just a matter of the Pharaoh's "free will choice"?

This provides the background of Paul's citation of Exodus 9:16. The portion of truth that here stings the pride of man is this: it is more important that God's name be magnified and His power made known than it is any single man get to "do his own thing." Pharaoh was surely never forced to do anything sinful (indeed, God probably kept him from committing many a sinful deed). He acted on the desires of his wicked heart at all times. But he is but a pot, a creature, not the Potter. He was formed and made and brought into existence to serve the Potter's purposes, not his own. He is but a servant, one chosen, in fact, for destruction. His destruction, and the process that led up to it (including all the plagues upon Egypt), were part of God's plan. There is simply no other way to understand these words.

Paul then combines the fact that God showed undeserved compassion and mercy to Moses (Exodus 33) with God's hardening of Pharaoh's heart (Exodus 5) and concludes that whether one is "mercied" or "hardened" is completely, inalterably, and utterly up to God. The verbs here are active: God performs these actions. He "mercies" *whom He wills* and He *hardens* whom He wills. The parallel between "mercy" and "hardening" is *inarguable*. We may like the "mercying" part more than the hardening, *but they are both equally a part of the same truth.* Reject one and you reject them both. There is no such thing as preaching God's mercy without preaching God's judgment, at least according to Scripture.

The passage reaches a crescendo in these final verses:

> You will say to me then, "Why does He still find fault?
> For who resists His will?" On the contrary, who are you,
> O man, who answers back to God? The thing molded
> will not say to the molder, "Why did you make me like
> this," will it? (Romans 9:19-20)

Paul well knew the objections man presents to the words he had just penned. If God has mercy solely based upon His good pleasure, and if God hardens Pharaoh on the same basis, all to His own glory and honor, how can God hold men accountable for their actions, for who resists His will? Paul's response is swift and devastating: Yes indeed God holds man accountable, and He can do so because He is the Potter, the one who molds and creates, while man is but the "thing molded." For a pot to question the Potter is absurd: for man to answer back to God is equally absurd. These words cannot be understood separately from the fundamental understanding of the freedom of the Sovereign Creator and the *ontological creatureliness* of man that removes from him any ground of complaint against God. Though already devastatingly clear, Paul makes sure there is no doubt left as to his point:

> Or does not the potter have a right over the clay, to make
> from the same lump one vessel for honorable use and
> another for common use? What if God, although will-
> ing to demonstrate His wrath and to make His power
> known, endured with much patience vessels of wrath pre-
> pared for destruction? And *He did so* to make known the
> riches of His glory upon vessels of mercy, which He pre-
> pared beforehand for glory, *even* us, whom He also called,
> not from among Jews only, but also from among Gen-
> tiles. (Romans 9:21-24)

The Potter's freedom pulses through these words, flowing in-

exorably into the sea of sovereignty, rushing any would-be proponent of free will out of its path. God has the perfect right to
do with His creation (including men) as He wishes, just as the
Potter has utter sovereignty over the clay. Just as God had demonstrated His wrath and power by wasting idolatrous Egypt, so
too He demonstrates His wrath upon "vessels of wrath prepared for destruction." Are these nations? Classes? No, these
are *sinners* upon whom God's wrath comes. They are said to
have been specifically "prepared for destruction." That is their
purpose.

Why are there vessels prepared for destruction? Because
God is free. Think about it: there are only three logical possibilities here.[2] Either 1) all "vessels" are prepared for glory (universalism); 2) all "vessels" are prepared for destruction; or 3)
some vessels are prepared for glory and some are prepared for
destruction and it is *the Potter* who decides which are which.
Why is there no fourth option, one in which the pots prepare
themselves based upon their own choice? Because pots don't
have such a capacity! Pots are pots! Since God wishes to make
known the "riches of His grace" to His elect people (the vessels prepared of mercy), there *must* be vessels prepared for
destruction. *There is no demonstration of mercy and grace where
there is no justice.*

The vessels of wrath, remember, *like* being vessels of wrath,
would never choose to be anything else, and they *detest* the
vessels that receive mercy. Indeed, during the writing of this
book I encountered an unbeliever who, upon hearing me mention the wrath of God, mocked and said, "Ah, yes, the wrath of
God! I LIKE IT!" This is the attitude of the vessel of wrath
prepared for destruction.

God's wonderful grace will be praised throughout eternity
because of the great contrast between the vessels of wrath and
the vessels of mercy. Why? *Because the only difference between
the vessels of wrath and the vessels of mercy is the sovereign grace
of God that changes the heart of the rebel sinner and turns him
from being a God-hater into a God-lover.* This is why there is no

basis for man's boasting, *ever*.

Given how clear and forceful this passage is, how can the Arminian escape its force? Dr. Geisler relies upon the standard Arminian explanations as he attempts to defuse this thoroughly Reformed proclamation in Romans 9.

A Most Difficult Task

CBF's response to Romans 9 is split up into various sections. This is unfortunate, since it would be most helpful to see an actual exegesis of the entire passage offered. One of the things that would be seen immediately were all the comments on Romans 9 to be placed in the same context is that the Arminian response is internally inconsistent. As we will see, *CBF* will argue that Romans 9:13, for example, is about *nations* not *people* (the standard Arminian stance). Yet, when we get down to the later verses in the passage, *CBF* switches over to talking about *persons*. When does the passage make this grand leap from *nations* to *persons?* We are not told, and of course, the text does not even begin to give us a reason for viewing it in that way. The Arminian interpretation faces insurmountable difficulties on many fronts.

We will address *CBF*'s comments not in the order presented in the book (Romans 9:16, for example, is addressed more than twenty pages *before* the rest of the chapter), but in the order of the text itself.

Upon the citation of Romans 9:11-13 Dr. Geisler writes, "This is a favorite passage of extreme Calvinists, especially those who believe in double predestination. For it appears to say that God not only loves just the elect, but also He even hates the non-elect."[3] Immediately we have a problem: the Calvinist "likes" the passage because it speaks of the inviolability of God's purpose in election and shows that His choices are not determined by anything in man. The quotation of Malachi 1:2-3 by the Apostle Paul is meant to contrast the gracious choice of Jacob over that of Esau. It is not an issue of proving that God loves the elect (that is a given), nor that God hates those He leaves to justice (Psalm 5:5 and 11:5 teach this no matter how one interprets Romans 9:13). Dr. Geisler states:

> Few scriptural texts are more misused by extreme Calvinists than this one. First of all, God is not speaking here about the *individual* Jacob but about the *nation* of Jacob (Israel). In Genesis when the prediction is made (25:23 NKJV), Rebekah was told, " 'Two nations are in your womb, two *peoples* shall be separated from your body . . . And the older shall serve the younger.' " So the reference here is not to *individual* election but to the *corporate* election of a nation—the chosen nation of Israel.[4]

A little later it is said,

> Third, God's "love" for Jacob and "hate" for Esau is not speaking of those men before they were born, but long after they lived. The citation in Romans 9:13 is not from Genesis when they were alive (c. 2000 B.C.) but from Malachi 1:2-3 (c. 400 B.C.), long after they died!

These two assertions provide the bulk of the argument that this section is speaking of nations, and the next quote provides the second prong, the idea that "hated" here really means "loved less."

> Fourth, the Hebrew word for "hated" really means "loved less." Indication of this comes from the life of Jacob himself. For the Bible says Jacob "loved also Rachel *more than* Leah...The Lord saw that *Leah was hated*" (Gen. 29:30-31)....So even one of the strongest verses used by extreme Calvinists does not prove that God hates the non-elect or even that He does not love them. It simply means that God's love for those who receive salvation looks so much greater than His love for those who reject it that the latter looks like hatred by comparison.
> A couple of illustrations make the point. The same lov-

ing stroke that makes a kitten purr seems like hatred if she turns the opposite direction and finds her fur being rubbed the wrong way.[5]

One is immediately struck by the fact that the key issues present in Reformed exegesis of the text *are utterly and completely ignored by CBF.* Aside from one footnote (addressed below), the entirety of the response to this section of Romans 9 can be summed up as 1) this refers to nations, not individuals, and 2) hated doesn't mean hated but "loved less." With all due respect to Dr. Geisler, this is a "non-response" that does not focus upon the text at all. There is no exegesis with which to interact. We will, however, respond to both assertions that are made.

First, we have already seen the inconsistency in claiming that the testimony of the passage to personal election unto salvation through the assertion that we are speaking *solely* of nations *not* of individuals cannot be substantiated. While Dr. Geisler will make reference to John Piper's work, and hence *must* know of the extensive discussion that work contains refuting this very concept, *not a single word is uttered in refutation.* As we pointed out in the Introduction, all that is provided is a footnote citing Piper's list of scholars who see this as having only national application. There is no footnote citing Piper's listing of the scholars who *do* see the passage referring to individual salvation (though the list begins on the same page). There is no discussion of the *pages* of argumentation provided by Piper *against* the position of *CBF.* As far as the reader of *CBF* would be concerned, Reformed theologians simply make the assertion and never substantiate it. It seems to us that given the claim on page 83 of *CBF* that Piper is "mistaken" in his views (specifically regarding the time frame of the act of divine election), it would be necessary for *CBF* to at least make an *attempt* to rebut *some* of Piper's material. For example, here is but one paragraph from Piper's work that gives an idea of the level of argumentation *CBF ignores*:

It is a remarkable and telling phenomenon that those who find no individual predestination to eternal life in Rom 9:6-13 cannot successfully explain the thread of Paul's argument as it begins in Rom 9:1-5 and continues through the chapter. One looks in vain, for example, among these commentators for a cogent statement of how the corporate election of two peoples (Israel and Edom) in Rom 9:12,13 fits together in Paul's argument with the statement, "Not all those from Israel are Israel" (9:6b). One also looks in vain for an explanation of how the pressing problem of eternally condemned Israelites in Rom 9:3 is ameliorated by Rom 9:6-13 if these verses refer "not to salvation but to position and historical task." I have found the impression unavoidable that doctrinal inclinations have severely limited exegetical effort and insight—not so much because the answers of these exegetes are not my own, but because of the crucial exegetical questions that simply are not posed by them.[6]

While these words were printed six years before *CBF* appeared (and obviously written long before that), they could not more thoroughly describe the "nations not people" assertion presented by Dr. Geisler. Since no effort is made to place this interpretation in the context so that we can see the relationship of 9:13 with the preceding context, we must simply say that the interpretation offered must be rejected on the basis that it makes Paul's entire argument muddled and incoherent. Until Arminian scholars are willing to step up and explain the passage *as a whole*, their efforts will remain unconvincing.

There are more reasons to reject *CBF*'s presentation. On page 83 an endnote appears that challenges Piper on the issue of the rejection of Esau. It is a classic example of out-of-context citation that should not appear in a work by a scholar of the rank of Norman Geisler. Here is what it says:

John Piper, widely held by extreme Calvinists to have the best treatment on Romans 9, makes this mistake.

Piper claims that "the divine decision to 'hate' Esau was made 'before they were born or had done anything good *or evil* (9:11).' " But, as shown on the previous page, the reference here is not to something said in Genesis about the *individuals* Jacob and Esau *before they were born.*[7]

One might think that this is being taken from the section of Piper's work specifically on the topic of Jacob and Esau. *It is not.* Instead, this short snippet is a partial sentence from a summary of a completely different topic, as we will show by providing the full (and useful) quotation:

> In sum then I have tried to demonstrate with three arguments that the phrase, "Whom he wills he hardens," describes God's freedom to choose the recipients of his hardening apart from any ground in their willing or acting. First, the parallel between 18a and 18b shows that the freedom of God to harden is parallel to his freedom to show mercy, which according to 9:16 has no ground in a person's willing or running. Second, the correspondence between the pairs, mercy/hardening (9:18) and love/hate (9:13), shows that Paul does not intend for us to view the hardening as a "divine reaction" to sin, since the divine decision to "hate" Esau was made "before they were born or had done anything good *or evil*" (9:11). Third, Paul's selection and adaptation of Ex 9:16, which summarizes the theme of Ex 4-14, shows that he understands God's activity to be grounded in *his own purposes*, not in the plans or actions of men.[8]

Does *CBF* attempt to respond to the actual argumentation Piper provides regarding 9:13? No. Does it attempt to respond to even *this* summary of Piper's argument which, if true, is utterly devastating to Geisler's entire thesis? No. Unfortunately, Piper is misrepresented yet again within just a few pages, this time in reference to Romans 9:15. We will examine *CBF*'s attempts to explain the "hardening" of Pharaoh's heart below, but in this section Piper is quoted as follows:

> John Piper stands the order and thought of the text on
> its head, claiming implausibly that "it is just as probable
> that 'the hardening of man by God appears as self-hard-
> ening'" (Piper, *The Justification of God*, 163). This is an
> almost classic example of reading one's theology into the
> text as opposed to reading the text.[9]

Is this a classic example of eisegesis? No, it is a classic example of misrepresentation through selective citation. The
quotation provided is not of Piper, first of all. This can be seen
in the fact that a second quotation mark appears in Geisler's
citation: Piper is actually citing an article titled "Die
Verstockung des Menschen durch Gott" by K.L. Schmidt. This
quotation comes at the end of a paragraph found in the middle
of an extensive section of argumentation that includes examination of original languages, charts of grammatical and syn-
tactical relationships, etc., that honestly asks about the nature
of the "hardening" spoken of with reference to Pharaoh. Secondly, *CBF* ignores *everything* documented in this section of
Piper's work, *even though the data offered is utterly contradictory to Geisler's conclusions.* The reader is directed to the original source for a more complete picture of how badly *CBF*
handles this scholarly source.

   Returning to Romans 9, we turn to the response offered to
9:15, where the "extreme Calvinist" is said to allege that "God
moved on his [Pharaoh's] heart to accomplish His purpose,
Pharaoh could not resist."[10] Of course immediately one would
have to correct this representation of the Reformed position:
Pharaoh could not *and would not desire to* resist. Pharaoh was
not a kind, gentle, godly man who was forced to act in a bad
way by a mean, nasty God. No, Pharaoh was a pagan idolater,
justly under the wrath of God, whose every breath and heart-
beat was his only as God extended mercy to him. His black-
ened, sin-filled heart was constantly being reined in by God's
common grace so that he was not nearly as bad as he could

have been. He did not have the first desire to submit to God or do right. To say that Pharaoh "could not resist" is to assume *he would ever want to.* CBF continues:

> While it is true that God predicted in advance that it would happen (Ex. 4:21), nonetheless the fact is that Pharaoh hardened his own heart first (7:13, 8:15, etc.), and then God only hardened it later (cf. 9:12, 10:1, 20, 27).

Piper completely refutes this single-sentence assertion over the course of *twelve pages* of scholarly argumentation.[11] We simply point out one major mistake: did God merely "predict" that He would harden Pharaoh's heart? To say that Pharaoh hardened his own heart first 1) ignores Exodus 5:1-2 and assumes that this is *not* the fulfillment of Exodus 4:21 and 2) assumes that the hardening of his heart by God is somehow "based upon" or dependent upon Pharaoh's actions. We have now seen, many times, that CBF's most fundamental presupposition is the absolute freedom of man and his ability to exercise "choice." This is a wonderful example of how that kind of philosophical presupposition can result in errors in exegesis. But the text provides an even greater example of how one's assumptions can lead to errors of interpretation:

> What is more, the Hebrew word "hardened" (*chazaq*) can and often does mean to "strengthen" (Judg. 3:12; 16:28), or even to "encourage" (cf. Deut. 1:38; 3:28). Taken in this sense, it would not carry any sinister connotations but would simply state that God made Pharaoh strong to carry through with his (Pharaoh's) will against Israel.[12]

It is difficult to respond to such an assertion. Even if one did not have the obvious context of Exodus to so clearly explain that the hardening of the heart of Pharaoh was specifically related to his refusal to let the people go *so that* God could bring judgment on Egypt, you would still have the immediate context of Romans 9. When Paul writes, "He has mercy on whom He desires, and He hardens whom He desires," there is an *obvious* parallel between "have mercy on" and "harden," and, of course, Paul is drawing his terminology from the Exodus account. Hence, *Paul* certainly did not understand it as "strengthen" for such makes absolutely *no sense* in Romans 9:18. Why this is even suggested is hard to see outside of the telltale comment that to suggest that God hardened Pharaoh's heart is somehow "sinister."

The second most amazing response[13] in *CBF* is found on page 59 where Norman Geisler responds to the use of Romans 9:16. Throughout the work Dr. Geisler focuses upon R.C. Sproul and singles him out for special criticism. He makes references to Sproul's use of Romans 9:16: "R.C. Sproul is incautiously triumphant about this, claiming: 'This one verse is absolutely fatal to Arminianism.'"[14] One paragraph is then provided in response to this tremendous passage. It reads,

> Again, the Greek word for "of" here is *ek*, which means "out of." It is a reference to the *source* of salvation, not the *means* by which we receive it—this means it is a *free act* of our will in receiving it (John 1:12; Eph. 2:8, etc.). All forms of Calvinism and Arminianism believe that God is the one who initiated salvation, even before the world began (Eph. 1:4). Only God can be the source of *God's* saving "mercy." However, as the Bible indicates later in Romans 9 (v. 22) and elsewhere, we can reject God's mercy (2 Peter 3:9; Acts 7:51).

First, the Greek term ἐκ does not appear in the text of Romans 9:16. Secondly, *CBF* says Romans 9 isn't about salvation to begin with, as we have already seen! Is there some massive change in the context between verses 13 and 16? No, there is not, but this is just another inherent problem with the Arminian attempts to get around the teaching of the passage. Thirdly, there is nothing *anywhere* in the text that provides a founda-

tion for the completely arbitrary claim that the passage is referring to the *source* of salvation in distinction from the *means*
of salvation. Are we to believe that Paul was concerned to prove
that salvation does not find its *source* in the will of man or the
works of man? Were his opponents actually suggesting such a
belief? Of course not. But so strong, so pervasive is the commitment to the concept of the autonomy of man that even a
passage that emphatically denies the role of the will of man
can be turned on its head so that CBF can claim, "this means
it is a *free act* of our will in receiving it." The term "eisegesis" is
too mild to describe such an assertion: no interaction with the
actual wording of the text is offered.

Even the use of the "imaginary objector" in 9:19 is brought
into the attempt to deflect this passage and rescue the Arminian
system. Geisler quotes the verse and interprets the Calvinistic
view as saying "This seems to imply that God's power in salvation is literally irresistible regardless of what one wills." Again,
we don't know how a discussion of nations became a discussion of salvation, but we certainly accept the assertion that
God's power in salvation *is* irresistible, as we will see in the
next chapter (dead men put up little resistance to anything).
He comments,

> So the idea that one cannot resist God's will may be no
> more part of Paul's teaching than the view that we should
> do evil so good may come.
> Furthermore, Paul clearly rejects the objector's stance
> in the very next verse, saying, "But who are you, O man,
> to talk back to [i.e., resist] God? (Rom. 9:20). His answer
> implies that the objector can and is resisting God by rais-
> ing this very question. But more importantly, the direct
> implication is that if it is irresistible, then we should not
> be blamed.[15]

We cannot help but notice how very difficult it is for the
Arminian scholar to provide any kind of textually-based response to this passage. The objector is voicing the obvious

argument men raise when faced with God's absolute sovereignty and freedom. Since the Arminian actually rejects the substance of the passage, it is easy to see why at this point they would try to find a way out of the final conclusion.

The point of Paul's response, "Who are you, O man, to talk back to God" is to emphasize the creatureliness of man. There is no reason, at all, for the insertion of the phrase, in brackets, "i.e., resist." The Greek term ἀνταποκρινόμενος means "talk back to, answer back to," not "resist." It strikes us as ironic that Dr. Geisler would chide Calvinists for allegedly "changing the Scriptures" when in this instance he inserts a phrase that has no basis in the text, and then bases his comments on his own inserted phrase! The objector is not "resisting God." What is more, it almost sounds as if Dr. Geisler is seriously suggesting that there is some connection between a person "resisting God" by answering back and the Calvinistic concept of irresistible grace in regeneration! Such would be a completely fallacious argument based upon equivocation, if in fact that is the intent. Finally, the real reason why the text has to be (to use Dr. Geisler's own term) manhandled comes out in the end: if it is true that God is this free, this sovereign, that He has mercy on whom He wills and hardens whom He wills, then "we can't be blamed." Of course, that's what the imaginary objector says: and the inspired Apostle refutes the objection in what follows.

CBF moves on to the rest of the passage,

> The image this conjures up in a Western mind is often deterministic, if not fatalistic, one where they have no choice but are overpowered by God.
>
> However, a Hebrew mind would not think this way, knowing the parable of the potter from Jeremiah 18. For in this context the basic lump of clay will either be built up or torn down by God, *depending on Israel's moral response to God.* For the prophet says emphatically, "If that nation I warned *repents* of its evil, then I will relent and not inflict on it the disaster I had planned" (18:8). Thus,

> the unrepentant element of Israel becomes a "vessel for
> dishonour" and the repentant group a "vessel for
> honor"....[16]

Just as we had to express our amazement at the insertion of
acts of "free will" into Romans 9:16, so too here we cannot
help but point out that the main point of the entire passage is
overthrown and literally contradicted all to maintain the supremacy of the free choices of men! Read Jeremiah 18 and see
if the point of the parable of the potter and the clay is that
there is something in the *clay* that determines what the potter
will do? The parable shows God's complete sovereignty over
the nation of Israel. He can do with the nation as He wishes.
He is not limited by the "free choices" of people. Surely he
calls the nation to repent beginning in verse 7, but upon what
principle of logic or hermeneutics are we to believe that the
actual point of the parable is that the clay can force the potter's
hand either by its sin or its repentance? Beyond this issue, may
we ask how any of *CBF*'s response is relevant to the text as it
stands? Where is there a discussion of vessels of honor and
dishonor in Jeremiah 18? Where is there a discussion of vessels of wrath and vessels of mercy? There is none. This leaves
the actual passage *untouched* and the point it communicates
unrefuted.

> Further, there is a different use of prepositions in "ves-
> sel *unto* honour" versus a "vessel *of* wrath" (Rom. 9:22).
> A vessel *of* wrath is one that has received wrath from
> God, just as a vessel of mercy has received mercy from
> God. But a vessel *unto* honor is one that gives honor to
> God. So a repentant Israel will, like a beautiful vessel
> unto [for] honor, bring honor to its Maker. But like a
> vessel of dishonor (literally, "no-honor"), an unrepen-
> tant Israel will not bring honor to God, but will rather be
> an object of His wrath.[17]

One cannot help but be struck by the consistency of this kind of interpretation: no matter how plainly the text emphasizes God's sovereignty, the interpretation finds a way to turn everything back upon the creature.

It is difficult to understand the argumentation provided regarding prepositions. When the idea is first introduced in verse 21 there is perfect parallelism between "vessel for honorable use" and vessel "for common use." In the same way, "vessels of wrath" is σκεύη ὀργῆς, and "vessels of mercy" is σκεύη ἐλέους. Both, again, are in perfect parallel (both "wrath" and "mercy" are in the genitive singular). There is no reason to parallel "vessel unto honor" (v. 21) with "vessels of wrath" (v. 22) as the text parallels "vessel unto honor" with a vessel "for common use" using the exact same language in verse 21. The only "difference in prepositions" is between the use of εἰς in v. 22 (in the phrase "vessels prepared *for* destruction") and ἐπί in v. 23 (in the phrase "*unto* vessels of mercy"), though this is not the difference to which Dr. Geisler points (seemingly basing his comments on the English translation, not the Greek text). There are easily discernable grammatical and lexical reasons why Paul would use "upon vessels of mercy" (the same preposition is used in Ephesians 2:7, "so that in the ages to come He might show the surpassing riches of His grace in kindness *toward us* in Christ Jesus"). But none of these issues actually speak to what Geisler asserts. A vessel of wrath is one *prepared for destruction* that will experience God's wrath: a vessel of mercy is one *prepared for glory*. These are the parallel statements. Nothing provided in CBF disproves the Reformed view of the passage.

So after "answering" Romans 9, CBF concludes,

> There is absolutely no reason to believe, as the extreme Calvinists do, either here or anywhere else in Scripture, that God predestines certain persons to eternal hell apart from their own free choice.[18]

We know by this point what underlies this assertion: it is the belief that man's free choice is the ultimate factor in the work of salvation. But after observing the methodology used throughout this section (and thus far in the book), we have to conclude that this is a statement of faith, not a conclusion based upon the text of Scripture. It comes not from exegesis but from a strong commitment to the presuppositions of Arminian theology. God created vessels of wrath. We may not like the idea, but we have no right to change the Word nor reject its teaching.

Having now seen that *CBF* has failed to respond to the biblical arguments used by Reformed believers to teach the total inability of man and God's unconditional election, we now turn to Christ's work of atonement and provide a response in defense of the glorious truth of the perfection of His work in the place of the elect.

Notes

1 John Piper, *The Justification of God* (Baker Book House, 1993), pp. 52-53.

2 Some argue for more than these three possibilities. R.C.H. Lenski inserts Satan into the context as the one who prepares these vessels of wrath. See my rebuttal at www.aomin.org/Lenskirep.html. Others argue the term should be translated as a middle so that these are vessels who "prepared themselves for destruction." See the rebuttal of this viewpoint by Daniel B. Wallace, *Greek Grammar Beyond the Basics* (Eerdmans, 1996), pp. 417-418.

3 *Chosen But Free*, p. 82.

4 Ibid.

5 Ibid., p. 83.

6 Piper, *The Justification of God* , p. 58.

7 Ibid., p. 83.

8 Ibid., p. 175.

9 *Chosen But Free*, p. 88.

10 Ibid., p. 88.

11 Piper, *The Justification of God*, pp. 159-171.

12 *Chosen But Free*, p. 87.

13 The most amazing response was given in reference to John 6:44 as we saw in chapter seven.

14 Ibid., p. 59.

15 Ibid., p. 89.

16 Ibid., p. 90.

17 Ibid, pp. 90-91.

18 Ibid., p. 91.

Chapter 10

The Perfect Work of Calvary

Modern evangelicals are mushy on the cross. While books about eschatology, Bible prophecy, or end-times theories fly off the shelves, and your average Sunday church-goer can discuss such things as rapture theories, the identity of the AntiChrist, etc., pitifully few could even begin to make a biblically-based presentation of the meaning of such terms as "atonement," "propitiation," "redemption" or the like. The preaching of our day on the work of Christ on Calvary is far more often based upon pure emotion than it is the clear and compelling teaching of the Bible. Sound unfair? Sound unkind? It is neither, I assure you.

The work of Christ on Calvary is the central theme of the message of the New Testament. Paul teaches that Christ is the focal point of history. At the core of the gospel message is the *exclusivisity* of the cross. The death of Christ is the *only* means of salvation, propitiation, forgiveness, and redemption. Christianity exists only when the preaching of the cross is its message. Once the death of Christ becomes *a way* and not *the way*, Christianity ceases to exist and the power of God is lost.

It has become traditional in evangelical Protestantism to preach the cross as follows: God so loved the world that He gave His Son to die upon the cross for every single individual in all the world. By exercising faith in Christ, you can receive the benefits of Christ's death on the cross. If you do not believe, Christ's death, even though offered in your place, will do you no good. You will still suffer for your sins. Christ truly wants to save you, if you will but believe.

Is this the message preached by the Apostles? Is this the preaching of the cross of Christ? Calvinists say "no," and they do so because of the biblical doctrine of atonement. In its simplest terms the Reformed belief is this: Christ's death saves sinners. It does not make the salvation of sinners a mere possibility. It does not provide a theoretical atonement. It requires no additions, whether they be the meritorious works of men or the autonomous act of faith flowing from a "free will." Christ's death saves *every single person* that it was *intended* to save.

It is right here that the first objection surfaces: those who do not believe God *intends* to save a particular people, but instead *tries* to save "the maximum number possible," will reject immediately the idea that Christ's death was intended to actually redeem the elect *perfectly*. Instead, the atoning work of Christ will have to be made a part of a hypothetical system, a "plan" that, if properly activated by the actions or will of man, results in salvation. But is this the *biblical* doctrine?

Beware! This topic is fraught with emotional pitfalls. We have so often heard certain things taught in a particular fashion that they have become part of the very fabric of our religious experience and belief. So when our personal traditions are challenged, we often respond with emotion rather than biblically-based thought and consideration. Love of the truth demands that we remember this: sentimentality is no replacement for doctrinal purity. To desire correct doctrine should be normative for every believer. Part of loving God is loving His truth and desiring to grow in it. And surely every believer can fully understand the need to know the truth about the "crosswork" of Christ so that we can stand firmly upon the basis of the Word in knowing that we have truly been redeemed and have peace with God.

Limited Atonement

It's the favorite target of Arminian preachers. "Calvinists are so far off that they preach that Christ's death is limited! They don't even believe Christ died for sinners, but just for them!" I have honestly seen this kind of rhetoric on the Internet and in self-published books from fundamentalists. Yet, almost never do we read a full, honest, biblically-based discussion of the *real* issues. Most of the time both sides will toss out passages that speak either of Christ dying for "all men" (resulting in the inevitable discussion of the meaning of "all" in various contexts), or of Christ dying for a specific people (resulting in a discussion of whether that group is fixed by God's decree or determined by the free act of faith). While both topics are important (and we have already seen that God does have a specific elect people that He intends to save), they skirt around the main issue. We do not determine the intention and result of the atonement by reasoning from such premises. There are direct, clear, compelling passages of Scripture that tell us what the *intention* and *result* of the atonement is, and to these we must look for our foundational understanding of the atoning work of Christ.

What does "limited atonement" mean? When a Calvinist uses the term, it means "Christ's intention in His death was the perfect and substitutionary atonement of all of His elect." The *scope* of His work is in perfect harmony with His *intention*, which is the salvation of His elect people who are entrusted to Him. It makes no sense for Christ to offer atonement for those the Father does not entrust to Him for salvation. Obviously, a person who does not believe the Father entrusts a particular people (the elect) to the Son has no reason to believe in particular redemption. But since it is His *intention* to save all those given to Him by the Father (John 6:37-39), He bears their iniquities in His body on the tree *in their place*. B.B. Warfield is correct when he asserts that the substitutionary aspect of the work of Christ on the cross is "as precious to the Calvinist as is his particularism, and for the safeguard of which, indeed, much of his zeal for particularism is due."[1]

A common, but not fully Reformed, assertion is that Christ's death was *sufficient* to save every single human being, but *efficient* to save only the elect. While the statement carries truth, it misses the most important issue: whether it was Christ's *intention* to make full and complete atonement for every single individual (making salvation theoretically possible but not actual) or whether it was His intention to make full atonement for all those given to Him by the Father (the elect). Both "sides" can use the statement: the Arminian can say it is true since the "elect" is determined not by God's choice, but by man's. Therefore this saying, popular since the scholastic period of church history, really says nothing to the point of debate.

Defining the Issues

This topic is so laden with emotion that it is absolutely necessary that we plot a clear course by providing an outline of the real issues. Keep these thoughts in mind as we examine this doctrine and *CBF*'s attempted refutation:

1) We must distinguish between the *scope* of the atonement, *the effect* of the atonement, and the *intention* of the atonement. That is, it is obviously a different thing to ask the question, "For whom did Christ die?" than it is to ask "What did Christ's death accomplish?" or "What did Christ intend to accomplish by His death?" Much confusion is found in the minds of believers when these different issues are not kept separate in one's thinking.

2) Saying the atonement is "limited" in one sphere is not the same as saying it is "limited" in all others. All people, with the possible exception of universalists (who posit salvation for all men, though normally not based upon the atoning work of Christ at the cross), "limit" the atonement in some fashion.

For example:

In Roman Catholicism, the work of Christ merits grace. This grace is mediated to men and women through the sacraments of the Church. The grace of justification, for example, is mediated through the sacrament of baptism, and, when one loses that grace through the commission of a mortal sin, through the sacrament of penance. This grace then places the believer in the "state of grace," so that he or she can now do "good works" that are meritorious before God and thereby earn the reward of eternal life. The death of Christ then is *necessary* to provide the key element or foundation of the "system" of salvation. Without it, there would be no grace to flow through the sacraments. In essence, it makes men *savable* (by inaugurating a system whereby men save themselves), but it does not actually *save*. One could surely not say that in Roman Catholicism the death of Christ is *sufficient* to fully and completely save any particular individual, nor would the phrase "substitutionary atonement" fit this viewpoint (the idea that Christ actually takes the penalty of sin due to each person for whom He dies). The lack of substitution explains the Roman Catholic concept of purgatory, the idea that sin can be forgiven and yet still require temporal punishment, etc. So, Rome would "limit" the atonement in its *effect* but not in its *scope*. They would say Christ intended to *provide the means of redemption*, but that His death, in and of itself, does not *redeem* outside of human actions.

Historic Arminians saw that believing in the idea of substitutionary atonement would not fit with their system of theology. Even though Arminians today may use this terminology, it does not strictly "belong" to them. Arminian scholar J. Kenneth Grider asserts that the idea of "substitutionary atonement" is foreign to Arminian thinking:

> A spillover from Calvinism into Arminianism has occurred in recent decades. Thus many Arminians whose theology is not very precise say that Christ paid the

penalty for our sins. Yet such a view is foreign to Arminianism, which teaches instead that Christ suffered for us. Arminians teach that what Christ did he did for every person; therefore what he did could not have been to pay the penalty, since no one would then ever go into eternal perdition. Arminianism teaches that Christ suffered for everyone so that the Father could forgive the ones who repent and believe; his death is such that all will see that forgiveness is costly and will strive to cease from anarchy in the world God governs. This view is called the governmental theory of the atonement.[2]

It is very difficult to understand *upon what basis* the Father could forgive those who "repent and believe," especially since there is no substitution and hence no payment of the penalty of sin. The atonement is a "demonstration" that "forgiveness is costly." Somehow this demonstration is meant to cause people to "cease from anarchy in the world God governs." But the main element of the position is a denial of substitutionary atonement, for it is understood that if Christ actually pays the penalty due to sin under God's law, then no person would ever enter into judgment, *given the idea that Christ's atonement is universal in scope.*

Modern Arminians are generally unaware of the history of Arminianism, and the fact that the phrases "Jesus took the place of sinners" or "Jesus died for us" or "Jesus' death paid the penalty of sin" are "borrowed" from Calvinism. Many an Arminian will confess belief in substitutionary atonement only to change the meaning of "atonement" into something merely theoretical. Robert Reymond described the logical ramifications of believing that Christ only made a theoretical atonement:

> It also follows necessarily, since Christ by his death *actually* procured nothing that guarantees the salvation of any man, and yet some men are saved, that the most one can claim for his work is that he in some way made all

men salvable. But the highest view of the atonement that one can reach by this path is the governmental view. This view holds that Christ by his death actually paid the penalty for no man's sin. What his death did was to demonstrate what their sin deserves at the hand of the just Governor and Judge of the universe, and permits God justly to forgive men if *on other grounds,* such as *their* faith, *their* repentance, *their* works, and *their* perseverance, they meet his demands. . . .But this is just to eviscerate the Savior's work of all of its intrinsic saving worth and to replace the Christosoteric vision of Scripture with the autosoteric vision of Pelagianism.[3]

There is, at least, consistency in the Arminian position. They recognize the intimate connection that exists between *substitution* and *forgiveness.* If Christ *became* a curse *in our behalf* (Gal. 3:13)[4] and if He sacrificially bore[5] in His body on the tree *our sins* (1 Peter 2:24),[6] there is only one possible result: the perfect salvation of all those for whom Christ died. Consistent Arminians, therefore, must reject substitutionary atonement and put in its place the governmental theory.

3) We must allow the words used by Scripture to carry their full weight and meaning. This means we must determine the meaning of such words as "propitiation" (ἱλαστήριον, *hilasterion*), "redemption" (λύτρωσις, *lutrosis*), "sacrifice" (θυσίας, *thusias*), "offering" (προσφοραν, *prosphora*) and the preposition "in the place of" or "for" (ὑπέρ, *huper*), as in Christ died "for" or "in the place of" His people.[7]

4) We must notice carefully the *objects* of the saving work of Christ. Does the Bible tell us something about the ones who receive the benefits of Christ's death?

5) Most importantly, we have to see that the work of Christ on the cross is directly related to other elements of His divine work of redemption, especially to His work as Mediator and Intercessor. For whom does Christ mediate and intercede? What does the Bible mean when it says Christ intercedes (ὑπερεντυγχάνω, *huperentungchano*) for us? These are issues rarely

touched upon in the debate over particular redemption, but they truly determine the truth of the doctrine.

Two Tremendous Passages

Two passages of Scripture speak with uncommon clarity and strength to the beauty of the truth of Particular Redemption: Romans 8:31-34 and the extended argument of the writer to the Hebrews in chapters 7 through 10. We will begin with the Apostle Paul. After proclaiming the "golden chain of redemption" in Romans 8:28-30, Paul applies this God-centered salvation and says,

> What then shall we say to these things? If God *is* for us, who *is* against us? He who did not spare His own Son, but delivered Him over for us all, how will He not also with Him freely give us all things? Who will bring a charge against God's elect? God is the one who justifies; who is the one who condemns? Christ Jesus is He who died, yes, rather who was raised, who is at the right hand of God, who also intercedes for us. (Romans 8:31-34)

Any treatment of soteriology must devote due time to this tremendous passage. After lauding the power of God in salvation and in bringing the elect into glory, Paul teaches the Romans that the very foundation of the Christian's confidence in the future is in understanding that God saves perfectly. It is important to see that the passage limits the audience to believers, those seen in the preceding verses as the predestined and called saints of God. Notice how the pronouns in the text prohibit us from wandering from the true meaning of the text:

> What then shall *we* say to these things? If God *is* for *us*, who *is* against *us*? He who did not spare His own Son, but delivered Him over for *us all*, how will He not also with Him freely give *us* all things? Who will bring a charge against *God's elect*? God is the one who justifies; who is

> the one who condemns? Christ Jesus is He who died, yes,
> rather who was raised, who is at the right hand of God,
> who also intercedes for *us*. (Romans 8:31-34)

These are *family* promises, given to those whom God chose on the basis of His own mercy and grace from all eternity. And from this we can see testimony to the particular redemption worked out in Christ. When Paul says "what shall *we* say to these things," and "If God is for *us*, who is against *us*?" he is clearly speaking of elect believers. So the rest of the pronouns likewise refer to the same group (and we will see verse 33 proves this identification).

With this in mind then, we look at verse 32. The Father did not spare, or hold back, His very own Son, but delivered Him over *for us all*. The word "delivered over" refers to the giving of the Son in sacrifice. The Greek word παρέδωκεν is used in this context by Paul, as in Ephesians 5:2 (where Christ gives Himself up *for us*), and 5:25 (where Christ gives Himself *for the Church*). It is also used in Matthew 27:26 of the delivering up of Jesus to be crucified. The Father delivered over the Son to die upon the cross *for us*. The preposition ὑπὲρ (*huper*) means "in the place of," and is *key* to the substitutionary concept of atonement. The Father gave the Son *in our place*, in the place of His *elect people*.

In light of the tremendous price paid for our redemption in Christ, Paul then asks, "how will He (the Father) not also with Him (Christ) freely give us all things?" To whom is Paul speaking? God's elect. Surely these words could not be spoken of every single human for two reasons: Christ is not "given" to the person who endures God's wrath in eternity, and, God obviously does not give "all things" to those who spend eternity in hell. If a person were to say, "Oh yes, God does," then it follows that this is an empty passage, one that says God *offers* all things, but very few actually *obtain* them. No, it is clear: God gives "all things" to those for whom He gave His Son as a sacrifice. That sacrifice was *for them*; it was made in their place.

Verse 33 connects particular redemption with the rest of

the work of salvation, especially justification. Paul asks, "Who will bring a charge against God's elect?" Here in the heavenly courtroom the declaration on the part of the divine Judge of the verdict upon those who are God's elect is pronounced: they are justified. There is no answer to Paul's question, since no one *can* bring a charge against God's elect. God is the one who justifies, and whom does He justify? His elect. Upon what basis? *The sole basis of justification for the elect is the perfect work of Christ performed in their place.* Just as God gave His Son for them, so too He proclaims them just *on the basis of the work of His Son.*

Since the Father is the one who justifies, who then can condemn? Once the divine sentence has been uttered, there can be no appeal to a higher court. This is why there can be no condemnation of those who are in Christ Jesus, for the number of those *in Him* is identical with the number of *the elect.* Can Christ Jesus bring a charge of condemnation against them? Certainly not, for He died and rose again and sits at the right hand of God, "who also intercedes" *for whom?* For us. Who is the "us"? The elect of God.

Intercession and Atonement

This brings us to a vital truth: *Jesus Christ intercedes for the elect of God.* His work of intercession is directly connected to His work of atonement. Indeed, upon what ground can Christ intercede except that perfect work accomplished on the cross? We will see in our review of Hebrews that Christ saves *completely* those for whom He intercedes. But since the work of intercession and the work of atonement are but *two different aspects* of His one atoning sacrifice, then it follows that *Christ saves all those for whom He dies.* The non-Reformed are again forced either to universalism (all are atoned for, hence all are saved) or to rendering the atonement less than perfect, less than truly salvific (Arminianism).

Christ *intercedes for us.* Can the redeemed heart, even for a moment, consider the possibility that this work could fail? Imagine it: Christ lays down His perfect, spotless, sinless life on the cross. He is raised from the dead, and stands before the Father and pleads that perfect sacrifice in the place of His people. Is it at all possible that Christ could intercede for someone and yet fail in His work and that person be lost? The Arminian says, "Yes, for all the work of God, from the decree of the Father to the sacrifice of the Son to the ministry of the Spirit, is limited by the finite will of the rebel sinner." But the Bible knows of no such message. No one can bring a charge of condemnation against the elect because the Father justifies them and the Son intercedes for them. The work of God in salvation is perfect.

The Testimony of Hebrews

This is the message of the writer to the Hebrews as well. From the first paragraph of the letter the writer demonstrates the superiority of Christ over the old shadows of the Jewish system. Every chapter expands upon this theme. In chapter seven the writer introduces the superior priesthood of Christ over the Jewish priests who offered sacrifice in the Temple. Here he enters into the heart of the work of Christ as High Priest for the people of God. The priesthood of Christ is superior to the old priesthood because He became a priest not on the basis of law but on the basis of an oath (7:15-21). This makes Him the "guarantee of a better covenant" (7:22). Then he writes,

> The *former* priests, on the one hand, existed in greater numbers because they were prevented by death from continuing, but Jesus, on the other hand, because He continues forever, holds His priesthood permanently. Therefore He is able also to save forever those who draw near to God through Him, since He always lives to make intercession for them. (Hebrews 7:23-25)

The old priests were imperfect on many levels. They could not save completely for they were prevented from continuing their ministry by death. Christ is not like them. He "continues forever," therefore, He holds His priesthood permanently. Because of this He has a capacity, an ability, that none of the old priests had: He is able to save εἰς τὸ παντελὲς, "forever" or "to the uttermost." Before expanding on this thought, we note that the Scriptures say He is able to save *a particular people* (those who draw near to God through Him) *because* He always lives to engage in that unique and wonderful work Paul mentioned in Romans 8:34, the work of intercession. Let us consider what these few words mean.

First, He *is able to save.* He has the ability to actually save human beings, deliver them from the dominion and penalty of sin, and bring them into eternal glory. This ability resides in *Him,* not in mere potentiality, but in reality. He is able to save *to the uttermost,* forever, completely, without fail.

If a person believes salvation is the work of God then these words fully explain why we glory in confessing Christ as the perfect Savior. This is the ground upon which we can understand His statement from the cross, "It is finished," rather than "it is now theoretically possible." Jesus is able *to save* not merely *make savable.*

Second, as we have seen, the Arminian says God decrees *to save,* but leaves the identity of who will be saved to the free choices of human beings. They might be tempted to insert this over-riding concern into this passage as well by pointing to the fact that Jesus saves "those who draw near to God through Him." "Obviously, drawing near to God involves an act of free will" would be the assertion, again placing the first power of choice in the hands of the sinner. But, of course, we have already seen that Jesus taught that no man is able to exercise this kind of "coming" unless it is granted by the Father (John 6:44, 65), and Paul taught the unregenerate man cannot do what is pleasing to God and that there is none who seeks after God (Romans 8:7-8, 3:10-11). But is anyone ready to say that the thought of this passage is dependent upon reading into a subordinate clause the concept of human free will and autonomy? That Christ's intercession is based upon human beings "enabling" Him to intercede for them? Christ makes intercession for those who draw near to God through Him. These are the elect (John 6:37 makes the same point). He intercedes *only* for them, not for *anyone else.*

Third, this leads us to another key truth: Christ *intercedes* for *all* for whom He *dies.* Just as the high priest could not intercede for anyone without a sacrifice, so too Christ does not intercede for anyone for whom He does not make atonement. Christ intercedes for *all* for whom He dies since intercession is simply the presentation of the finished work of Calvary before the Father. The scope of the atonement, then, is the scope of intercession. Yet, we saw in Romans that Christ intercedes for God's elect, and here the same group is in view, those who come unto God by Him. And since His act of intercession is given as the explanation for Christ's ability to save forever, it follows inexorably that Christ's death *saves all those for whom it is made.* This is clearly the Reformed doctrine, *not* the Arminian doctrine. And if the Arminian says, "just because Christ intercedes for someone does not mean they will be saved," we respond with the context of the passage: the writer is demonstrating the *superiority* of Christ to the old priests. The old priests could indeed intercede for an individual to no effect: if Christ can likewise intercede to no effect, how is this an argument for Christ's superiority? It isn't. Therefore, the passage cannot be made consistent with the Arminian view.

This truth of the superiority of Christ continues on through the next chapters, all cementing our belief in the particularity of the redemptive work of Christ. In chapter 8 of Hebrews we are told that Christ inaugurates a "better covenant, which has been enacted on better promises." The New Covenant differs from the Old *primarily in the perfection of the work of the Mediator.* In the New Covenant God works *internally:* He writes His law upon their hearts, He enters into a personal relationship with *all* of them so that they all know Him, and He is merciful to their iniquities and remembers their sins no more (Hebrews 8:10-13).

This better covenant leads to a better divine service, a heavenly one, and a heavenly tabernacle, where Christ enters into the holy place:

> But when Christ appeared *as* a high priest of the good things to come, *He entered* through the greater and more perfect tabernacle, not made with hands, that is to say, not of this creation; and not through the blood of goats and calves, but through His own blood, He entered the holy place once for all, having obtained eternal redemption. For if the blood of goats and bulls and the ashes of a heifer sprinkling those who have been defiled sanctify for the cleansing of the flesh, how much more will the blood of Christ, who through the eternal Spirit offered Himself without blemish to God, cleanse your conscience from dead works to serve the living God? (Hebrews 9:11-14)

Christ enters the holy place "once for all." This is a temporal statement (once for all time) not a statement of scope (once for all individuals).[8] He enters once, not like the old priest who had to enter each year, and He does so *having obtained eternal redemption*. The old priest could never claim that: the old priest had to enter over and over and over again, proving the inadequacy of that system. But we need to realize that the person promoting the universal view of atonement encounters a real problem here. Such a person is promoting a *theoretical* redemption. What, exactly, had Christ "obtained" in their view? Are we to understand these words to mean that Christ had obtained "the savability" of mankind? Is this what "eternal redemption" means? Not at all.

The writer provides further evidence of what it means to "obtain eternal redemption." He says that Christ "at the consummation of the ages has been manifested to put away sin by the sacrifice of Himself" (9:26). What does it mean to "put away" sin? If His self-sacrifice *puts away* sin, how can any man for whom Christ died be held accountable for those sins? Such involves "double jeopardy," the punishment of Christ and the punishment of the man *for the same sins!* This is not the intention of Scripture.

This comes to full fruition in chapter ten when the argument reaches a crescendo. The repetitive nature of the sacrifices of the old system shows that they are imperfect (Hebrews 10:1-4). This throws the *uniqueness* of the sacrifice of Christ into the forefront:

> By this will we have been sanctified through the offering of the body of Jesus Christ once for all. And every priest stands daily ministering and offering time after time the same sacrifices, which can never take away sins; but He, having offered one sacrifice for sins for all time, SAT DOWN AT THE RIGHT HAND OF GOD, waiting from that time onward UNTIL HIS ENEMIES BE MADE A FOOTSTOOL FOR HIS FEET. For by one offering He has perfected for all time those who are sanctified. (Hebrews 10:10-14)

What does the *one* offering of the body of Jesus Christ *accomplish?* The setting apart of believers. The passage does not say, "By the one offering of the body of Jesus Christ it has been made possible for people to be sanctified if they will only exercise free will." The atonement of Christ *accomplishes* something with certainty, and unless one sees the truth of the elect of God running through the pages of Scripture such passages will make no sense.

The contrast is repeated by reference to the ineffective repetitive sacrifices of the old priests. Christ does not stand daily, but is *seated* at the right hand of God. The priest could not sit down because his work was never done. Christ's is done, "for by one offering He has perfected for all time those who are sanctified." The one-time offering of Christ *perfects* forever those who are sanctified. No additions necessary on the part of man. No sacraments or works of merit are needed. Christ's perfect offering does what the old sacrifices could never do: as Jesus said, "It is finished." It is perfect, complete, done.

The beautiful consistency of the Scriptures as God-breathed revelation bears out this understanding of the intention of the writer to the Hebrews. One of the passages that (needlessly) troubles many Christians comes at the conclusion of Hebrews chapter 10. The book of Hebrews is written to demonstrate the superiority of Christ to those in the congregation who might be tempted to return to the old ways of the Jewish system. Not knowing who in the gathered people are truly of the elect requires the elder in the congregation to issue warnings and plead with all to hear well the truth of God. This comes out in Hebrews 10:26-29:

> For if we go on sinning willfully after receiving the knowledge of the truth, there no longer remains a sacrifice for sins, but a terrifying expectation of judgment and THE FURY OF A FIRE WHICH WILL COMSUME THE ADVERSARIES. Anyone who has set aside the Law of Moses dies without mercy on *the testimony of* two or three witnesses. How much severer punishment do you think he will deserve who has trampled under foot the Son of God, and has regarded as unclean the blood of the covenant by which he was sanctified, and has insulted the Spirit of grace? (Hebrews 10:26-29)

This strong warning passage is often cited as evidence that one can lose salvation. But taken in its own context such is not the case at all. It is a warning to anyone who would have a "knowledge of the truth" and yet, despite this, go back to the old ways, the old sacrifices. There are no more sacrifices, now that the final and perfect sacrifice has been offered. To go back is to treat the blood of Christ as a "common" thing.[9] The error that is often made in regards to this passage is to understand "by which he was sanctified" to refer to the person who goes on sinning willfully against the blood of Christ. Grammatically, the phrase "by which he was sanctified" can refer to 1) the apostate, 2) Christ, the Son of God, or 3) to a general concept best rendered, "by which sanctification is provided." But remembering yet again the argument of the writer we see that the writer is referring to *Christ* as the one who is sanctified, set apart, shown to be holy, by His own sacrifice, and that this is why it is such a terrible thing to know of the power and purpose of Christ's blood and yet treat it as "common," like any of the sacrifices of goats and bulls offered under the old system. John Owen mentions the view that the "he" refers to the apostate,[10] but then says,

> But the design of the apostle in the context leads plainly to another application of these words. It is Christ himself that is spoken of, who was sanctified and dedicated unto God to be an eternal high priest, by the blood of the covenant which he offered unto God, as I have showed before. The priests of old were dedicated and sanctified unto their office by another, and the sacrifices which he offered for them; they could not sanctify themselves: so were Aaron and his sons sanctified by Moses, antecedently unto their offering any sacrifice themselves. But no outward act of men or angels could unto this purpose pass on the Son of God. He was to be the priest himself, the sacrificer himself,—to dedicate, consecrate, and sanctify himself, by his own sacrifice, in concurrence with the actings of God the Father in his suffering. See John xvii. 19; Heb. ii. 10, v. 7, 9, ix. 11, 12. That precious blood of Christ, wherein or whereby he was sanctified, and dedicated unto God as the eternal high priest of the church, this they esteemed "an unholy thing;" that is, such as would have no such effect as to consecrate him unto God and his office.[11]

The dire warning of this passage, then, comes from understanding that there is no more sacrifice for sins. Christ has offered Himself once and has, thereby, perfected those for whom He dies. To treat that perfect sacrifice, then, as "common" by going back to the repetitive sacrifices of the old system is to spit in the very face of the Son of God. What kind of punishment, indeed, is fitting in such a situation!

The Divine Substitute

This God-honoring, Christ-exalting understanding of a finished, perfect work runs throughout the Bible, and if it were not for the traditions that so easily cling to our thinking, we would see it everywhere. Indeed, everyone has heard what the angel said about the coming Messiah:

> She will bear a Son; and you shall call His name Jesus, for He will save His people from their sins. (Matthew 1:21)

Why is the Lord even named "Jesus"? Because *He will save His people from their sins.* We are not being trite to point out the obvious: He is not called Jesus because He will make savable a vague, indistinct general group of people who exercise their free will to enable Him to redeem them. He is called Jesus because 1) He *has* a people, *His* people, and 2) He *will* save them from their sins. He does not *try* to save them, *seek long and hard* to save them, but He *saves them.* He saves them by making propitiation for their sins:

> Therefore, He had to be made like His brethren in all things, so that He might become a merciful and faithful high priest in things pertaining to God, to make propitiation for the sins of the people. (Hebrews 2:17)

Propitiation is the sacrifice *that brings forgiveness and takes away wrath.* What "people" is here in view? It is the "many sons" of 2:10, those He "sanctifies" (2:11), "My brethren" (2:12), "the children God gave Me" (2:13), those "subject to slavery all their lives" (2:15), "the descendant of Abraham" (2:16), "His brethren" (2:17). In light of this we understand the statement of Hebrews 2:9, "so that by the grace of God He might taste death for everyone." Another passage often cited without context by Arminians yet defined so plainly in the text.[12]

Is it not the message of the Bible that Christ *saves* sinners? By what warrant do we read the following verses and change their meaning to "wants to save" or "makes savable" or "saves synergistically with the assistance of the sinner himself"?

> For the Son of Man has come to seek and to save that which was lost. (Luke 19:10)

> It is a trustworthy statement, deserving full acceptance, that Christ Jesus came into the world to save sinners, among whom I am foremost *of all.* (1 Timothy 1:15)

> Just as the Son of Man did not come to be served, but to serve, and to give His life a ransom for many. (Matthew 20:28)

> As a result of the anguish of His soul,
> He will see *it and* be satisfied;
> By His knowledge the Righteous One, My Servant, will justify the many,
> As He will bear their iniquities.
> (Isaiah 53:11)

> I am the good shepherd; the good shepherd lays down His life for the sheep....even as the Father knows Me and I know the Father; and I lay down My life for the sheep. (John 10:11-15)

When we keep in mind the biblical teaching of the *power* and *completeness* of Christ's atonement we can see in these passages the particularity that is so vehemently denied by the Arminian. And how can we not see the particularity of the following words:

> I have been crucified with Christ; and it is no longer I who live, but Christ lives in me; and the *life* which I now

> live in the flesh I live by faith in the Son of God, who
> loved me and gave Himself up for me. (Galatians 2:20)

Consider for a moment how precious it is that the Christian can say, "I have been crucified with Christ." This is *personal* atonement, *personal* substitution. We revel in the awesome love of our Savior who loved us *as individuals* and gave Himself up *for us*. For me! Me, the hate-filled sinner who spurned Him and His love! How much less glorious is the idea, "Christ loved a generic group and died so as to give them the opportunity to possibly join the group and hence receive certain benefits."

But let us ask this question: can the justly condemned sinner who stands upon the parapets of hell in eternity to come, screaming in hatred toward the halls of heaven, say, "I was crucified with Christ! He loved me and gave Himself up for me!" Surely not! Can such a person say, "My sins have been punished twice! First they were perfectly atoned for on the cross of Christ, and now I am undergoing punishment for them again here in hell!" The very idea causes us to recoil in horror. You see, particular redemption means *personal redemption*. Christ died *in my place*, not generically, but *individually*. What a glorious Savior!

We have now seen many passages that teach the truth of particular redemption. Many of these passages are not even mentioned in *CBF*. Yet, we read these words in that work:

> Not only are there no verses that, properly understood, support limited atonement, but there are numerous verses that teach unlimited atonement, that is, that Christ died for the sins of all mankind. Extreme Calvinists have not offered any satisfactory interpretations of these texts that support limited atonement.[13]

We assume the last phrase should read, "that support *unlimited* atonement." We know that the first assertion is untrue, as the preceding discussion proves. But what about the rest? Do

Reformed theologians have no satisfactory explanations for the texts that are cited in support of universal atonement? Let's find out.

Notes

1   B.B. Warfield, *The Plan of Salvation* (Eerdmans, n.d.), p. 94.

2   J. Kenneth Grider, "Arminianism" in *Evangelical Dictionary of Theology*, Walter Elwell, ed., (Baker, 1984), p. 80.

3   Robert Reymond, *A New Systematic Theology of the Christian Faith* (Thomas Nelson, 1998), p. 479

4   This is the clear assertion of the text: "in our behalf" or "in our place" renders the strong phrase ὑπὲρ ἡμῶν. Likewise, "became" renders γενόμενος, "being made" a curse in our place. If He became the curse in our place, how can we then bear the curse ourselves?

5   The Scripture here is without question: Christ *bore, carried away, took away* the sins of God's people in His body. The term Peter uses, ἀναφέρω, is closely connected with sacrifice both in the New Testament (Hebrews 7:27, 9:28), but as the normal translation of the Hebrew term עָלָה, "to offer sacrifice" in the LXX. If Christ has borne our sins, how can we then be punished for them?

6   We note as well that this passage gives us the purpose of Christ's bearing our sins: "so that we might die to sin and live to righteousness." If Christ bears the sins of the reprobate, His intention for them is frustrated by their never dieing to sin and living to righteousness. Obviously, His purpose is fulfilled in the elect.

7   For a full and most helpful substantiation of this meaning of *huper*, see Daniel B. Wallace, *Greek Grammar Beyond the Basics* (Eerdmans, 1996), pp. 383-389

8   The Greek term is ἐφάπαξ, "once for all time." It is a temporal adverb.

9   The Greek term translated "unclean" is κοινὸν, common, and by extension, unclean.

10 The person familiar with Owen's comments on this passage in *The Death of Death in the Death of Christ* should be aware that Owen takes a different view in his commentary on Hebrews. Owen wrote *The Death of Death* when he was 32 years of age. The commentary on Hebrews, comprising seven volumes, was written more than two decades later. The mature Owen, engaging in a purely exegetical work, takes a different view than he did earlier. It does not seem that Owen was even aware of the viewpoint that here Christ is spoken of when he wrote *The Death of Death.*

11 John Owen, *Commentary on the Book of Hebrews* (Banner of Truth Trust, 1996), 4:545-546.

12 *CBF* likewise provides exactly two sentences of commentary on page 203, "Christ died for everyone, not just the elect. This is the plain meaning of the text." No discussion of context, no discussion of the meaning of propitiation.

13 Ibid., p. 192.

Chapter 11

Particular Redemption

CBF does not discuss the biblical doctrine of the atonement, nor does it interact with the Reformed doctrine on the issue. There is no discussion of the passages we examined in the previous chapter regarding the work of Christ in the book of Hebrews. No attempt is made to explain how "propitiation" can be merely theoretical when it refers to the actual taking away of wrath. The relationship between intercession and atonement is likewise left untouched. No positive, Scripturally-based presentation is made of what the atonement actually accomplishes. And while such works as John Owen's *The Death of Death in the Death of Christ* are mentioned, their substantial exegetical presentations are not even noted, let alone refuted. Other works, such as Gary Long's *Definite Atonement* are ignored, even though that work provides extensive responses on such key passages as 2 Peter 2:1.

The arguments leveled against particular redemption, as we noted earlier, are often really objections against particular *election*. We will see this come out a number of times in the responses noted below.

The exegesis offered by *CBF* on this topic is often tremendously strained, or based upon objections that are shallow at best. Note this use of Romans 5:6 where it is said that "Christ died for the ungodly." *CBF* asserts:

> But it is not only the elect that are ungodly and en-
> emies of God, but also the non-elect. Therefore, Christ
> must have died for the non-elect as well as for the elect.
> Otherwise, He would not have died for all the ungodly
> and enemies of God. Further, if Paul meant Christ died
> only for the "elect" he could easily have said it and avoided
> any misunderstanding. The word "elect" was a regular
> part of New Testament vocabulary...."[1]

In other words, "Unless the Bible uses the exact phrase 'Christ
died *only* for the elect,' then it can't possibly be true." A moment of reflection reveals that Romans 5:6 is perfectly in harmony with the Reformed position and the doctrinal truths we
saw in the preceding chapter. Christ died for the ungodly. The
elect, until they are regenerated, are fallen sons of Adam as are
all others. They are ungodly. Hence, the statement "Christ died
for the ungodly" is perfectly true. Further, all the elect, until
they are brought to faith in Christ, are enemies of God, walking in the rebellious ways of the world (Eph. 2:1-3). Hence,
saying Christ reconciled those who were enemies of God by
His death is perfectly true and harmonious with the biblical
teaching of particular redemption. There is nothing in the context that demands us to believe that the statement "Christ
died for the ungodly" means "Christ died for every single ungodly person who has ever, or will ever, live." Nor is there any
reason to believe that the reconciliation spoken of here (personal reconciliation of human beings to God, not the broader
use of the term with regard to all creation used by Paul in
Colossians 1:20) is merely theoretical and non-salvific. This
kind of argumentation leads to such troubling conclusions as
asserting that it is the "plain teaching of other Scriptures" that
"Not all Christ died for will be saved." This is the reasoning
offered:

> The doctrine of limited atonement claims that all Christ
> died for will be saved. But the above passages and many
> others reveal that: (1) Christ died for all, and (2) All will

not be saved (cf. Matt. 25:41; Rev. 20:10). Thus, not all Christ died for will be saved. The doctrine of limited atonement is contrary to the clear teaching of Scripture.[2]

Such simplistic arguments ignore the vast mountain of Reformed literature let alone the "plain teaching" of Hebrews 7-10 and Romans 8:31-34. Will readers of CBF be familiar enough with the exegesis offered by Reformed writers to recognize that the issues are not being dealt with in a truly scholarly and fair manner?

The Issue of Calvin's View of the Atonement

Before entering into the specific responses offered by CBF on the doctrine of particular redemption, it is important to respond to the oft-repeated claim made by Dr. Geisler that John Calvin was not a Calvinist. The *only* ground offered by CBF upon which the distinction between "extreme Calvinists" and "moderate Calvinists" can be based is the assertion that Calvin did not believe in limited atonement. This comes out a number of times in CBF, first in a footnote on page 20 where the phrase "extreme Calvinist" is first used:

> We use the term "extreme" rather than "hyper" since hyper-Calvinism is used by some to designate a more radical view known as "superlapsarianism," which entails double-predestination,...denies human responsibility..., or nullifies concern for missions and evangelism.
> We should note that theologians we classify as extreme Calvinists consider themselves simply "Calvinists," and would probably object to our categorizing them in this manner. In their view, anyone who does not espouse all five points of Calvinism as they interpret them is not, strictly speaking, a true Calvinist. Nonetheless, we call them "extreme" Calvinists because they are more extreme than John Calvin himself...and to distinguish them from moderate Calvinists.

In passing we note that supralapsarianism[3] is not the equivalent of hyper-Calvinism. Be that as it may, how is it that "extreme" Calvinists are more radical than John Calvin? One, and only one reason, is ever offered:

> Even John Calvin was not an extreme Calvinist on this point, for he believed that by Christ's death "all the sins of the world have been expiated." Commenting on the "many" for whom Christ died in Mark 14:24, Calvin said, "The word many does not mean a part of the world only, but the whole human race." This means that people like Jonathan Edwards, John Gerstner, and R.C. Sproul, who believe in limited atonement, are more extreme than John Calvin! Hence, they have earned the title "extreme Calvinists."[4]

Knowing that such a statement can be challenged, Dr. Geisler included an appendix titled "Was Calvin a Calvinist?" This appendix amounts to a grand total of five pages of citations. There is not the *first attempt* to interact with a *single* Reformed work on the subject. Other than a reference to R.T. Kendall's *Calvin and English Calvinism to 1649*, no work of scholarship is cited, referenced, or noted (including the responses written by Calvinists to Kendall's work). Only *two* of the passages cited by Reformed authors who believe Calvin *did* hold to a particular view of the atonement is cited, and even then, it garners no response nor discussion, as we will see. Yet, despite the complete failure to interact with *any* viewpoint other than his own, Dr. Geisler concludes the appendix with these words:

> Whatever else Calvin may have said to encourage extreme Calvinism's T-U-L-I-P, he certainly denied limited atonement as they understand it. For Calvin, the Atonement is universal in *extent* and limited only in its *application*, namely, to those who believe.[5]

Please note the use of the word "certainly." We honestly cannot understand how one can make such a statement without dealing in-depth with the readily available works that argue for just the opposite conclusion. And when we take just a few moments to examine some of Calvin's statements, we will see that it is "certain" that Calvin did *not* deny limited atonement. And if that is the case, the entire nomenclature of "moderate Calvinist" versus "extreme Calvinist" collapses.

An in-depth analysis of Calvin's view of the atonement is beyond the scope of our response to *CBF*. However, the reader is directed to the following works for the necessary information upon which to make an informed decision:

> William Cunningham, *The Reformers and the Theology of the Reformation*, (Banner of Truth, 1989), pp. 395-408.

> Robert Peterson Sr., *Calvin and the Atonement* (Mentor, 1999).

> Paul Helm, *Calvin and the Calvinists* (Banner of Truth, 1998).

> Jonathan Rainbow, *Will of God and the Cross : An Historical and Theological Study of John Calvin's Doctrine of Limited Redemption* (Pickwick Publications, 1990).

It should be noted that some scholars conclude that we simply cannot decide what Calvin's view was. Others say we can, and argue for both sides. But even the most cursory examination of Calvin *must* provide more than a few isolated quotations that do not even begin to take into consideration the *consistency* of Calvin's theology. What Calvin believed about election, the deadness of man in sin, and the work of intercession *must* be considered. *CBF* does not even attempt a fair review of Calvin on this point.

The Fall, 1985 issue of the *Westminster Theological Journal* contained a twenty-nine page article written by Roger Nicole

titled "John Calvin's View of the Extent of the Atonement."
Nicole offers the following arguments in favor of the belief
that Calvin *did* hold to a definite atonement:

1   Calvin's strong emphasis upon the divine purpose points
    us in this direction. "It seems difficult to imagine that
    Calvin would posit as the purpose of Christ an indefinite,
    hypothetical redemption, when at so many other points it
    is plainly apparent that the specific elective purpose of God
    is the controlling feature of his outlook."[6]
2   Calvin often asserts that God's purpose in election is ulti-
    mate and that we cannot go behind it. "To assume a hypo-
    thetical redemptive purpose more inclusive than the elec-
    tion of grace is doing precisely what he precludes."[7]
3   "Calvin makes it quite plain that he views repentance and
    faith and all other recreative benefits of salvation to have
    been merited for the elect by Christ. What Christ accom-
    plished on the cross is not so much to secure the salvability
    of all humans, as actually to accomplish the salvation of
    those whom he does redeem."[8]
4   Calvin often connected in the same statement benefits that
    are given to the elect alone together with references to the
    effects of the death of Christ.
5   Calvin closely connects the priestly work of Christ in His
    death with His work as intercessor. This is brought out
    especially with reference to Calvin's comments on John
    17:9:

> He openly declares that he does not pray for the world,
> because he has no solicitude but about his own flock,
> which he received from the hand of the Father. I reply,
> the prayers which we offer for all are still limited to the
> elect of God. We ought to pray that this man, and that
> man, and every man, may be saved, and thus include the
> whole human race, because we cannot yet distinguish
> the elect from the reprobate; and yet, while we desire the
> coming of the kingdom of God, we likewise pray that

God may destroy his enemies. Besides, we learn from these words, that God chooses out of the world those whom he thinks fit to choose to be heirs of life, and that this distinction is not made according to the merit of men, but depends on his mere good-pleasure. For those who think that the cause of election is in men must begin with faith. Now, Christ expressly declares that they who are given to him belong to the Father; and it is certain that they are given so as to believe, and that faith flows from this act of giving. If the origin of faith is this act of giving, and if election comes before it in order and time, what remains but that we acknowledge that those whom God wishes to be saved out of the world are elected by free grace? Now since Christ prays for the elect only, it is necessary for us to believe the doctrine of election, if we wish that he should plead with the Father for our salvation. A grievous injury, therefore, is inflicted on believers by those persons who endeavor to blot out the knowledge of election from the hearts of believers, because they deprive them of the pleading and intercession of the Son of God.[9]

"But if oblation and intercession are recognized to be coextensive, they will both be universal or both be particular. The clear-cut particularity of intercession becomes therefore a telling argument for the equal particularity of the atonement."[10]

6 Calvin's interpretation of the most popular texts used to promote a universal saving intent shows that he had in mind the particular elective purpose of God. "This is explicitly brought to the fore in the commentaries in Ezek 18:32; John 3:16; 2 Pet 3:9. In the commentaries and sermons on 1 Tim 2:4 and Titus 2:13 the word 'all' is interpreted to refer to 'all kinds or classes of men.' In relation to John 1:29 and 1 John 2:2 the word 'world' is viewed as intending to transcend a nationalistic Jewish particularism." Obviously, the question is, if Calvin disagrees with the universalist on every one of these passages (all of which are

cited with frequency by Norman Geisler and interpreted *consistently* in opposition to Calvin), why should he then do a sudden flip-flop and *agree* on this universal intention of the atonement? Such makes no sense at all.

7   The majority of the passages cited by Arminians who seek to enlist Calvin's support "may be alleviated by the consideration that Calvin meant to place special emphasis on the indiscriminate call of the gospel." This is seen throughout Calvin's writings, even in the passage cited above regarding John 17:9.

8   "There are in Scripture as well as in Calvin passages where the particular intent of Christ's death is stressed." These include Matthew 1:21, John 15:13, Titus 2:14, etc., where Calvin's comments provide a particular, not universal, interpretation.

9   Calvin's statement in response to Heshusius is especially telling: "I should like to know how the wicked can eat the flesh of Christ which was not crucified for them, and how they can drink the blood which was not shed to expiate their sins."[11]

10 Calvin's use of terms such as "reconciliation," "redemption," and "propitiation" are inconsistent with a universalistic conclusion. "The language of Calvin does not fit a mere potential blessing which remains ineffective pending some performance by the sinner, which would then make it truly operative: it connotes a basic act of God, who then sees to it that it is implemented unto the salvation of all those he purposed to save."[12]

11 Calvin fully understood and taught the concept of penal substitution. "It is difficult to imagine that Calvin failed to perceive the necessary link between substitution and definite atonement, or that, having perceived it, he carried on without giving regard to this matter!

12 Calvin's Trinitarian view would lead him to believe in a full unity amongst the divine Persons. "But universal atonement introduces a fundamental disjunction between the universal intent of the Son who gave himself for all and the particular purpose of the Father who elected only some people, and

the Holy Spirit, who confers regeneration, faith, and repentance to the elect only."

13 Finally, how does one explain the swift move of Reformed thought from an alleged universal view of Calvin to the particular view of the first generation of his disciples?

At the very least one thing is obvious: given CBF's failure to interact with *any* of these arguments the assertion that Calvin "certainly" did not believe in particular redemption is left without any foundation whatsoever. Therefore, since this statement is the *only* basis for the "moderate/extreme" Calvinist distinction, we must conclude the distinction is arbitrary and erroneous.

Two quotes from Calvin should suffice to demonstrate that Dr. Geisler has misunderstood his use of the word "world" and "all men" in many of the passages he cites. CBF cites 1 Timothy 2:4 as supportive of a universal desire on God's part for salvation, and that this is its "plain meaning."[13] If Calvin likewise saw this passage in a universalistic fashion, this would lend support to Geisler's theory. Yet, read Calvin's own words:

> *And may come to the acknowledgment of the truth.* Lastly, he demonstrates that God has at heart the salvation of all, because he invites all to the acknowledgment of his truth. This belongs to that kind of argument in which the cause is: proved from the effect; for, if "the gospel is the power of God for salvation to every one that believeth" (Romans 1:16), it is certain that all those to whom the gospel is addressed are invited to the hope of eternal life. In short, as the calling is a proof of the secret election, so they whom God makes partakers of his gospel are admitted by him to possess salvation; because the gospel reveals to us the righteousness of God, which is a sure entrance into life.
>
> Hence we see the childish folly of those who represent this passage to be opposed to predestination. "If God" say they, "wishes all men indiscriminately to be saved, it is false that some are predestined by his eternal purpose

to salvation, and others to perdition." They might have had some ground for saying this, if Paul were speaking here about individual men; although even then we should not have wanted the means of replying to their argument; for, although the: will of God ought not to be judged from his secret decrees, when he reveals them to us by outward signs, yet it does not therefore follow that he has not determined with himself what he intends to do as to every individual man.

But I say nothing on that subject, because it has nothing to do with this passage; for the Apostle simply means, that there is no people and no rank in the world that is excluded from salvation; because God wishes that the gospel should be proclaimed to all without exception. Now the preaching of the gospel gives life; and hence he justly concludes that God invites all equally to partake salvation. But the present discourse relates to classes of men, and not to individual persons; for his sole object is, to include in this number princes and foreign nations. That God wishes the doctrine of salvation to be enjoyed by them as well as others, is evident from the passages already quoted, and from other passages of a similar nature. Not without good reason was it said, "Now, kings, understand," and again, in the same Psalm, "I will give thee the Gentiles for an inheritance, and the ends of the earth for a possession." (Psalm 2:8-10.) In a word, Paul intended to shew that it is our duty to consider, not what kind of persons the princes at that time were, but what God wished them to be. Now the duty arising: out of that love which we owe to our neighbor is, to be solicitous and to do our endeavor for the salvation of all whom God includes in his calling, and to testify this by godly prayers.[14]

This is the *very* interpretation that Dr. Geisler identifies as "implausible." If this interpretation of "all men" is read into the passages cited from Calvin, however, it becomes plain that Calvin did not hold the unlimited view of the atonement that CBF claims. As to the word "world," Calvin's view is exemplified by his comments on 1 John 2:2. This passage is quoted by *CBF*. Yet, for some reason, it is *seems* as if *CBF* thinks this quotation affirms a *universal* view of atonement. It is highly educational to note that Dr. Geisler inserted a whole series of italics into his rendition of Calvin's words. Why is it educational? *Because he emphasizes the portions that seem to support his thesis, but ignores the direct statements that contradict him.* Calvin scholars for centuries have cited this passage as evidence of Calvin's particularism. But note how Geisler cites the passage:

> He put this in for amplification, that believers might be convinced that *the expiation made by Christ extends to all who by faith embrace the Gospel.* But here the question may be asked as to *how the sins of the whole world have been expiated.* I pass over the dreams of the fanatics, who make this a reason to extend salvation to all the reprobate and even to Satan himself. Such a monstrous idea is not worth refuting. Those who want to avoid this absurdity have said that *Christ suffered sufficiently for the whole world but effectively only for the elect.* This solution has commonly prevailed in the schools. Although *I allow for the truth of this,* I deny that it fits this passage. For John's purpose was only to make this blessing common to the whole Church. Therefore, under the world 'all' [in 1 John 2:2] he does not include the reprobate, but refers to all who would believe and those who were scattered through various regions of the earth. For, as is meet, the grace of Christ is really made clear when it is declared to be the only salvation of the world" (Comments on 1 John 2:2).[15]

Dr. Geisler then provides this interpretation:

> Calvin clearly denies universalism and affirms the sufficiency of Christ's death for the whole world, even though he denies that this particular passage can be used to teach this.[16]

There is a clear error being committed here by Dr. Geisler. If he wished to italicize the important element of the quote, he would have italicized this statement: "Therefore, under the world 'all' [in 1 John 2:2] he does not include the reprobate, but refers to all who would believe and those who were scattered through various regions of the earth." This is the key affirmation! Here Calvin completely contradicts Dr. Geisler's interpretation. In fact, as we will see below, *CBF* identifies the idea expressed by Calvin (and earlier by Augustine) as "an obvious case of *eisegesis* (reading into the text)" that "does not deserve an extensive treatment."[17]

Further, Geisler italicizes the assertions of *others* rather than Calvin, yet then interprets these as being *Calvin's* view! Calvin believes John's assertion is meant to give confidence to *all believers* that Christ is their propitiation, but that this does *not* mean that Christ's death is offered for the reprobate. If we interpret this in Calvin's context his words are clear: it is without question his assertion that when John says "the whole world" he is saying this does *not* include the reprobate. This means he does *not* believe Christ died for every single human being. Dr. Geisler italicizes the statement of the schoolmen about the sacrifice being "sufficient" for the world, but "efficient" for the elect, despite the fact that Calvin denies this is the meaning of the passage!

In conclusion, then, we see that the assertion that Calvin "certainly" denied limited atonement, and that this means that those who hold this view are "extreme Calvinists" is utterly without substantiation, either in Calvin's words or in the readily available scholarly sources.

John 17:9

We saw in the previous chapter that the Lord Jesus in His High Priestly prayer immediately before His sacrifice on Calvary prayed for those whom the Father had given Him. He specifically differentiated between the objects of His prayer and "the world." This distinction, introduced in a particularly poignant salvific context, causes Arminian exegetes no end of trouble.

> Several important things should be noted in response to this. First, the fact that Christ only prayed for the elect in this passage does not in itself prove that He never prayed for the non-elect at any time. If, as extreme Calvinists admit, Jesus as a man could have had negative answers to His prayers, then He could have prayed for some people who were not elect, even if it is not recorded in Scripture. Many things Jesus did are not recorded (cf. John 21:25).[18]

Such a response completely misses the reason the passage is cited by Reformed exegetes. The context of John 17:9 *is the Lord's High Priestly prayer.* It is pure misdirection to even introduce the idea of prayers receiving negative answers: *is it CBF's assertion that the Father will give a negative answer to the Son's intercession for His people?* We would surely hope not, for such would be as unbiblical a position to take as could be imagined! But the explanation continues to miss the mark:

> Second, Christ prayed for non-elect persons. His prayer, " 'Father, forgive them for they know not what they do' " (Luke 23:34 KJV) undoubtedly included people who were not elect.[19]

Given that Dr. Geisler posits that it is certain that Calvin did not believe in particular redemption, his words might carry some weight here:

> If any one think that this does not agree well with Peter's sentiment, which I have just now quoted, the answer is easy. For when Christ was moved by a feeling of compassion to ask forgiveness from God for his persecutors, this did not hinder him from acquiescing in the righteous

judgment of God, which he knew to be ordained for reprobate and obstinate men. Thus when Christ saw that both the Jewish people and the soldiers raged against him with blind fury, though their ignorance was not excusable, he had pity on them, and presented himself as their intercessor. Yet knowing that God would be an avenger, he left to him the exercise of judgment against the desperate. In this manner ought believers also to restrain their feelings in enduring distresses, so as to desire the salvation of their persecutors, and yet to rest assured that their life is under the protection of God, and, relying on this consolation, that the licentiousness of wicked men will not in the end remain unpunished, not to faint under the burden of the cross.[20]

Then note these words that are added:

It is probable, however, that Christ did not pray for all indiscriminately, but only for the wretched multitude, who were carried away by inconsiderate zeal, and not by premeditated wickedness. For since the scribes and priests were persons in regard to whom no ground was left for hope, it would have been in vain for him to pray for them. Nor can it be doubted that this prayer was heard by the heavenly Father, and that this was the cause why many of the people afterwards drank by faith the blood which they had shed.[21]

CBF continues,

Further, Jesus indirectly prayed for the world by asking us to "'pray the Lord of the harvest to send out laborers into His harvest'" (Luke 10:2 KJV), yet knowing that not all would be saved (Matt. 13:28-30). In fact, He wept for unbelievers (Matt. 23:37) and prayed that unbelievers would be saved (John 11:42).[22]

God has ordained the *means* as well as the ends: the prayer of

Luke 10:2 is that the Lord would send out workers into the harvest. To confuse this with a prayer by our High Priest in behalf of the world in general is to stretch a passage far beyond the breaking point. We have seen the error of this use of Matthew 23:37, and John 11:42 speaks of the Lord praying to the Father with reference to being "heard" by the Father so that people would believe. Obviously, this has *nothing* to do with Jesus praying for unbelievers, since, of course, that would require the assumption that none of those gathered around were of the elect.

> Third, even if Jesus had not prayed for the non-elect, still other passages of the New Testament reveal that the apostle Paul did, and he exhorts us to do the same.[23]

Of course, there is a vast difference between Paul and the Lord Jesus: Paul is not our High Priest. Paul is not our Intercessor. Paul does not have supernatural knowledge concerning the *identity* of the elect. Of course Paul prays in a way different than the incarnate Lord! The fact remains that when praying as our High Priest *specifically* about the salvation of the elect Christ *excludes* those who are *not* His. CBF has failed to provide a reason to reject the Reformed understanding of this passage. So why does CBF miss the important elements of passages such as this? The concluding comment on John 17:9 reveals the reason: "The important thing is that Jesus wanted everyone to be His children (Matthew 23:37; 1 Tim. 2:4-6; 2 Peter 3:9)."

Mark 10:45 and Real Versus Potential Atonement

In the context of responding to Mark 10:45 CBF deals with the vital difference between the Reformed belief in an *actual* atonement and the inconsistent Arminian (i.e., the position of CBF that claims to affirm substitutionary atonement: historic Arminianism recognizes the inconsistency of holding to this view and therefore adopts the governmental view) position that renders the atonement a mere potentiality. This will serve to address a number of key issues that define the debate. In reference to substitutionary atonement Dr. Geisler says,

> But extreme Calvinists insist that logic demands that if Christ died for all, then all would be saved. For if Christ was substituted for their sin, then He paid for it and they are free. But the Bible teaches that all will not be saved....Therefore, they argue that Christ could not have died for the sins of all mankind.[24]

This accurately summarizes the position we have put forward: that the Bible's teaching on the *intention* and *effect* of the atonement precludes us from believing that Christ died to make men *savable*, but that He actually *saved* those for whom He substituted. In fact, it is our assertion that the word "substitution" should not be used of a merely *potential* atonement, for such would destroy the *personal aspect of the death of Christ*. Dr. Geisler begins by dismissing the Reformed understanding as being based upon mere "speculative inferences." But seemingly he recognizes this is not enough and continues:

> Second, the inference is not logically necessary. That a benefactor buys a gift and freely offers it to someone does not mean that person *must* receive it. Likewise, that Christ paid for our sins does not mean we *must* accept the forgiveness of sins bought by His blood.[25]

By now the errors of the Arminian view here enunciated should be clear. They are: 1) rejection of the biblical doctrine of the positive decree of God; 2) rejection of the biblical doctrine of the deadness of man in sin and his inability to do anything that is pleasing to God (including "acceptance of forgiveness of sins"); 3) rejection of the biblical doctrine of the atonement, including its *intention* and *result*. The result is a theoretical atonement that saves no one: His blood may "buy" forgiveness, but our choice determines whether the entire work of Christ in our behalf will be a success or a failure.[26] This empties the word "paid" of its meaning. If someone pays my bill, I no longer owe the money. The Arminian view leaves us with a contractual situation where Christ *offers* to pay the bill based upon the performance of the free act of faith. The true consequences of this come out in this key passage:

> Finally, that Christ's death made everyone *savable* does not thereby mean that everyone is *saved*. His death on the Cross made salvation *possible* for all men but not *actual*—it is not actual until they receive it by faith. This should not be difficult for an extreme Calvinist to understand. For even though the elect were *chosen* in Christ, the Lamb slain before the creation of the world (Rev. 13:8; Eph. 1:4), nonetheless, they were not actually *saved* until God regenerated and justified them. Before the moment in time when they were regenerated, the elect were not saved actually but only potentially. Salvation, then, can be *provided* for all without it being *applied* to all. There is enough Bread of Life put on the table by Christ for the whole world, even though only the elect partake of it. The Water of Life is there for "whoever" (all) to drink (John 4:14), even though many refuse to do so.[27]

Given how tremendously popular this type of argument is, we need to provide a thorough response. First, this is a vitally important claim:

> Finally, that Christ's death made everyone *savable* does not thereby mean that everyone is *saved*. His death on the Cross made salvation *possible* for all men but not *actual*—it is not actual until they receive it by faith.

There is an element of truth here in the sense that until the point of regeneration, the benefits of Christ's death are not applied to the elect. But, the *vast chasm* that separates this teaching and the Reformed doctrine *must* be understood. *The certainty of the application of the benefits of Christ's work is found in the fact that the elect are known personally to God due to His decree: therefore, Christ substitutes for them personally in His death, assuring the application of the benefits of His death in the life of each individual who has received God's sovereign grace in eternity past.* The salvation of the elect is therefore *certain* not because God passively knows who will believe, but because God's decree makes the elect a reality (even before we, who live long after the cross, are born) so that *they can be intimately joined with Christ in His death upon the cross.* As Paul said, "I have been crucified with Christ." This is the statement *of every one of the redeemed,* but may we never teach that this is a statement that can be uttered by the rebel God-hater in hell!

Contrast this with the view enunciated by Dr. Geisler: given his assertion of the overriding freedom of the will of man and the fact that the "list" of the elect is not made up without reference to the free actions of man, it follows that the death of Christ must be only *potential.* It cannot actually *make certain* the application of that death *to any particular person* since the final decision for salvation is not an eternal decree but *the free choices of men in time.* Dr. Geisler teaches that it is Christ's intention and desire to save every single individual person so that He "substitutes" for them. But how can this be? If He takes the place of every single individual, does this result in *savability* or *salvation*? Are we to understand that the difference between "savability" and "salvation" is "the act of free will called faith"? What does "faith" do to change a mere possibility into reality? If men are always free, does this not mean that at any time a person may "activate" this "substitutionary atonement" and thereby become saved? Why would this be different with reference to a person in hell? If Christ truly substituted for all those in hell, why could they not, if they remain free, simply "activate" the substitution that was made for them?

The assertion above confuses the issue as well. The death

of Christ took place in time. We live long after that time. Hence, the work of salvation must be applied to us in our time-frame. The real question is, "Does the death of Christ make it certain that any single individual will, during their lives, receive the benefits of the substitutionary atonement of Christ, so that they will enter into that personal relationship with Him having been forgiven all their sins at Calvary?" The Reformed say yes, the Arminians say no. The Arminian says it is possible for any person at any time to "actuate" the potential salvation that is offered, but there is no guarantee that anyone will do so. It is all up to man. Next,

> This should not be difficult for an extreme Calvinist to understand. For even though the elect were *chosen* in Christ, the Lamb slain before the creation of the world (Rev. 13:8; Eph. 1:4), nonetheless, they were not actually *saved* until God regenerated and justified them. Before the moment in time when they were regenerated, the elect were not saved actually but only potentially. Salvation, then, can be *provided* for all without it being *applied* to all.

The problem with this argument is that it misses the entire point: we are not saying that God *completed and applied the entire work of salvation to the elect at the cross.* Such would be impossible since most of the elect were not yet born. What we *are* saying is that the elect were *joined to Christ* in His death so that they can all say "I was crucified with Christ." What we *are* saying is that the unregenerate man in hell can *never* say "I was crucified with Christ." What we are saying is that it is equivocation to say "Before the moment in time when they were regenerated, the elect were not saved actually but only potentially." What does "potentially" mean? That there was some *doubt* involved?

You see, Dr. Geisler differentiates between the terms "potential" and "applied," but in the process inserts great confusion. The death of Christ *obtained eternal redemption,* not *possibly*, but *with certainty*. The elect were joined with Christ *so that no possibility exists of their not receiving the benefits of their being joined to Christ*. He *procured* actual forgiveness of sins *in their place*. Yes, this great benefit will be applied to them in time, *but that does not reduce the certainty of its application to a mere possibility*.

The sins of the elect people of God were nailed to the cross of Christ *and no others*. This is the difference, then: the Arminian says all sins committed by all men are nailed to the cross of Calvary and borne in His body on the tree. The Reformed says if this is so then they cannot be borne *by anyone else at any time*. It is not a matter of Christ "potentially" bearing sin: either He bore it or He didn't. If He did, those sins are forgiven. The fact that the elect will only come to know of this great benefit when God, by His grace, regenerates them, brings them out of darkness and into His light, and gives them the knowledge of what Christ did for them long before they were born, does not make His work in their behalf a mere potentiality.

We cannot help but agree wholeheartedly with the words of Charles Spurgeon:

> Let the Christian feel that the teaching which lowers the work of Christ, makes it dependent upon the will of man as to its effect, puts the cross on the ground, and saith, "That blood is shed, but it may be shed in vain, shed in vain for you," — let us all feel that such teaching cometh not from the Spirit of God. That teaching it is which, pointing to the, cross, saith, "He shall see of the travail of his soul, and shall be satisfied;" that teaching which makes the atonement a true atonement which put away the vindictive justice of God for ever from every soul for whom that atonement was offered, exalts Christ, and, therefore, it is a teaching which comes from the Spirit of God. When your heart is brought to rest upon what Christ has done, when, laying aside all confidence in your own works, knowledge, prayings, doings, or

believings, you come to rest upon what Christ has done in its simplicity, then is Jesus Christ exalted in your heart, and it must have been the work of the Spirit of divine grace. The person, then, and the work of Christ are exalted.[28]

Dr. Geisler continues the theme a few pages later:

The first thing to note is that this objection is a form of special pleading, based on a different view of substitution. Of course, if substitution is automatic, then everyone for whom Christ is substituted will automatically be saved. But substitution need not be automatic; a penalty can be paid without it automatically taking effect.[29]

Is this true? What if the substitution involves *death*? If a person bears the sins of another, upon what basis can the penalty for those sins be brought to bear a second time? This is why historic Arminians reject substitutionary atonement and why the "moderate Calvinist" who uses this Reformed phrase finds himself in such contradiction. Ponder for a moment these words in light of the Bible's teaching on the meaning of the term "propitiation":

For instance, the money can be given to pay a friend's debt without the person being willing to receive it. Those, like myself, who accept the substitutionary atonement but reject limited atonement simply believe that Christ's payment for the sins of all mankind did not automatically save them; it simply made them savable. It did not automatically apply the saving grace of God into a person's life. It simply satisfied (propitiated) God on their behalf (1 John 2:2), awaiting their faith to receive God's unconditional gift of salvation, which was made possible by Christ's atonement.[30]

This is *not* substitutionary atonement. It is another instance where a historic term is being redefined. If God is propitiated in behalf of *all men*, upon what basis can God punish them in hell for eternity? How can a truly propitiatory, substitutionary atonement make men "savable" but not actually save? Remember, we are not here speaking of the fact that God applies the work of Christ in the elect's life at a point in time: the real issue is the assertion of what the death of Christ does (or doesn't do) for the non-elect. If God is "satisfied on their behalf" then what is left? The autonomous act of faith, evidently. So is God satisfied or not? Does Christ's death result in 99% satisfaction, with the 1% satisfaction coming from man's faith? *CBF* equates "satisfaction" with propitiation. Yet, propitiation means "the sacrifice that brings forgiveness of sins and removes wrath." So, why is the non-elect person lost for eternity if, in fact, the wrath of God was poured out on Christ *in their place?* We are left with the utterly untenable conclusion that God extracts double-payment for these sins: He punished them first in Christ, and then He will punish them for eternity in the non-elect, who could have avoided this if they had simply exercised their free will and believed.

Let us add one further difficulty to Dr. Geisler's position. Let us say there is a man named John Green. Given the position enunciated in *CBF*, God, in His perfect foreknowledge of the "free acts" of human beings, knows perfectly (but did not decree) that John Green will *not* accept Christ. Despite the best efforts of the Holy Spirit, it is known, perfectly, that John Green will die rejecting the gospel and end up in hell as a result. The view promoted in *CBF* would lead us to believe that even though God the Father knew, infallibly, that John Green would *never* accept the work of Christ in his behalf, still God the Father causes Jesus Christ to suffer in John Green's place, bearing his sins and their penalty on the cross. This is despite the fact that God likewise knows that He will exact the same penalty for the same sins from John Green in eternity to come! Why would God lay John Green's sins on Jesus *knowing full well that Christ's work would fail in his behalf?*

Later in the work Dr. Geisler again attacks the teaching that it was Christ's intention to *procure salvation for His people* (Matthew 1:21) by dying in *their* place upon the cross. He teaches that it was God's intention instead to procure salvation for all who would believe, and, since God wanted everyone to believe, Christ died to provide salvation for all people. We noted at the beginning of our examination of the atonement that it is a highly emotional issue, and this comes out in the conclusion offered by Dr. Geisler regarding the Reformed proclamation of the atonement: "It is the denial that God really wants all persons to be saved that is such a hideous error of extreme Calvinism."[31] We leave the reader to determine if such words are warranted.

John 1:29

> The next day he saw Jesus coming to him and said, "Behold, the Lamb of God who takes away the sin of the world!" (John 1:29)

CBF presents this passage as a proof-text for universal atonement by saying:

> In light of the context and other uses of the word "world" in John's gospel, it is evident that the word "world" here does not mean "the church" or "the elect" but all fallen human beings.[32]

To which we reply that if the Lamb of God takes away the sin of every single individual then *that sin is gone* and can no longer be held against anyone. Obviously, given the teaching of the Bible regarding *how* Christ takes away sin (by bearing it in His body on the tree) we cannot help but point to the fact that John uses the term "world" in many different ways. It cannot be assumed that "world" means the same thing in every context. In John "world" is used of those for whom Christ does not pray (John 17:9), so obviously its meaning here cannot simply be assumed. We will address this usage of "world" as it is found in the more famous passage relevant to this issue, 1 John 2:2.

I John 2:2

The final passage[33] we will examine is the most often cited by proponents of a universal, non-specific atonement.

> My little children, I am writing these things to you so that you may not sin. And if anyone sins, we have an Advocate with the Father, Jesus Christ the righteous; and He Himself is the propitiation for our sins; and not for ours only, but also for *those of* the whole world. (1 John 2:1-2)

The understanding presented by the Arminian is as follows: Christ is the propitiation for the sins of all Christians, and not for Christians only, but also for every single person in all places and at all times. The Reformed understanding is that Jesus Christ is the propitiation for the sins of all the Christians to which John was writing, and not only them, but for all Christians throughout the world, Jew and Gentile, at all times and in all places.

If there was not so much emotional energy involved in the debate the means of determining which interpretation is the proper one would be agreed to by all: the meaning of "propitiation" would be examined. The meaning of "Advocate" would be deduced. And then John's writings would be studied to see how he uses the phrase "the whole world" and what other phrases/descriptions could be paralleled with it. For example, such a study would find the following passage, also from the pen of John, relevant:

> And they sang a new song, saying, "Worthy are You to take the book and to break its seals; for You were slain, and purchased for God with Your blood *men* from every tribe and tongue and people and nation. You have made

them *to be* a kingdom and priests to our God; and they will reign upon the earth." (Revelation 5:9-10)

Such a passage is relevant for it 1) speaks of Christ's death and His blood; 2) speaks of Christ's "purchasing" men for God; 3) presents a specific description of the *extent* of this work of redemption, that being "men from every tribe and tongue and people and nation." We suggest that this passage, then, sheds significant light upon 1 John 2:2, for it is obvious that the passage in Revelation is not saying that Christ purchased *every* man from every tribe, tongue, people and nation. Yet, obviously, this is a parallel concept to "the world" in 1 John 2:2. Similarly we can find yet another passage in John's writings that provides parallel information:

> But one of them, Caiaphas, who was high priest that year, said to them, "You know nothing at all, nor do you take into account that it is expedient for you that one man die for the people, and that the whole nation not perish." Now he did not say this on his own initiative, but being high priest that year, he prophesied that Jesus was going to die for the nation, and not for the nation only, but in order that He might also gather together into one the children of God who are scattered abroad. (John 11:49-52)

Again we note the exegetical relevance: 1) the death of Christ is in the context; 2) the object of the death of Christ is discussed and identified; 3) a generic term "people" is more closely identified as "the children of God who are scattered abroad." Clearly the point of the passage is that Christ dies with a *specific purpose in mind*, so that He might gather together into one the children of God who are scattered abroad. Nothing is said about making them "savable." His death enables Him to gather them together in one (fulfilling John 6:38-39). And we likewise see the direct relevance to 1 John 2:2 and the meaning of "the whole world."

How does *CBF* rebut the Reformed position? Let's examine the attempt:

> The groundless claim of extreme Calvinists is that "world" here refers to "Christian world" namely, to the elect. The later St. Augustine said John here "means 'of the world,' all the faithful scattered throughout the whole earth." This is such an obvious case of *eisegesis* (reading into the text) that it does not deserve an extensive treatment.[34]

The fact that Dr. Geisler either is unaware of the comments we just provided (which are found in any number of Reformed works on the subject) or chooses to ignore them does not make the claim, drawn from honest and contextual exegesis of the text, "groundless." And given the large number of examples of eisegesis we have identified thus far in *CBF*, we believe this accusation is more than premature and unfair. He continues:

> One needs only to make a study of the generic use of the word "world" (*cosmos*) in John's writings to confirm that he speaks here of the fallen, sinful world (cf. John 1:10-11; 3:19).

We are not told why these passages are exegetically relevant outside of the appearance of the word "world." *Why* should we accept the claim that, for example, John 3:19 is somehow relevant to the meaning of the word "world" at 1 John 2:2? Indeed, that passage says light has come "into the world." Does that mean "every single individual living on planet earth" or "this worldly system"? We are given no substantial arguments upon which to decide.

> In fact, John defines his use of the term "world" only a few verses later. In the same chapter, he claims Christ's death is a satisfaction for the "whole world." He says, "Do not love the world or anything in the world. If anyone loves the world, the love of the Father is not in him. For *everything in the world—the cravings of sinful man,*

the *lusts of his eyes* and the *boasting of what he has and does*—comes *not from the Father* but from the world" (2:15-16). This is clearly a description of the fallen, sinful world that includes the non-elect—for whom Christ died (v. 2).[35]

We must respectfully point out that this is a tremendous example of misinterpretation of a passage. Nowhere in 1 John chapter 2 do we have John teaching that "Christ's death is a satisfaction for the whole world." The passage cited tells us *not to love the world!* Does Dr. Geisler not see the result of his assertion? If this use of "world" is to be taken in the extensive, universal sense of every single individual, this passage now tells us not to love all men! Is this what he seriously wishes to suggest? We would hope not. When the passage says that these evil impulses come not from the Father but from the world, the antithesis points to the world as the *present evil system* not the universal population of mankind. We here have a classic example of what Dr. Geisler accuses the Reformed of: eisegesis, reading into the passage a meaning that it could never have borne when first written.

The Great Spurgeon Question

Charles Spurgeon believed in particular redemption. He also openly preached on the particular redemptive work of Christ. In a well-known sermon he made these comments:

> I have hurried over that, to come to the last point, which is the sweetest of all. Jesus Christ, we are told in our text, came into the world "to give his life a ransom for *many*." The greatness of Christ's redemption may be measured by the EXTENT OF THE DESIGN OF IT. He gave his life "a ransom for many." I must now return to that controverted point again. We are often told (I mean those of us who are commonly nicknamed by the title of Calvinists — and we are not very much ashamed of that; we think that Calvin, after all, knew more about the gospel

than almost any man who has ever lived, uninspired) —
We are often told that we limit the atonement of Christ,
because we say that Christ has not made a satisfaction
for all men, or all men would be saved. Now, our reply to
this is, that, on the other hand, our opponents limit it:
we do not. The Arminians say, Christ died for all men.
Ask them what they mean by it. Did Christ die so as to
secure the salvation of all men? They say, "No, certainly
not." We ask them the next question — Did Christ die
so as to secure the salvation of any man in particular?
They answer " No." They are obliged to admit this if they
are consistent. They say "No, Christ has died that any
man may be saved if" — and then follow certain conditions of salvation. We say, then, we will just go back to
the old statement — Christ did not die so as beyond a
doubt to secure the salvation of anybody, did he? You
must say "No;" you are obliged to say so, for you believe
that even after a man has been pardoned, he may yet fall
from grace, and perish. Now, who is it that limits the
death of Christ? Why, you. You say that Christ did not
die so as to infallibly secure the salvation of anybody, We
beg your pardon, when you say we limit Christ's death;
we say, "No, my dear sir, it is you that do it. We say
Christ so died that he infallibly secured the salvation of
a multitude that no man can number, who through
Christ's death not only may be saved, but are saved, must
be saved, and cannot by any possibility run the hazard of
being anything but saved. You are welcome to your atonement; you may keep it. We will never renounce ours for
the sake of it.[36]

Spurgeon's presentation has had such force over the years that
CBF felt compelled to attempt a response:

However, this inverted logic is a good example of
Spurgeon's eloquence gone to seed. It is an upside down
logic indeed that can get anyone to think twice about
the assertion that limited atonement is more unlimited

than unlimited atonement! For one thing, the first assertion diverts the issue, for it is not a question of *securing* salvation of all (this is universalism) but of *providing* salvation for all (as in moderate Calvinism and Arminianism), as opposed to extreme Calvinism, which holds that Christ died to *provide* and to *secure* the salvation of only the elect. So first, Spurgeon in the case of (1) gives the right answer to the wrong question! Further, in the case of (2) he gives the wrong answer to the right question, for both the moderate Calvinist and traditional Arminian opponents of extreme Calvinism surely do believe that Christ died to secure the salvation of the elect and that God foreknew from all eternity exactly who they would be.[37]

We suggest that it is *CBF*, not Spurgeon, who has "gone to seed," but not with eloquence. Instead, this is what happens when free-willism "goes to seed" on the subject of the atonement. Let's see if *CBF* actually touches on Spurgeon's argument.

First, Geisler confuses categories when he attempts to avoid the truth in Spurgeon's statement that the Arminian limits the atonement. Indeed, the response ignores the obvious fact that the Arminian limits the *effect* of the atonement by saying it is made in behalf of millions who will be lost for eternity. We have already discussed this unbiblical limitation and how it is utterly contrary to the meaning of "propitiation" and "atonement." "Unlimited atonement" is unlimited only in relation to scope, *but not in relation to accomplishment.* On the other hand, "limited atonement" is limited in scope, but is *unlimited* in its results. This is obviously Spurgeon's point, but it is either missed, or misrepresented, by *CBF*.

Next, these words again confirm one of the main assertions of our work: that there is no meaningful difference between Geisler's "moderate Calvinism" and Arminianism. When we find them saying the same things all the time, why bother differentiating them?

The difference between the biblical atonement *that actually saves* and the theoretical atonement of Arminianism (and, we are forced to point out, Roman Catholicism) is seen clearly in the response offered to Spurgeon's assertion that Christ died to *secure* the salvation of His people. Geisler sees the truth that Arminians have seen all along: that if Christ's death *actually saves in and of itself,* then we must either embrace universalism, or, particular redemption (Calvinism). Hence, their choice is to deny that Christ's death saves outside of the addition of the "free will choice" of man, rendering the atonement theoretical instead.

We have already examined the error of exchanging the divine truth that Christ died *to infallibly secure the salvation of the elect* with the idea that He died *to make salvation a theoretical possibility based upon the free actions of men.* This comes out yet once again as the *real* objection to particular redemption surfaces: the identity of the elect must be based upon God's foreknowledge of their free actions. It *cannot* be based upon God's decree, for it is were, then salvation is totally of God, and not of man.

Thanks be to God He saves perfectly in Christ!

Notes

1 *Chosen But Free*, p. 197.
2 Ibid., p. 203.
3 We assume that Dr. Geisler is referring to *supralapsarianism* not "superlapsarianism." For a discussion of this issue, see Robert Reymond, *A New Systematic Theology of the Christian Faith*, (Thomas Nelson: 1998), pp. 479-502.
4 *Chosen But Free*, p. 50.
5 Ibid., p. 160
6 Roger Nicole, "John Calvin's View of the Extent of the Atonement," *WTJ* V47 #2, p. 220.
7 Ibid.
8 Ibid.
9 John Calvin, *Commentary on the Gospel of John*, in *The Comprehensive John Calvin Collection* (Ages Digital Library, 1998).
10 Nicole, "John Calvin's View," pp. 221-222.
11 *CBF* cites this very passage on page 160 and provides a footnote in response that reads, "Calvin seems to have verbally overstated his point here in the heat of the battle against Heshusius's heretical claim that even the wicked can receive benefit from Communion 'by the mouth bodily without faith.' In context his point is clear, namely, only those who believe actually enter into the benefits of Christ's death." Dr. Geisler is reading his own universalism into a particularlist such as Calvin while ignoring all the evidence that runs counter to this conclusion.
12 Nicole, pp. 223-224.
13 *Chosen But Free*, p. 201.
14 John Calvin, *Commentary on 1 Timothy*, in *The Comprehensive John Calvin Collection* (Ages Digital Library, 1998).
15 *Chosen But Free*, p. 159, italics inserted by Dr. Geisler.
16 Ibid., p. 160.
17 Ibid., pp. 194-195.
18 Ibid., p. 78.
19 Ibid.
20 John Calvin, *Commentary on the Gospel of Luke* in *The Comprehensive John Calvin Collection* (Ages Digital Library, 1998).
21 Ibid.
22 *Chosen But Free*, pp. 78-79.
23 Ibid., p. 79.
24 Ibid., p. 80.

25 Ibid., p. 80.

26 We cannot help but point out that Rome's view is frighteningly similar: Christ's death merits grace that then allows us, through the sacraments, to work out our own salvation.

27 *Chosen But Free*, p. 81.

28 "The Spirit's Office Toward Disciples," a sermon preached April 23, 1865, *The Charles H. Spurgeon Collection* (Ages Digital Library, 1998).

29 *Chosen But Free*, p. 85.

30 Ibid., p. 85.

31 Ibid., p. 205.

32 Ibid., p. 192.

33 2 Peter 2:1ff, discussed on pp. 195-197, is fully discussed in both John Owen's *The Death of Death in the Death of Christ* and more importantly in Gary Long's *Definite Atonement* (Backus Books, 1977). Dr. Geisler's *entire discussion* of the meaning of ἀγοράζω and δεσπότης is answered in full by Long's book, written twenty-two years prior. This is noteworthy, for Geisler's discussion ends with, "In view of this New Testament usage, the burden of proof rests on the extreme Calvinists to prove that Peter is using this term in any other than a redemptive sense here." Long provided the evidence in full. For a summary see my own comments at www.aomin.org/2PE21.html.

34 *Chosen But Free*, p. 194-195.

35 Ibid., p.195.

36 "Particular Redemption," a sermon preached February 28, 1858 *The C.H. Spurgeon Collection*, (Ages Digital Library, 1998).

37 *Chosen But Free*, p. 204.

Chapter 12

Irresistible Grace is Resurrection Power

> Before we believed in Jesus, we were not capable of those
> sacred actions which are now our daily delight. We could
> not pray. We may have "said our prayers," as so many do,
> but, the living breath of true God-inspired prayer was
> not in us. How could it be in us while we were still dead
> in trespasses and sins? We could not believe. How could
> we do so, when we had not received the gift of faith from
> the ever-blessed Spirit? The fact is, we were under a ter-
> rible bondage; and just as a corpse is under bandage to
> death, and cannot stir hand or foot, lip or eye, so were we
> under bondage to sin and Satan. But we are under that
> deadly bondage no longer; for we are living men, and
> free men in Christ Jesus our Lord, who has overcome
> that death for us.[1]

The doctrine of irresistible grace is easily understood. Once
we understand the condition of man in sin, that he is dead,
enslaved to a corrupt nature, incapable of doing what is pleasing to God, we can fully understand the simple assertion that
God must raise the dead sinner to life. This is all, really, the
phrase means: it has nothing to do with sinners rebelling against
God and "resisting" Him in that way. It has nothing to do with
the fact that Christians often resist God's grace in their lives
when they sin against Him. No, irresistible grace means one

thing: God raises dead sinners to life.

When we discussed man's deadness in sin we emphasized the fact that even though spiritually dead and alienated from God, the unregenerate sinner is still very *active* in his or her rebellion against God. In our actions and in our thoughts we reject God's sovereign right to rule over us and our natural duty to serve and honor Him. So being dead in sin does not mean we are *passive* in our rebellion.

Instead, the key issue has to do with *abilities and inabilities*. Man is *incapable* of doing what is pleasing in God's sight. It is this *inability* that renders the myth of "free will" an empty phrase: who cares if the will is "free" when the nature that provides it with the desires upon which it acts is corrupt and evil?

Irresistible grace, then, is simply the assertion that God's grace, expressed in the sovereignly free act of regeneration, is irresistible. When God chooses to raise one of His elect to life He can do so without asking permission of the dead creature. This is seen clearly in the raising of Lazarus from the dead:

> Jesus said to her, "Did I not say to you that if you believe, you will see the glory of God?" So they removed the stone. Then Jesus raised His eyes, and said, "Father, I thank You that You have heard Me. I knew that You always hear Me; but because of the people standing around I said it, so that they may believe that You sent Me." When He had said these things, He cried out with a loud voice, "Lazarus, come forth." The man who had died came forth, bound hand and foot with wrappings, and his face was wrapped around with a cloth. Jesus said to them, "Unbind him, and let him go." Therefore many of the Jews who came to Mary, and saw what He had done, believed in Him. (John 11:40-45)

On the level of spiritual capacity the unregenerate man is just like Lazarus: dead, bound, incapable of "self-resurrection." It would be patently absurd to demand that Jesus first ask Lazarus for "permission" to raise him to spiritual life. Corpses are not known for engaging in a great deal of conversation. No, before Lazarus can respond to Christ's command to come forth, something must happen. Corpses do not obey commands, corpses do not move. Jesus changed Lazarus' condition first: Lazarus' heart was made new; his mind revitalized. Blood began once again to course through his veins. What was once dead is now alive, and can now hear the voice of his beloved Lord, "Come forth!"

The term "irresistible" then must be understood as speaking to the *inability of dead sinners to resist resurrection to new life.* Since they are dead it is an empty (though often repeated) cavil to accuse this doctrine of being tantamount to "forcing" someone to be saved or engaging in "divine rape." One can just imagine a reporter from Jerusalem shoving a microphone in the face of the newly resurrected Lazarus and saying, "Lazarus, do you feel your rights were violated by Jesus in forcing you back to life? Did He ask you if you wanted this to happen first? Do you plan any legal action?" The bewildered Lazarus would look at the reporter and say, "Are you kidding me? I was dead! Jesus rescued me and called me to life! Those were the most precious words I ever heard, when He called my name and said, 'Come forth!' I owe everything to Him!"

This is the testimony of every believer. Out of the darkness of death Christ called us. His call did not come without power, no indeed! When Christ calls Lazarus the result is resurrection power! So it is today. When Christ the Great Shepherd calls His own, they hear His voice because He is the very source of life and He raises them up to spiritual life. It is absurd to call this gracious deliverance of the slave from the dungeon an unkind act of "force."

The Scriptural testimony to this truth comes from the many passages we examined regarding total depravity and inability, together with those that teach the absolute sovereignty of God. Even if we could not present further direct biblical teaching, these two truths alone would be enough to establish the necessity of irresistible grace. But, of course, there is a positive testimony to this truth in the Bible.

The Testimony of Scripture

Just as John's writings bear eloquent testimony to the deadness of man in sin (John 6:44, 6:65, 8:47), so too do they testify to the necessity of the regenerating work of God. Jesus said to Nicodemus:

> Truly, truly, I say to you, unless one is born again he cannot see the kingdom of God. (John 3:3)

Every Christian knows the truth of these words, but how often do we consider the order of the actions of "born again" and "see the kingdom of God"? That is, by tradition it is taught that a person sees the kingdom of God, desires to enter into it, and then believes, resulting in regeneration. Yet, Jesus taught that the unregenerate person cannot even *see* the kingdom of God. Does this mean simply that the unregenerate person cannot enter into the kingdom in some future day unless born again? While true, is that *all* it means? We suggest the passage goes beyond this. As we will see in the rest of John's testimony, spiritual birth *precedes all actions of the spiritual life*, including, here, seeing the kingdom of God. Jesus parallels "seeing" the kingdom with "entering" the kingdom in the same passage:

> Jesus answered, "Truly, truly, I say to you, unless one is born of water and the Spirit he cannot enter into the kingdom of God. That which is born of the flesh is flesh, and that which is born of the Spirit is spirit. Do not be amazed that I said to you, 'You must be born again.'" (John 3:5-7)

The contrast between flesh and spirit, unregenerate and regenerate, spiritually dead and spiritually alive, is complete, making the new birth an absolute *necessity*. You *must* be born again.

The relationship of faith and regeneration is central to the topic of irresistible grace. Arminians contend strongly that faith results in regeneration: Calvinists contend just as strongly that one must be born again to be able to do something that is clearly a function of the spiritual man and that is pleasing to God: have saving faith. The Arminian says the natural man is capable of true, saving faith, the Calvinist denies this. Does the Bible speak to the issue of what comes first, regeneration or faith?

The Scriptures tell us that we are saved by grace through faith. Of this there is no doubt. But the question properly focuses upon the *nature* of this faith and the relationship it bears to regeneration. The previous considerations regarding man's deadness in sin point to the obvious conclusion that man must first be made *capable* of such a spiritual activity as saving faith, and the fact that the glory for salvation goes solely to a sovereign, life-giving God bears upon this issue as well. But there are Scriptural passages that bear directly upon the topic:

> Whoever believes that Jesus is the Christ is born of God,
> and whoever loves the Father loves the *child* born of Him.
> (1 John 5:1)

Generally such a passage would be understood to present the following order of events: 1) Believe that Jesus is the Christ, and 2) you are born of God. Yet, the original readers of this text would not jump to such a conclusion. In reality, the most literal rendering would be, "Every one believing (present tense participle, ὁ πιστεύων, emphasizing both the on-going action as well as the individuality of saving faith, "each believing person") that Jesus is the Christ has been born of God (a perfect passive verb, γεγέννηται, "has been born by the agency of God"). In John, "the one believing" is very common, and it is no accident that the emphasis falls upon the *on-going action* of faith. The one believing that Jesus is the Christ *has been born of God*. If a person is now believing that Jesus is the Christ in a true and saving fashion, they are doing so because, as a completed action in the past, they were born again through the work and agency of God. The verb "to be born" is passive: they were caused to be born by another, that being God. They did not cause their own spiritual birth. And what is the *inevitable* result of being born of God? Belief that Jesus is the Christ. Just as all those who are given by the Father to the Son come to the Son (John 6:37), so too all who are spiritually reborn through the work of God have as the object of their faith the Lord Jesus Christ.

Some Arminian exegetes might object to this interpretation. A means of testing the consistency of the exegesis offered of this passage would be to ask how such a person interprets these words from John:

> If you know that He is righteous, you know that everyone also who practices righteousness is born of Him. (1 John 2:29)

Every consistent Protestant would say, "the reason one practices righteousness is because they have already been born of Him. We do not practice righteousness so as to be born, but instead the birth gives rise to the practice of righteousness." And such is quite true. But, this means that in 1 John 5:1 the belief in Jesus as the Christ is the *result* of being born of Him. The verbal parallel is exact: in 1 John 2:29 "the one practicing righteousness" is a present participle; in 1 John 5:1 "the one believing" is a present participle. In both passages the exact same verb in the exact same form is used (γεγέννηται). Therefore, sheer consistency leads one to the conclusion that divine birth *precedes* and is the *grounds* of *both* faith in Christ as well as good works.

The testimony to the fact that God's work of grace precedes any human action can be found all through the text of Scripture. Luke knew it well:

> A woman named Lydia, from the city of Thyatira, a seller of purple fabrics, a worshiper of God, was listening; and the Lord opened her heart to respond to the things

spoken by Paul. (Acts 16:14)

It is no response to say that the opening of Lydia's heart was a mere "moving" of God upon her that in essence brought her to a moral neutral point, leaving the final decision to her. The obvious question is, *why would God have to open her heart and to what end?* The text tells us why He engaged in this supernatural action: so that Lydia would "respond" to the things spoken by Paul. God had a specific purpose in what He was doing, that being the acceptance of the preached Word. But if saving faith in response to the preaching of the Gospel is the ability of every man and woman, why did God have to open Lydia's heart? Obviously, such a question begins with a flawed assumption, as we have seen. God had to take out that heart of stone and put in Lydia a heart of flesh (Ezekiel 36:26) so that she would respond to the message of the Cross. All of the Corinthians were reminded of this truth by Paul:

> For consider your calling, brethren, that there were not many wise according to the flesh, not many mighty, not many noble; but God has chosen the foolish things of the world to shame the wise, and God has chosen the weak things of the world to shame the things which are strong, and the base things of the world and the despised God has chosen, the things that are not, so that He may nullify the things that are, so that no man may boast before God. But by His doing you are in Christ Jesus, who became to us wisdom from God, and righteousness and sanctification, and redemption, so that, just as it is written, "LET HIM WHO BOASTS, BOAST IN THE LORD." (1 Corinthians 1:26-31)

God has cut out *every* ground of boasting by choosing to save in a way that confounds the wisdom of men. No man can boast before God. Notice a small phrase that is often overlooked: "But by His doing you are in Christ Jesus...." The text reads, ἐξ αὐτοῦ, "by means of Him, from Him." Is it by my act of free will, or God's act of free will, that I am in Christ Jesus?

Every believer must ask this question. It is not enough to limit God's free will to making a *plan* available. The question is not "Is God ultimately the source of the plan of salvation?" Even the Judaizers in Galatia, who were placed under the curse of God as false teachers in Galatians 1:6-9, could say *that*. The question is, *Who, ultimately, is responsible for my union with Jesus Christ?* God is *both* the one who is the origin and source of salvation in general, *and the one who powerfully, purposefully, and perfectly draws His elect people into blessed union with Jesus Christ.* The Arminian simply cannot allow this freedom to God. The Scripture knows no other doctrine. Paul knew this truth doctrinally and experientially:

> But when God, who had set me apart *even* from my mother's womb and called me through His grace, was pleased to reveal His Son in me so that I might preach Him among the Gentiles, I did not immediately consult with flesh and blood, (Galatians 1:15-16)

If anyone knew that the idea of "free will" was a myth, it was Paul. It was not free will that knocked Paul to the ground on the road to Damascus. It was not free will that blinded him. Paul was not "seeking after God" nor the Savior, Jesus Christ on that day when God chose to reveal His Son to him. No, God determined the day and the hour, and Paul was only happy to oblige. He preached a powerful grace, a grace that saves rebel sinners hard of heart, a grace that stops the elect in their tracks and changes them. He knew nothing of a grace that tries and tries, and fails and fails. It is powerful grace, purposeful grace, sovereign grace that lies at the base of his words to Titus:

> He saved us, not on the basis of deeds which we have done in righteousness, but according to His mercy, by the washing of regeneration and renewing by the Holy Spirit, whom He poured out upon us richly through Jesus Christ our Savior, (Titus 3:5-6)

Saving grace that brings the gift of faith. A mighty God

who saves His elect. This is the biblical presentation.

The Gift of Faith

Sovereign grace is offensive to the Arminian for it crushes human pride and exalts the Potter's freedom. The necessary corollary to irresistible grace is the biblical truth that faith is a gift from God. Since this is a subject particularly reprehensible to CBF, we will here only present some of the more obvious passages that teach this truth and leave a fuller defense of the Reformed position for the next chapter where we respond to Dr. Geisler's assertions.

Paul began many of his epistles with thanksgiving to God for the love *and the faith* of the Christians to whom he was writing. For example:

> We give thanks to God, the Father of our Lord Jesus Christ, praying always for you, since we heard of your faith in Christ Jesus and the love which you have for all the saints; (Colossians 1:3-4)

> We ought always to give thanks to God for you, brethren, as is *only* fitting, because your faith is greatly enlarged, and the love of each one of you toward one another grows *ever* greater; (2 Thessalonians 1:3)

Why should we thank God for the faithfulness of Christians? Why should God be thanked when we hear of the faith of others, or see their faith increasing? If faith is something within the capacity of every unregenerate hater of God, why should we thank God when one person exercises it? Unless, of course, faith finds its origin in God Himself and is, as we believe, a gift? That is what Paul taught:

> Peace be to the brethren, and love with faith, from God the Father and the Lord Jesus Christ. Grace be with all those who love our Lord Jesus Christ with incorruptible *love.* (Ephesians 6:23-24)

Christian peace, Christian love, and Christian faith, all come "from God the Father and the Lord Jesus Christ." Note how love and peace and faith appear in this famous passage, also showing that they come not from us, but from God:

> But the fruit of the Spirit is love, joy, peace, patience, kindness, goodness, faithfulness, (Galatians 5:22)

While the translation speaks of "faithfulness," the Greek word is simply "faith." Paul taught this even more explicitly to the Philippians:

> For to you it has been granted for Christ's sake, not only to believe in Him, but also to suffer for His sake, (Philippians 1:29)

Here Paul speaks of two things that have been "granted" to Christians. The term "granted" is the Greek term ἐχαρίσθη from the term *charizomai*, "to give as a gift." And what has been "granted" to believers? The eye seems drawn to the final phrase, "to suffer for His sake." This is what seems to take up the mind when reading the passage. It has been *granted as a gift* to suffer for Christ! What a strange thought for many today who have not experienced persecution and suffering, but it surely was not to those to whom Paul was writing. But just as suffering is not something brought about by our "free will," neither is the first thing granted to us: to believe in Christ. This is the normal term used for saving faith (πιστεύειν). God has *granted* to us to believe in Christ. Why would this be if, as we are told, anyone can πιστεύειν, can "believe"?

The writer to the Hebrews knew something about the origin of faith that is vital to understand as well:

> Therefore, since we have so great a cloud of witnesses surrounding us, let us also lay aside every encumbrance and the sin which so easily entangles us, and let us run

with endurance the race that is set before us, fixing our
eyes on Jesus, the author and perfecter of faith, who for
the joy set before Him endured the cross, despising the
shame, and has sat down at the right hand of the throne
of God. (Hebrews 12:1-2)

Jesus is described as the "author and perfecter" of faith. The
Greek words chosen by the author are most interesting: ἀρχηγὸν
καὶ τελειωτὴν. *Archegon* refers to the origin, source, beginning,
and then by extension, author. *Teleiotes* refers to one who completes and perfects. Consider what this means: Jesus is the
origin and source of faith, the goal of faith, the one who completes and perfects faith. It surely does not seem that much
room is left for the pot to boast about contributing his free will
act of faith, does it? For the Christian these are precious words.
When we are weak, when we are discouraged, when it seems
that we cannot possibly go on, what is our sole confidence?
Christ. God will not abandon His own. We are kept indeed by
the power of faith, but it is not a merely human faith, but a
divine faith, a gift from God! Why do some stumble and fall
while others persevere? Is it that some are better, stronger, than
others? No. The reason lies in the difference between having
saving faith and a faith that is not divine in origin or nature.
Many are those who make professions not based upon regeneration, and the "faith" that is theirs will not last. Jesus taught
this truth in the parable of the soils in Matthew 13:3-9, 18-23.
Some of the seed that was sown resulted in immediate growth.
But the growth produced no fruit and did not last. These are
those who have false, human faith that does not last. But those
with true faith produce fruit and remain.

Once this truth is understood, we can see it being mentioned often in Scripture. Listen closely to how Peter refers to
faith:

And on the basis of faith in His name, *it is* the name
of Jesus which has strengthened this man whom you

see and know; and the faith which *comes* through Him
has given him this perfect health in the presence of you
all. (Acts 3:16)

Faith comes through whom? Christ. That's why Peter could
write years later:

who through Him are believers in God, who raised Him
from the dead and gave Him glory, so that your faith and
hope are in God. (1 Peter 1:21)

We are believers *through Him*, not through ourselves. Faith is
a gift, the universal possession of all believers. Just a few other
passages that testify to this truth:

And the grace of our Lord was more than abundant, with
the faith and love which are *found* in Christ Jesus. (1
Timothy 1:14)

Simon Peter, a bond-servant and apostle of Jesus Christ,
to those who have received a faith of the same kind as
ours, by the righteousness of our God and Savior, Jesus
Christ: (2 Peter 1:1)

Indeed, repentance is likewise styled a gift in Scripture, and
given the intimate relationship between saving faith and repentance, this further proves the Reformed position:

The Lord's bond-servant must not be quarrelsome, but
be kind to all, able to teach, patient when wronged, with
gentleness correcting those who are in opposition, if perhaps God may grant them repentance leading to the
knowledge of the truth, and they may come to their senses
and escape from the snare of the devil, having been held
captive by him to do his will. (2 Timothy 2:24-26)

Or do you think lightly of the riches of His kindness and
tolerance and patience, not knowing that the kindness
of God leads you to repentance? (Romans 2:4)

Ephesians 2:8-9

Despite the richness of the testimony of Scripture seen above, many focus almost solely upon the citation of Ephesians 2:8-9 when it comes to the debate between Arminians and Calvinists. And while the teaching of this verse is important, it is surely not the main basis upon which the truth of the divine nature of saving faith is to be based. The blessed words are well known:

> For by grace you have been saved through faith; and that not of yourselves, *it is* the gift of God; not as a result of works, so that no one may boast. For we are His workmanship, created in Christ Jesus for good works, which God prepared beforehand so that we would walk in them. (Ephesians 2:8-10)

This passage cuts the ground out from underneath every and all systems of works-salvation, any teaching that tells us that our performances, our works, our efforts, are necessary to bring salvation. And it is an empty cavil to say that Paul speaks here only of the bare *provision* of the possibility of salvation. He says his readers *have been saved* by grace through faith, not "made savable." They have already entered into the state of salvation and continue therein. The means of their salvation is said to be grace, free grace. They have been saved *through faith*.

To this point all is agreed, at least on basic issues. The debate begins with the next phrase, "and that not of yourselves, it is the gift of God." The basic issue is, "to what does the word 'that' refer?" The Greek term is τοῦτο, the neuter singular demonstrative pronoun. The basic rule of thumb is to look for a singular neuter noun in the immediate context as the antecedent of the pronoun. Yet, there are no neuter singular nouns in the first phrase of Ephesians 2:8. "Grace" is feminine singular; "have been saved" is a masculine participle; "faith" is feminine singular. So to what does τοῦτο refer?

The simple answer is: the entirety of the phrase "for by grace you have been saved by faith." It is good Greek grammar to use a neuter pronoun to "wrap up" a phrase or a series of thoughts into a single whole. Paul's point is that the entirety of the work of salvation does not find its basis in men but in God: true salvation is the gift of God, not the work of man. All of it is free, all of it is divine, not human.

So what of the claim that Ephesians 2:8 teaches that faith is a gift of God? It is common for Arminians to triumphantly point out that since "faith" is feminine and "that" is neuter, it *cannot* be that faith is a gift. But this is only partially true. The Arminian would have to admit that the grace mentioned in 2:8 is a gift: yet, it is feminine singular as well, which, if we follow their reasoning, would mean that grace is not a gift anymore than faith is. Such argumentation is too shallow to allow a meaningful conclusion to be drawn.

There is no reason, contextual or grammatical, to accept the fact that two of the three substantival[2] elements (grace and salvation) are a "gift," while the third, faith, is a strictly human contribution. Paul's entire theology, including the fact that he specifically refers to faith as something that is "granted" to us (Philippians 1:29), would indicate that all three elements together constitute a singular gift of God, for surely grace is His to freely give; salvation is His to freely give, and likewise, saving faith is the gift of God given to His elect.

A Sobering Thought

Half a century ago, J.I. Packer and O.R. Johnston wrote a tremendous introduction to Martin Luther's *Bondage of the Will*. These words are even more vital today than they were when they were penned:

> These things need to be pondered by Protestants to-day. With what right may we call ourselves children of the Reformation? Much modern Protestantism would be neither owned nor even recognized by the pioneer Re-

formers. *The Bondage of the Will* fairly sets before us what they believed about the salvation of lost mankind. In the light of it, we are forced to ask whether Protestant Christendom has not tragically sold its birthright between Luther's day and our own. Has not Protestantism today become more Erasmian than Lutheran?...Have we not grown used to an Erasmian brand of teaching from our pulpits—a message that rests on the same shallow synergistic conceptions which Luther refuted, picturing God and man approaching each other almost on equal terms, each having his own contribution to make to man's salvation and each depending on the dutiful co-operation of the other for the attainment of that end?—as if God exists for man's convenience, rather than man for God's glory? Is it not true, conversely, that it is rare to-day to hear proclaimed the diagnosis of our predicament which Luther—and Scripture—put forward: that man is hopeless and helpless in sin, fast bound in Satan's slavery, at enmity with God, blind and dead to the things of the Spirit? And hence, how rarely do we hear faith spoken of as Scripture depicts it—as it is expressed in the cry of self-committal with which the contrite heart, humbled to see its need and made conscious of its own utter helplessness even to trust, casts itself in the God-given confidence of self-despair upon the mercy of Christ Jesus— 'Lord, I believe; help Thou my unbelief!' Can we deny the essential rightness of Luther's exegesis of the texts? And if not, dare we ignore the implication of his exposition?[3]

And so we must now provide a biblically-based response to the strong, at times strident denial of the sovereign work of God in the regeneration of His elect found in *CBF*. This doctrine is especially pernicious in the view of Dr. Geisler, as is the idea that saving faith is a gift of God. But what do the Scriptures say? Let's see.

Notes

1   C.H. Spurgeon, "Salvation as it is Now Received" Preached June 23, 1872, *The C.H. Spurgeon Collection* (Ages Digital Library, 1998), 700.

2   Taking the participle σεσωσμένοι in the sense of a substantive referring to salvation as a whole.

3   Martin Luther, *The Bondage of the Will*, translated by J.I. Packer & O.R. Johnston, (Fleming H. Revel, 1957), pp. 59-60.

Chapter 13

Irresistible Grace

It is our honest opinion that *CBF* shows the greatest dislike and uses the strongest language in denying the Reformed doctrine of irresistible grace than in any other area of its presentation. The idea that God would sovereignly change a sinner from a God-hater to a God-lover by the exercise of divine power seems especially reprehensible to Dr. Geisler. Given his stated view that he believes this to be an act of "dehumanization," we can certainly understand his feelings. But feelings do not determine truth, and all Christians must submit their feelings to the higher authority of Scripture. Dr. Geisler consistently identifies the Reformed view as involving coercion, force, or to use a term that appeared in one of his earlier writings (but mercifully not in *CBF*), "divine rape."[1]

Throughout *CBF* Dr. Geisler makes reference to the "earlier" Augustine and the "later" Augustine and how on these issues the "earlier" Augustine was more moderate while the later Augustine wrote in support of a fully Calvinistic view of predestination and regeneration. It is a measure of how *CBF* views the Calvinistic position that the constant explanation offered for Augustine's change in view is not his growth and maturity, nor the fact that he was forced to work through these issues by his monumental battle with Pelagius. No, Augustine did not mature with time and look more deeply at these things (though that is what Augustine claimed in his *Retractiones*).

Instead, Augustine's actions with reference to the Donatist controversy, wherein he acquiesced to the use of physical force so as to suppress "heresy," are made the *sole* basis of the change in his thinking. Geisler writes:

> Since Augustine came to believe that heretics could be coerced to believe *against* their free choice, he saw no problem in God doing the same for the elect.[2]

Our concern here is not to debate Augustine[3] nor his views, but rather to document the strident claims made by *CBF* regarding this doctrine. The act of sovereignly freeing the elect from the shackles of sin, raising them to spiritual life, giving them a new nature, and suppressing the madness of rebellion in their heart (for which the elect express eternal gratitude) is likened to the forceful suppression of the Donatists in North Africa. But this is not the full extent of the expression of dislike of this doctrine in *CBF*:

> But since God only gives the desire to some (not all), this leads to another problem.
> Second, "irresistible grace" on the unwilling is a violation of free choice. For God is love (1 John 4:16), and true love is persuasive but never coercive. There can be no shotgun weddings in heaven. God is not a cosmic B.F. Skinner who behaviorally modifies men against their will.[4]

For God to be truly loving He must in essence become one of the pots. All of the objections voiced by Dr. Geisler are based upon the idea that God interacts with man on the same level as a man would interact with a prospective wife. The utter sovereignty of God in His dealings with men has no place in this system of thought. We would ask the proponent of this form of "moderate Calvinism" if the following passages make God 1) a Sovereign free to do with His creation as He will, or 2) a cosmic B.F. Skinner:

He turned their heart to hate His people,
To deal craftily with His servants.
(Psalm 105:25)

For it was of the LORD to harden their hearts, to meet
Israel in battle in order that he might utterly destroy
them, that they might receive no mercy, but that he might
destroy them, just as the LORD had commanded Moses.
(Joshua 11:20)

Why, O LORD, do You cause us to stray from Your ways
And harden our heart from fearing You? Return for the
sake of Your servants, the tribes of Your heritage.
(Isaiah 63:17)

I will make an everlasting covenant with them that I will
not turn away from them, to do them good; and I will
put the fear of Me in their hearts so that they will not
turn away from Me. (Jeremiah 32:40)

We need to realize that God is the Potter, we the pots. Much
of the presentation in *CBF* places God on the level of man in
regards to His relationship to us. The illustrations of a man
wooing a potential mate, a doctor performing an operation on
someone (see below), etc., all miss the fundamental Christian
assertion that God is God and man is a creature. The Potter
has the right to make the pots for whatever purposes He sees
fit. Human analogies that do not properly reflect the Creator/
creation distinction only blur, not clarify, biblical truth.

Arminians teach that God sends his grace to "persuade"
men to believe, but they deny that God can actually raise a
man to spiritual life without his assistance and agreement. They
deny that there is an elect people, based solely on the choice
of God, to whom God will infallibly apply the benefits of
Christ's atonement. Grace is limited to being effective on the
"willing," i.e., it is submitted to the power and will of man and
his decisions. It becomes a mere "wooing" force. The Reformed
Christian who has sought to share the gospel of grace with

Roman Catholics recognizes that this is the same view of grace found in the Roman communion, and it is deeply troubling to find it expressed within what is called Protestantism. Note the words of *CBF*:

> Further, moderate Calvinists do not deny that God's grace works on the unregenerate to move them to faith. It only denies that any such work is irresistible on the unwilling, or that God gives faith only to the elect, without which no one can be saved.[5]

Given that there is no such thing as a God-seeker, none who understands, and none who can do what is pleasing to God (i.e., all are unwilling until changed by grace), this view of grace as a force that "moves" only the willing to faith (but does not actually impart faith) is simply unbiblical, despite its great popularity today.

In objecting to the sovereign work of God in regenerating His people, *CBF* raises the serious objection that the Reformed position denies the omnibenevolence of God. The Calvinist's God is unloving, we are told by many an advocate of Arminianism. But is this so?

The Issue of Omnibenevolence

All through this section of *CBF* the same objection is raised: God could not "force" someone (i.e., resurrect someone without asking their permission) into the kingdom of God without violating His loving nature. Note these words:

> But if God's grace can be resisted, then it is not irresistible. Irresistible force used by God on His free creatures would be a violation of both the charity of God and the dignity of man. God is love. And true love never forces itself on anyone, either externally or internally. "Forced love" is a contradiction in terms.[6]

"Forced love" for the Arminian is resurrection life for the Calvinist. Lazarus was glad Jesus "forced" His love upon him, and we are eternally thankful that He raised us from spiritual death as well. But Dr. Geisler, using this imbalanced and unfair caricaturization of God "forcing" unwilling men into the kingdom, raises a more serious objection:

> In fact, if God is one indivisible being without any parts, as classical Calvinists believe, then His love extends to *all* of His essence, not just part of it. Hence, God cannot be partly loving. But if God is all-loving, then how can He love only some so as to give them and only them the desire to be saved? If He really loves all men, then why does He not give to all men the desire to be saved? It only follows that, in the final analysis, the reason why some go to hell is that God does not love them and give them the desire to be saved. But if the real reason they go to hell is that God does not love them, irresistibly regenerate them, and give them the faith to believe, then their failure to believe truly would result from God's lack of love for them.[7]

The final sentences should be reread. Here is *CBF*'s summary of the Reformed position. Men go to hell because God did not love them and save them. It is God's fault for not being loving enough, if, in fact, the Calvinists are right about predestination and election.

What can be said in response to this? The single most fundamental rebuttal of this erroneous argument is simply this: *Arminians should well consider why they demand that God have less freedom in His actions and His love than they grant to the creature man.* As we will see immediately below, the key problem with Geisler's attack is that it demands that God's love be indiscriminate. While man has the freedom to love those closest to him with a particular love that is not given to anyone else, God is not granted this freedom. If He is to be "all loving" then His love is to have no distinctions, no freedom, no particularity. Love all the same or love none at all is the argument.

Second, it is pure misrepresentation to say that Calvinists believe men are sent to hell simply because God did not love them. Men are sent to hell out of pure, holy, and unfettered justice that demands the punishment of their vile sins. God is under no compulsion or obligation to show mercy, grace, or redeeming love to *any* person, let alone the myriads to whom He has shown Himself gracious. And, hell exists, and men will be punished therein, to demonstrate both His perfect justice *as well as* the glory of His grace upon those that He freely chose to bring to Himself. There is a single five-letter word that will separate the vilest sinner screaming epithets at God from the parapet of hell and the most adoring saint in heaven showering Him with praises: G R A C E. Nothing else.

So convinced is Dr. Geisler that the Reformed viewpoint is susceptible to criticism at this point that he devotes an entire section to the following accusation:

The Extreme Calvinists' God is Not Really All-Loving[8]

For God to be all loving, He could not possibly have the freedom to save *some* but not *all.* It should be remembered that in Geisler's view, God *wants* to save every single person, *but is incapable of doing so.* He loves every single individual equally, but, despite this love and all that He has done to save every person, millions perish. One could easily argue that a God that would create a universe well knowing that in the final outcome millions of the objects of His love would end up in eternal punishment and all His best efforts would be frustrated would not be considered a very wise or, in fact, a very loving God. Why create, and set His love upon, creatures that He knows, infallibly, will destroy themselves in rebellion and will thwart His every effort to save them? This issue aside, we return to the argument:

> In fact, God is not really loving at all toward them with regard to their salvation. If He were, then they would be part of the elect, for according to extreme Calvinists,

whomever God really wants to be saved will be saved. R.C. Sproul's response to "the problem," though, is a bit shocking. He argues that to say God should have so loved the world, as He did the elect, is to assume that "God is obligated to be gracious to sinners . . . God may owe people justice, but never mercy."

But how can this be? Both justice and mercy (or love) are attributes of an unchangeable and infinite God. God by His very nature manifests to all His creatures what flows from all His attributes. So, whereas there is *nothing in the sinner* to merit God's love, nonetheless, *there is something in God* that prompts Him to love all sinners, namely, God is all-loving (omnibenevolent). *Hence, extreme Calvinism is in practice a denial of the omnibenevolence of God.*[9]

Here we touch upon the heart of the error inherent in this argument (we will see an expansion of this in the "parable" discussed below). The definition of omnibenevolence is both untenable and unbiblical. The definition offered demands that God's love be 1) equally distributed to all men without any reference to their actions or behavior; 2) be of the same *kind* to all men (i.e., God cannot choose to show redemptive love to one and not another). There cannot be any *choice* in God's love. If He loves one, He must love all, equally, in the same fashion.

But let us point out that such a definition is untenable. Let's replace the word "love" with the word "grace." Is God all gracious? By the same definition given above, God would have to show equal grace to every single individual in the world. Hence, either all would be saved, or, all would be lost, but in any case, all would receive the exact same "amount" or "kind" of grace. God could not say "I will have mercy on whom I have mercy" if this definition is true, since it demands that all receive equal love, equal grace, equal mercy, equal justice, etc. But such removes from God an attribute that Dr. Geisler zealously demands be given to man: *freedom of choice.* CBF denies to the Potter what it gives to the pots.

God created us with the ability to love. We love those who are closest to us with a special, discriminating love. A mother loves her children with a love utterly unlike that she might have for a cousin, or a co-worker. The love of husband and wife is likewise of a totally different kind than the love that exists between a sister and a brother, or that between very close friends. We exercise choice in our love relationships, knowing how costly true love is, and how precious it is. Even the Lord Jesus had special relationships amongst the disciples. The Scripture speaks of the "disciple Jesus loved" (John 20:2). This shows His freedom to have a closer relationship with one than with the others.

But what is common to humans seemingly is denied to God. While someone might argue that in humans the ability, or desire, to discriminate and choose in the matter of love is a result of sin, it surely cannot be said that the Lord Jesus, in loving the Apostle John with a special love, was somehow in error or suffering from the taint of sin. How then can CBF make the claim that unless God loves each and every individual with redeeming love that He cannot love any at all? This is tantamount to claiming God cannot have grace upon whom He chooses to have grace: that there is no freedom in God to have mercy on whom He has mercy, let alone to harden whom He would harden (Romans 9:18).

At this point Dr. Geisler reproduces a "parable" that he feels illustrates how the Reformed view of God's freedom and love is in fact not "omnibenevolent." Here's the illustration as it appears in CBF:

> Suppose a farmer discovers three boys drowning in his pond where he had placed signs clearly forbidding swimming. Further, nothing their blatant disobedience he says to himself, "They have violated the warning and have broken the law, and they have brought these deserved consequences on themselves." Thus far he is manifesting his sense of justice. But if the farmer proceeds to say, "I will make no attempt to rescue them," we would im-

mediately perceive that something is lacking in his love And suppose by some inexplicable whim he should declare: "Even though the boys are drowning as a consequence of their own disobedience, nonetheless, out of the goodness of my heart I will save one of them and let the other two drown." In such a case we would surely consider his love to be partial and imperfect.[10]

The reason we note that this is the form it took in *CBF* is that Dr. Geisler used this exact parable in the 1985 Basinger & Basinger work on predestination and free will,[11] with one interesting difference: in the 1985 edition the final assertion that the love of the farmer (here meant to represent the Calvinist's God) is "imperfect" is not included. Why is any of this relevant?

Two years after Dr. Geisler's essay appeared in the Basinger & Basinger work, C. Samuel Storms wrote *Chosen for Life: An Introductory Guide to the Doctrine of Divine Election*. In it he provided a *devastating* critique of the parable of the farmer. The critique extends for six pages and provides the careful reader with a multitude of reasons to reject the parable as having any merit whatsoever. *CBF* does not contain a single citation of or reference to Storms' work. Obviously, it is possible Dr. Geisler never saw this work, even though it was published by Baker (a major Christian publisher). But such seems unlikely. My response to this parable will follow the outline of Storms and draw heavily from his insights.

The major problem with this parable is not what it does say but what it *doesn't* say. It is the entire blocks of truth that are ignored that allows one to conclude that the loving God who redeems an unworthy people is in fact less than all loving. There are all sorts of hidden assumptions that lead to the completely erroneous conclusion presented in *CBF*.

Consider especially the fact that the parable uses a mere creature (the farmer) to represent the holy God. Immediately, as we consider the example of the farmer, we do so on a human plane. The farmer would have limited knowledge; would be sinful himself and in need of mercy; and may himself have jumped into some other farmer's pond when he was but a kid. We expect certain things of human beings that we have no right to expect of the infinite, holy, almighty God. All these things enter into an evaluation of the attitudes of God based upon how we feel about a fellow human being (the farmer). Storms notes,

> Related to this is the tendency to think that if he really wanted to, it would not affect the farmer in the least simply to take down the sign, suspend the punishment, and turn his pond into a swimming hole for everyone to enjoy. But again, God's retributive justice is not like an old hat that he can discard if he so chooses. Retributive justice is as much a part of God's nature as love is.[12]

To make the parable even semi-workable one would have to change the farmer into the greatest and most noble king and ruler of all time. Then, at least, there would be some meaningful comparison, though still very limited.

Along with what Storms calls a "straw God" the parable likewise trivializes sin. Can anyone seriously think that some "good ol' boys" swimming in a pond is to be likened to the depth of the depraved heart of mankind? If the parable wished to be serious the sin would have to be made realistic: the great king returns to his castle from doing good amongst the people of the land to find a group of men robbing, raping, and murdering his family and friends. They have intentionally set fire to the castle and, if they do not quickly escape, they will perish in the flames. At least this would capture a *little* more of the seriousness of sin and the horrific nature of it. But let's add something more: these are subjects of the great king who have benefited greatly at his hand. He has provided them with great material blessings in the past. They have sat at his table and enjoyed his hospitality. And yet they treat him in this fashion. Unlike the parable, these rebels have sinned against the king (in the parable they sin against a "No Swimming" sign) *personally*. And, it should be noted that this is not the first time. They have a *long* track record of rebellion, and they have often found mercy at the hand of the king.

But let's move even further. These "good ol' boys" are not even described in Geisler's parable. We are told nothing about them other than the fact that they are drowning. To again insert some level of biblical truth, we would have to be informed that these men who are found by the king engaging in heinous crimes against his very own family in the king's castle are not crying out for deliverance from their activities. Despite the mounting flames and heat they continue in their violent behavior, destroying everything that reminds them of the king and his rule. They are enjoying themselves immensely. They *love* their rebellion and their sin. They even make excuses for it and, in fact, get mad at anyone who would call their activities sinful! Indeed, they so enjoy their activities that they encourage others to *join* them in their attack upon the king!

But the truth is even further removed from the offered parable. If we ask "how do these rebels respond to the attempt to deliver them from their rebellion?" there is only one answer: they mock the king's attempts. Should he seek to open a way for them through the flames so as to save them, they would each, invariably, laugh at him and mock his actions. They would throw debris in his face and run away into the smoke, cursing his name. Indeed, if they had the power, they would pull the king into the burning building and make sure he perished in the flames, laughing with glee the entire time! They would surely *never* cry out for deliverance or seek escape from the danger that surrounds them. This is part of the error brought into the parable by Geisler's insistence that the unregenerate man *can* do what is pleasing to God, in direct contradiction to Romans 8:7-8. No rebel sinner (outside of the grace of God bringing them spiritual life) is crying out for help. Even if the proverbial "life ring" were cast into the pond, or a squad of firemen made it to the rebels in the smoke, they would not cooperate with the rescue effort, and even at this, we are missing an important element of biblical truth: they lack the capacity (due to spiritual death) to take advantage of any kind of "assistance" even if they desired to do so! On every level, the parable fails to correspond to the reality of biblical teaching.

But there is more. The parable contains an implicit swipe at the sovereign will of God in election. Storms rightly protests:

> When the farmer is finally portrayed as seeking their deliverance, he does so on an "inexplicable whim." A "whim"? This sort of needless caricature portrays God's solemn, most blessed, and altogether gracious determination to save as little more than a bothersome afterthought, with no purpose or design. What the author of this illustration calls a "whim" the Word of God calls "the kind intention of His will" (Eph. 1:5b).[13]

The conclusion of Geisler's parable is the assertion that such a "God" as the farmer has a "partial and imperfect" kind of love. To be *truly* loving, it seems, the king would not have the freedom to show mercy to *some* of the rebels: he would have to show equal mercy to *all* the rebels. If he is all-loving, the king would have to offer pardon, on equal basis, to all the rebels who were busy joyously trashing his castle and killing his family. But, in reality, there is more, much more. For how can the king provide forgiveness for these rebels anyway? The law must be satisfied. He must send his one and only son to pay the price of their sin. Going back to the pond illustration, Storms lays it out clearly:

> Divine, biblical love, on the other hand, entails that the farmer casts his own son into the pond, knowing full well that if his son makes an effort to save the boys he will die. The son swims to the three boys, notwithstanding their vehement and hostile cries that he get out of the water and leave them alone. As he reaches the three, he extends his arms in love to but one of them. Though that one boy is vile and reprehensible in every respect, the son of the farmer brings him back safely to shore, but in doing so he himself drowns. The two remaining

boys laugh and mock that the farmer's son has drowned. Their glee is beyond control. The one boy for whom the son gave his life to save is suddenly brought to tears as he senses the magnitude of the love that has been shown him, while he was yet hateful and full of blasphemy. The farmer lifts the boy up, dries him off, cleans the mud and filth from his body, and clothes him in the garments of his own dear son. They embrace in everlasting love. The young boy falls to his knees in gratitude, tears flowing. The two who remain in the water continue hurling their taunts at the farmer, declaring that even if they could start anew, they would dive defiantly into the middle of the pond without a moment's hesitation.[14]

So what are we to make of Dr. Geisler's assertion that a God who saves *some* rebel sinners (but not all) through the miracle of divine grace, freeing them from the shackles of sin, giving them a new heart and a new nature, despite their hatred of Him and His ways, is a denial of omnibenevolence? Once all the false assumptions are stripped away we can all see the error of the presentation. It is based upon a false view of God's holiness, a false view of His freedom, a false view of the sinfulness and capacities of man, and a complete misunderstanding of the *freedom* of God to show mercy *as He wills* not as we *demand.* The king would have a perfect right to ring the burning castle with his best troops to make sure the rebels cannot escape, and stand there in perfect majesty and let the flames consume his enemies. It is love beyond degree if the king sends his only son into the burning structure to save *any* of the rebels. There is no logical or rational argument that can be mustered to say that the king must send his son to save *every single one* of the rebels or else be "imperfect" in his love. What *CBF* calls "imperfection" the Bible says is merely God's freedom to show grace to whom He will show grace, and justice to whom He will show justice. "Omnibenevolence" does *not* mean God's grace becomes something that can be demanded by all. Grace, to be grace, must be *free* and *freely given.*

If one is going to argue that God must have the very same kind of love for every rebel sinner to have love for *any*, then it would of necessity follow that God must either save all, or save none. To avoid these two conclusions, evangelicals, including Dr. Geisler, are willing to say that God *tries* to save as many as He can, but fails to do so in many instances, due to the lack of cooperation by the creature.

Redefinition of Terms

Despite CBF's strong dislike of irresistible grace, the work attempts to redefine the phrase so that the "moderate Calvinist" moniker can be maintained. To do this it is said that "Thus, grace is only irresistible to the willing, not to the unwilling."[15] Of course, if someone is "willing" the term "irresistible" no longer has meaning. Why even combine these terms in a meaningless fashion such as this? The Reformed say this grace is irresistible because man is dead in sin and God is the sovereign Creator: the Arminian says man is alive and able to put up a fight and God's grace cannot change him without his assistance. How is this conflict of beliefs aided by redefining the term irresistible and stripping it of all theological meaning? Geisler is saying God's grace is dependent upon free will just as the Arminian is. Why not just admit this and move on? Instead, this meaningless statement becomes an interpretive device used to overthrow any biblical evidence to the contrary. For example, even when faced with the overwhelming statement of Romans 9:21, "Or does not the potter have a right over the clay, to make from the same lump one vessel for honorable use and another for common use?" he writes,

> Irresistible grace operates the way falling in love does. If one willingly responds to the love of another, eventually they reach a point where that love is overwhelming. But that is the way they willed it to be. Even if Paul agreed with the objector that God's work is irresistible, it would not support the hard line of extreme Calvinism,

since God uses irresistible saving grace only on the willing, not the unwilling.

We have seen no substantiation of this theological maxim outside of mere assertion, yet, it enters into the very interpretation of the passage and becomes *the determining factor* in how it is to be understood! He goes on,

> Finally, even if one could show that God is working here (1) irresistibly, (2) on individuals, (3) for eternal salvation—all of which are doubtful—it would not follow necessarily that He works irresistibly *on the unwilling*. Indeed, as we have seen, God does not force free creatures to love Him. Forced love is both morally and logically absurd.[16]

In reality our exegesis of Romans 9 showed that Paul is speaking of God's utter freedom to sovereignly choose individuals for eternal salvation, all to his glory. None of this is doubtful (*CBF* surely gave us no substantial counter-exegesis). But despite working with a text that *shouts* the freedom of God and the creatureliness of man, the commentary concludes with yet another assertion of the existence of "free creatures" and their abilities.

Smoke and Mirrors?

Under the banner "Grace is Irresistible Only on the Willing" (i.e., "God Cannot Save Anyone Without Man's Help") we read the following:

> Some extreme Calvinists use a kind of smoke-and-mirror tactic to avoid the harsh implications of their view. They claim that God does no violence toward a rebellious will; He simply gives a new one. In R.C. Sproul's words, "If God gives us a desire for Christ we will act according to that desire." This sounds reasonable enough until the implied words are included: "If God gives us

> a[n irresistible] desire for Christ we will [irresistibly] act
> according to that desire." Now it can be seen that ex-
> treme Calvinists are using word magic in an attempt to
> hide the fact that they believe God forces the unwilling
> against their will.[17]

One thing we do not do is hide our beliefs, and given that Dr.
Geisler is in this very section talking about "irresistible grace
on the willing," we suggest that making allegations of "word
magic" might not be overly wise. But one thing is for certain:
Calvinists believe God changes the heart of the dead sinner by
grace and changes him from being a God-hater into a God-
lover. Is this not what the Bible says? Do we not read of God
taking out the heart of stone and giving us a heart of flesh
(Ezek 36:26)? What is this if not a complete change of the
individual? More "word magic" takes place when we are told
that God "forces the unwilling" when the accurate statement
is that God renews the heart and the mind. By using unfair
words and ignoring the continuity of the biblical doctrines of
the sovereignty of God and the deadness of man in sin, *CBF*
produces a tremendously unfair and inaccurate critique that
quickly breaks down into simply mockery:

> What extreme Calvinists want to do is to avoid the
> repugnant image of a reluctant candidate being forced
> into the fold or captured into the kingdom....But no
> matter how well the act of "irresistible grace" is hidden
> by euphemistic language, it is still a morally repugnant
> concept.
>   The problem with the idea of "irresistible grace" in ex-
> treme Calvinism, according to this analogy, is that there
> is *no informed consent* for the treatment. Or, better yet,
> the patients are dragged kicking and screaming into
> the operating room, but once they are given a head
> transplant, they (not surprisingly) feel like an entirely
> different person![18]

What *CBF* calls a "head transplant" the Bible calls a "new creature." We are thankful, so very thankful, that God has the free-

dom, and the will, to change the hearts of sinners, not as they "enable Him" but as He freely wills. We are thankful that God did powerfully subdue the insane rebellion that filled our hearts and caused us to live as if He and His law did not matter a bit. We are thankful He inscribed His law upon our hearts and gave us a love for Christ, for without all of this gracious work on our behalf, we would be lost and undone. There is a vast difference between free grace and grace that is dependent upon man for its power. We are thankful God's grace is not fettered by man's actions, will, or desires.

Is Faith a Gift?

> It is an intramural debate among those opposed to extreme Calvinism whether faith is a gift or not. The Bible is seriously lacking in any verses demonstrating that faith is a gift. But if it is a gift, then it is one offered to all and can be freely accepted or rejected.[19]

Along with his attack upon irresistible grace comes not only an in-text denial of the gift of divine faith, but an entire appendix as well. We are told that the Bible is "seriously lacking" in "any" verses demonstrating that faith is a gift. Yet, it takes an entire appendix to respond to at least some of them, and a number we have already presented are completely ignored by CBF.

John 3:3, 6-7

We made mention of the Lord Jesus' teaching on the new birth in John 3. CBF addresses this as well:

> The dispute is over whether this comes by an act of God apart from the recipient's free choice. On this point the text both here and elsewhere indicates that this new birth comes through an act of faith on the part of the recipient. According to this very passage, it is "whoever

believes" that gets eternal life (John 3:16). And in 1 John
5:4 it is "everyone born of God overcomes the world This
is the victory that has overcome the world, even *our faith.*"
Although prompted—not coerced—by grace, the act of
faith is an act of the believer, not a gift from God only to
the elect.[20]

None of this touches upon whether regeneration precedes faith
or whether faith is a gift of God. The phrase "free choice" is
such a mantra for the Arminian that it appears over and over
again, even when the phrase *nowhere appears in the texts being
examined!* But most importantly the reader should fully understand the assertion that in the above quotation grace is limited
to prompting. By using the term "coerce" to cover over the
beautiful act of regeneration the reader is kept from fully weigh-
ing the two sides fairly. Nothing in the text leads to the conclusion that faith is not a gift given by God to His elect people.
This is simply a reiteration of what *must* be if *CBF*'s central
affirmation—the freedom of the will of unregenerate men—is
to be maintained. And we are not engaging in any kind of ad-
hominem argumentation to point out something else: this is
Rome's view of grace, not Geneva's. That is, Rome likewise
limits grace to a prompting, aiding force which can, and often
does, fail to accomplish its goal. This is what divided the pio-
neer Reformers from the Roman Catholics. On this issue, as
we have already noted, *CBF* is firmly planted on the other side
of the Tiber River from the Protestant Reformation.

Ephesians 2:8-9

Regarding faith being a gift at Ephesians 2:8-9, *CBF* notes,

> Zealous defender of extreme Calvinism R.C. Sproul is
> so confident that this is what the text means that he
> triumphantly concludes: "This passage should seal the
> matter forever. The faith by which we are saved is a gift
> of God. But even John Calvin said of this text that "he
> does not mean that *faith* is the gift of God, but that

salvation is given to us by God, or, that we obtain it by the gift of God."[21]

Did John Calvin agree with Norman Geisler's assertions here? The short citation provided might give that idea, but it would be a mistake to think so. Here is the full context, by which a person can judge for themselves how Calvin interpreted the passage:

> Ought we not then to be silent about free-will, and good intentions, and fancied preparations, and merits, and satisfactions? There is none of these which does not claim a share of praise in the salvation of men; so that the praise of grace would not, as Paul shews, remain undiminished. When, on the part of man, the act of receiving salvation is made to consist in faith alone, all other means, on which men are accustomed to rely, are discarded. Faith, then, brings a man empty to God, that he may be filled with the blessings of Christ. And so he adds, not of yourselves; that claiming nothing for themselves, they may acknowledge God alone as the author of their salvation.... This passage affords an easy refutation of the idle cavil by which Papists attempt to evade the argument, that we are justified without works. Paul, they tell us, is speaking about ceremonies. But the present question is not confined to one class of works. Nothing can be more clear than this. The whole righteousness of man, which consists in works, — nay, the whole man, and everything that he can call his own, is set aside. We must attend to the contrast between God and Man, between grace and works. Why should God be contrasted with man, if the controversy related to nothing more than ceremonies?
> Papists themselves are compelled to own that Paul ascribes to the grace of God the whole glory of our salvation, but endeavor to do away with this admission by another contrivance. This mode of expression, they tell us, is employed, because God bestows the first grace. It is really foolish to imagine that they can succeed in this

way, since Paul excludes man and his utmost ability,—
not only from the commencement, but throughout,—
from the whole work of obtaining salvation.

But it is still more absurd to overlook the apostle's in-
ference, lest any man should boast. Some room must
always remain for man's boasting, so long as, independently of grace, merits are of any avail. Paul's doctrine is
overthrown, unless the whole praise is rendered to God
alone and to his mercy. And here we must advert to a
very common error in the interpretation of this passage.
Many persons restrict the word gift to faith alone. But
Paul is only repeating in other words the former sentiment. His meaning is, not that faith is the gift of God,
but that salvation is given to us by God, or, that we obtain it by the gift of God.[22]

As the reader can see, if just the preceding two sentences had
been quoted, the real meaning would be seen. Specifically,
Calvin is refuting those who say that the term "gift" is to be
restricted to faith *alone*. This is *not* the Reformed view, as was
seen in the previous chapter. To cite Calvin as if he would
agree with the denial that faith is a gift in this passage is to
completely misrepresent these words of the Genevan Reformer.
Instead, make special note of two of the phrases provided by
Calvin in response to Rome's claims: "nay, the whole man,
and everything that he can call his own, is set aside. We must
attend to the contrast between God and Man, between grace
and works;" and "since Paul excludes man and his utmost ability, — not only from the commencement, but throughout, —
from the whole work of obtaining salvation." We suggest that
the person who honestly wishes to know where Calvin would
stand on the debate today would find these to be the key
affirmations, for if Geisler's position is correct, and "anyone
can believe," then Calvin's entire position is overthrown. Would
not such a faith be something the man could "call his own"?
Calvin says it is set aside. Would this not be part of man's
"utmost ability" especially at the very "commencement" of

salvation"? Paul excludes it from the whole work of obtaining salvation, Calvin teaches. There is, in fact, very little in "moderate Calvinism" that Calvin would ever call his own.[23]

Philippians 1:29

We presented this passage in the previous chapter as clear evidence of the nature of faith as a gift from God. *CBF* attempts to argue otherwise:

> There are several indications here that Paul had no such thing in mind. First, the point is simply that God has not only provided us with the opportunity to trust Him but also to suffer for Him. The word "granted" (Greek: *echaristhe*) means "grace" or "favor." That is, both the opportunity to suffer for Him and to believe on Him are favors with which God has graced us.[24]

We must again object to the retranslation of the passage without the slightest foundation being provided. How does "granted to you to believe in Him" become "granted to you the opportunity to believe in Him"? And are we really to believe that Paul was teaching the Philippians that God had *granted them the opportunity to suffer?* Such is pure eisegesis. "To believe" and "to suffer" are perfectly parallel in the passage: if the one is a matter of a mere opportunity to believe based upon our own free will actions, does it not follow that the suffering is likewise to be viewed as something we can choose, or not choose, to endure? No, the "simple meaning" of the passage is that God has granted faith to his elect people and that those people well know the path to glory: it is the path of suffering, trod by their Savior.

> Further, Paul is not speaking here of initial faith that brings salvation but of the daily faith and daily suffering of someone who is already Christian.

We are not told how Dr. Geisler proves this from the text, but

again, if this is so, it means that unregenerate men can exercise saving faith that brings forgiveness of sins without receiving this faith as a gift from God, but, the regenerate man for
some reason *is not as capable of producing daily faith!* Are we to
believe that the faith that accepts the promises of Christ unto
salvation is somehow "easier" than the faith the Christian needs
for every day living? Surely not!

> Finally, it is noteworthy that both the suffering and
> the believing are presented as things that we are to do.
> He says it is granted for "you" to do this. It was not
> something God did for them. Both were simply an op-
> portunity God gave them to use "on the behalf of Christ"
> by their free choice.

Here in three sentences we have both straw-man argumentation and eisegesis. First, the Reformed does not argue that we
do not exercise faith. Instead, it is argued that we are not capable of exercising saving faith until enabled by God (John
6:65). That ability is a gift from God given to His elect as part
of the work of regeneration. So, to say "It was not something
God did for them" is to completely misrepresent the debate.
Finally, while the text says God granted them "to believe" and
"to suffer," *CBF* must change this to "the opportunity to exercise your free will in faith" and "to choose to suffer."

1 Corinthians 12:8-9

> For to one is given the word of wisdom through the Spirit,
> and to another the word of knowledge according to the
> same Spirit; to another faith by the same Spirit, and to
> another gifts of healing by the one Spirit, (1 Corinthians
> 12:8-9)

This passage plainly says that faith is a gift given by the Spirit.
How does *CBF* respond?

> To be sure, faith *is* referred to here as a gift from God.

However, Paul is not talking about faith given to *unbelievers* by which they can be *saved*. Rather, it is speaking of a special gift of faith given to some *believers* by which they can *serve*. One can plainly see the difference by looking at the context.[25]

We have only one question to ask in response: if the unregenerate, spiritually dead, slave-to-sin natural man outside of Christ is capable of saving faith, why would a regenerate, born again, freed-from-sin spiritual man in Christ need a *gift of faith*?

Acts 5:31

He is the one whom God exalted to His right hand as a Prince and a Savior, to grant repentance to Israel, and forgiveness of sins. (Acts 5:31)

This passage is cited as evidence that God "grants" repentance on the basis of the work of Christ. *CBF* responds:

If this is so, then all Israel must have been saved, since both were given "to Israel."[26]

This is obviously untrue. The point of the passage is not the definition or extent of the term "Israel," but the fact that repentance and forgiveness are both gifts (over against the Arminian contention that repentance is something unregenerate man is able to do on his own). What is not addressed is the obvious question: why would Christ have to *grant* what is, in the Arminian view, an inherent *ability* that all men already have? The response continues:

This clearly does not mean that all Gentiles will be saved but that all have the opportunity to be saved. Likewise, it means that all have the God-given opportunity to repent (cf. 2 Peter 3:9)

Second, the *opportunity* to repent is a gift of God. He graciously allows us the opportunity to turn from our

sins, *but we must do the repenting*. God is not going to
repent for us. Repentance is an act of our will supported
and encouraged by His grace.

Where did the term "opportunity" come from in the text of
Acts 5:31? It does not appear. So upon what exegetical basis
are we to determine that "grant repentance" actually means
"grant opportunities for repentance"? What is granted in the
text? Repentance itself. Since Dr. Geisler chides Reformed
writers for allegedly changing Scripture when they paraphrase
something, why does he here provide a paraphrase that actually changes the meaning of the text?

Next, if Jesus merely grants the *opportunity* to repent, may
we ask why He does not grant this to every single individual?
Indeed, it cannot be said that every single Jew who has ever
lived has heard the gospel, hence, even if we take the passage
in this a-contextual manner, it leaves us with a contradiction,
for it then pictures the exalted Christ granting "opportunities"
of repentance to only some.

Next, no one is arguing that God repents for us. This is
straw-man argumentation. The question is, can the unregenerate man who is still in the flesh repent so as to please God?
Paul said no (Romans 8:7-8). So does this passage not refer to
the *ability* to repent as "repentance"? Surely it does. So, Acts
5:31 teaches us that since Christ is now exalted He, graciously,
grants repentance and forgiveness of sins. Both are divine gifts
for which we must be eternally grateful. Geisler concludes,

> Further, if repentance is a gift, then it is a gift in the
> same sense that forgiveness is a gift. But forgiveness was
> obtained by Jesus on the Cross for "everyone who be-
> lieves" (Acts 13:38-39), not just for the elect. Hence,
> by the same logic, all men must have been given saving
> faith—a conclusion emphatically rejected by extreme
> Calvinists.

We have seen how the biblical doctrines of God's sovereignty,
man's deadness in sin, God's unconditional election, etc., all

stand together. We can likewise see how the strong commitment to the free will of man on the part of *CBF* determines
every interpretation of every verse that is raised against the
idea. We have seen in the words of Jesus that *all* who are given
to Him by the Father *will* come to Him in faith (John 6:37).
Hence, "everyone who believes" is a phrase that must consistently be seen as coextensive with the elect. But none of this is
even slightly relevant to what would have to be shown to deflect this passage: that repentance (not the mere opportunity)
is not a gift given by the exalted Christ.

Acts 16:14

What of the Lord's opening of Lydia's heart to respond to
the things spoken by the Apostles in Acts 16:14?

> Moderate Calvinists do not deny that God moves upon
> the hearts of unbelievers to persuade and prompt them
> to exercise faith in Christ. They only deny that God does
> this coercively by irresistible grace and that He only does
> it on some persons (the elect). The Holy Spirit is con-
> victing "the world [*all men*, not just some; cf. John 3:16-
> 18; 1 John 2:15-17] of sin, righteousness and judgment"
> (John 16:8). And God does not force anyone to believe
> in Him (Matt. 23:37).[27]

First, where does the text speak of "moving upon the hearts of
unbelievers to persuade and prompt them to exercise faith in
Christ"? The text says the Lord opened the heart of Lydia "to
respond to" the gospel message. There is nothing about persuading or prompting here (i.e., no exegetical response is offered). Secondly, if this opening of the heart was not done on
specific persons (Lydia), why, then, were not all who heard
converted? Was Lydia "better" or more "spiritual" than the
others? Why did the Holy Spirit succeed in persuading her,
but not everyone else? Next, upon what basis does Dr. Geisler
confuse conviction of the entire world with regeneration of the

elect? Are the two the same thing? Surely not. It is the Reformed contention that the Holy Spirit regenerates the elect at the very time the Father has decreed. That surely involves conviction of sin, but it is not *limited* to it. Finally, we have seen the misuse of Matthew 23:37 with tremendous frequency in *CBF*, so we only note again that since *CBF assumes* one particular interpretation of this passage but does not *prove* that interpretation nor defend it against the objections we have raised, the entirety of the work suffers greatly.

2 Peter 1:1

We cited 2 Peter 1:1 in presenting our belief in the divine nature of saving faith. Dr. Geisler says of this passage,

> Peter claims only that they have "received" or "obtained" (NKJV) their faith, but does not inform us as to exactly how they got it. Using such a vague, undefined statement as this to support their belief only demonstrates how desperate the extreme Calvinists are to find support of this unscriptural dogma.[28]

The only "desperation" here is on the part of someone attempting to find some *substance* in *CBF*'s attempts at exegesis. The text describes the faith these Christians have as something they "received" or "were given." The Greek term is defined by one lexical source as "what comes to one, always apart from one's own efforts"[29] and by another as "to receive, with the implication that the process is related somehow to divine will or favor."[30] So the text makes explicit reference to a faith given by divine favor to all Christians. If this is not relevant to the topic at hand, what possibly could be? Claiming Calvinists are "desperate" while 1) ignoring such passages as 1 John 5:1 and 2) providing non-substantive responses to passages such as this, is hardly helpful.

In Conclusion

Finally, on page 189 we find a major title which reads, "Saving Faith is Something All Can Exercise." This is followed by:

> Nowhere does the Bible teach that saving faith is a special gift of God only to a select few. Further, everywhere the Bible assumes that anyone who wills to be saved can exercise saving faith. Every passage where the Scriptures call upon unbelievers to believe or repent to be saved implies this truth.

This truly does summarize the main problem with *CBF*: we have now seen that the attempted response to the biblical teaching that saving faith is a gift of God given to his elect involves 1) skipping over certain passages such as 1 John 5:1 and Hebrews 12:2, and 2) providing non-substantive responses to passages such as 2 Peter 1:1 and Philippians 1:29. So we are left with unfounded "implications" rather than direct biblical teaching. And these implications all come from the same source: the over-riding belief in creaturely freedom, a freedom that, sadly, is more important than the confession of the Potter's freedom to do with His creation as He sees fit, all to His glory and honor.

Notes

1   Specifically the phrase used was, "God is not a divine rapist" in reference to a denial of "irresistible force." David Basinger & Randall Basinger, *Predestination & Free Will* (InterVarsity Press, 1985), p. 69.

2   *Chosen But Free*, p. 47.

3   We simply point out that many Augustine scholars do not make the connection, and such great Protestant scholars as B.B. Warfield viewed the Reformation as simply the victory of Augustine's doctrine of grace over Augustine's doctrine of the church, leading one to recognize that the Donatist controversy informed Augustine's view of ecclesiology while the Pelagian controversy informed his view of grace.

4   *Chosen But Free*, p. 48.

5   Ibid., p. 66.

6   Ibid., p. 49.

7   Ibid.

8   Ibid., p. 85.

9   Ibid., p. 86.

10 Ibid., p. 49.

11 *Predestination & Free Will*, David Basinger & Randall Basinger, ed., (InterVarsity Press, 1985), pp. 69-70.

12 C. Samuel Storms, *Chosen for Life: An Introductory Guide to the Doctrine of Divine Election* (Baker Book House, 1987), p. 126.

13 Ibid., p. 128.

14 Ibid., p. 130.

15 *Chosen But Free*, p. 89.

16 Ibid., p. 90.

17 Ibid., pp. 96-97

18 Ibid., p. 97.

19 Ibid., p. 35.

20 Ibid., p. 60.

21 Ibid., p. 182.

22 John Calvin, *Commentary on the Epistle to the Ephesians*, in *The Comprehensive John Calvin Collection* (Ages Digital Library, 1998).

23 Besides this, Calvin elsewhere teaches the very thing CBF denies. When refuting the teachings of the Council of Trent on justification Calvin, as the other Reformers, emphasized the foundational difference between Rome and the Bible by pointing to this very truth: that faith is a gift of God. He wrote, "What they say of faith might perhaps hold true, were faith itself, which puts us in possession of righteousness, our own. But seeing that it too is the free gift of

God, the exception which they introduce is superfluous." John Calvin, *Acts of the Council of Trent With the Antidote*, in *The Comprehensive John Calvin Collection*.

24 *Chosen But Free*, p. 183.
25 Ibid., p. 185.
26 Ibid., p. 185.
27 Ibid., p. 186.
28 *Chosen But Free*, pp. 187-188.
29 *Analytical Lexicon to the Greek New Testament*, 1994, Timothy and Barbara Friberg, found in BibleWorks 4.0, Hermeneutika Software, 1998.
30 *Louw-Nida Greek-English Lexicon of the New Testament Based on Semantic Domains*, 2nd Edition, Edited by J. P. Louw and E. A. Nida, (United Bible Societes,1988), found in BibleWorks 4.0, Hermeneutika Software, 1998.

Chapter 14

The Potter's Freedom Defended

There are few truths more precious to the Reformed believer than the doctrines of grace. These are not issues of mere debate. They are the very essence of the meaning of grace. God's freedom, His proper right of kingship, His unchanging nature, and eternal decree, are precious. In a world where men fancy themselves demigods the Calvinist says, "God reigns, and I gladly serve Him."

The freedom of God's grace is the greatest joy that can be known. To know, both in mind and heart, that God freely chose to redeem me from the pit and draw me to Himself, is an awesome thing. It brings deep humility to know that I did not differ one wit from the person who remains in his or her sin. I am no better than another. I was no more intelligent, no more spiritual, no more wise, than anyone else. It was not something I did, not something I accomplished, not something I would ever have chosen had He not been gracious to me. I know the depth of sin and depravity that yet remains in my heart, and knowing it, realize my utter impotence to break its chains outside of grace.

Grace is a wonderful word that speaks of God's freedom and God's power. I cannot earn grace, merit grace, purchase grace, or force grace. It is free or it is not grace. Yet the grace of God that brings His elect safely into eternal rest is not merely some persuasive power that may or may not accomplish the ends for which God intends it. Grace is no servant of man, dependent upon the creature for its success. No, saving grace is God's own power. Saved, and kept, by grace. That is the Christian's hope.

The Reformed believer cannot help but stop in wonder at the words of Paul, "I have been crucified with Christ; and it is no longer I who live, but Christ lives in me; and the *life* which I now live in the flesh I live by faith in the Son of God, who loved me and gave Himself up for me." He loved *me!* The mighty Son of God loved me, the rebel sinner, unworthy of even the first portion of His grace! And He loved me so perfectly, so completely, that He gave Himself up for me on the cross of Calvary, in some mysterious way joining me with Himself so that His death is my death! My sins borne in His body on the tree, bringing perfect redemption whole and free! How can this possibly be?

The doctrines of grace touch every aspect of the Christian life, and determine, truly, whether our faith will be God-centered, or man-centered. If we realize that all things are meant to result in His glory, and that we are but vessels of mercy, made for honor and glory, we will live our lives so as to reflect the glory of the divine and majestic Creator who made us and sustains us. Our lives will be seen not as our own, directed by our sovereign and autonomous will for whatever ends *we* choose. We will live for the One who formed us and made us and sustains us every moment.

What Difference Does It Make?

Dr. Geisler provided a chapter in *CBF* titled, "What Difference Does It Make?" In this chapter he notes that "belief affects behavior, and so ideas have consequences."[1] In this he is quite correct. And, since the vast majority of the argumentation in *CBF* is directed at Calvinism and is written in support of Arminianism, it is obvious that he believes the practical implications of Calvinism are important indeed, in a strongly negative sense. Immediately before noting what he calls "practical consequences of extreme Calvinism," he writes, "Likewise, false doctrine will lead to false deeds."[2] In concluding our refutation of CBF we would like to note these alleged concerns.

The first concern voiced is that Calvinism leads to "failing to take personal responsibility for our actions." This is false. Calvinism has historically been in the forefront of every meaningful revival, such as the Great Awakening, that included as a part of its fabric personal behavior and a concern for holiness. The greatest impetus that exists for personal holiness and godly behavior is a recognition of one's creatureliness, the sovereignty of God, His glory, and our debt to grace. The heart that has been touched by grace and knows truly the depth of its own depravity and the greatness of God's power that was necessary to renew that heart is quite concerned to take responsibility and glorify the God who has so graciously saved.

Next we are told that Calvinism blames God for evil. This is false. Calvinism's God is so great, so powerful, and so free, that He can answer the "big questions" without being stripped of His freedom and His ability to positively decree whatsoever comes to pass. It is the reverse position that is so lamentable. Dr. Geisler, in this section, speaks of a speaker at a conference that recognized that God had been involved in the death of his son, and CBF, sadly, provides a surface level response that shows no interest in entering into the depths of this topic. We read,

> I thought to myself, "I wonder what he would say if his daughter had been raped?" Would he not be able to come to grips with the matter until he concluded victoriously that "God raped my daughter!" God forbid! Some views do not need to be refuted; they simply need to be stated.[3]

As one who has worked as a hospital chaplain and faced death directly in the most difficult situations therein, I can only say that such responses betray a tremendous lack of familiarity with the great Reformed writers of the past who have spoken to the matter of suffering with such power and depth that we all can benefit greatly from listening to their words. If God is not sovereign over all things, including the very moment of death, then death does indeed have the final victory, the final power. You simply cannot honestly look at someone and say, "God has a purpose in your life" when you then have to say on the other hand, "God had nothing to do with the death of your loved one." The greatest joy in death, the greatest comfort in sorrow, is knowing that there is *nothing* that is purposeless, *nothing* that is mere chance.

Arminianism simply cannot provide this kind of comfort. If indeed, the ultimate authority in what takes place amongst men is the autonomous free will of man (rather than the all-wise decree of the Almighty Creator of time and space), then to say there is purpose in *anything* is at best a guess and at worst a lie. Calvinists affirm the biblical truth:

> Whatever the LORD pleases, He does,
> In heaven and in earth, in the seas and in all deeps.
> (Psalm 135:6)

Sadly, the Arminian reads this as, "Man does whatever he pleases, and God handles the rest, as long as it does not impinge upon the ultimate freedom of the creature."

God works all things after the counsel of His will, including those things that involve the creature, man. As the Bible testifies:

> The LORD nullifies the counsel of the nations;
> He frustrates the plans of the peoples.
> The counsel of the LORD stands forever,
> The plans of His heart from generation to generation.
> (Psalm 33:10-11)

God's purpose is always just, holy, and good. All things resound to His glory, even when we cannot see how this will be.

Even the greatest atrocities in history the Calvinist knows were not purposeless nor senseless. Even if we cannot see the purpose, we have the promise of God that a purpose did, and does, exist. God is still on His throne.

It is so very sad, then, to read the following:

> Actually, there is no real difference on this point between the extreme Calvinists and fatalistic Islam in which Allah says, in the holy book (the Qur'an), "If We [majestic plural] had so willed, We could certainly have brought Every soul its true guidance; But the Word from Me Will come true. 'I will Fill Hell with jinn and men all together'" (Sura 32:13).[4]

CBF then cites from Puritan writer William Ames who concludes by saying, "Reprobation is the predestination of certain men so that the glory of God's justice may be shown in them."[5] It is clearly Dr. Geisler's purpose to say that these two statements are parallel. Yet, to make such a statement shows tremendous disregard for simple accuracy, let alone respect for Ames or any who believe as he. Allah does not redeem rebel sinners out of grace and mercy. Allah does not give His Son for *utterly undeserving men and women.* Allah does not do these things to bring glory to his grace! To ignore this fundamental, definitional difference is to engage in the rankest sort of ad-hominem argumentation that is far below the kind of material we would expect to come from Dr. Geisler's pen.

Next, Dr. Geisler alleges that Calvinism lays the ground for universalism. This is false. Just the opposite is true. Arminianism has opened that door, not Calvinism. Universalists detest the concept of justice, holiness, and glory that is part and parcel of Reformed theology. Universalists are great proponents of free willism, not the freedom of God nor the glory of God.

It is then said that Calvinism undermines trust in the love of God. This is false, and just the opposite is true. Calvinism presents a love that is powerful and effective, not a love that tries and tries and tries but fails because it is dependent upon the synergistic cooperation of the objects of that love. The love proclaimed in Scriptural Calvinism is a love that saves, a love that lasts, the love about which we sing, "Oh love that will not let me go...."

Indeed, at this point a most strange and incomprehensible statement is made by Dr. Geisler. He says that extreme Calvinism "has been the occasion for disbelief and even atheism for many."[6] A footnote is appended at this point which reads,

> Charles Darwin called hell a "damnable doctrine"...And renowned agnostic Bertrand Russell said, "I do not myself feel that any person who is really profoundly humane can believe in everlasting punishment."[7]

We have no idea how this footnote is related to the assertion. Have men fled into atheism out of hatred for the sovereign God? Of course. Men flee into all sorts of idolatry as they suppress the truth of God that is within them (Romans 1:18-20). But what does the hatred of hell, a doctrine we would assume Dr. Geisler believes, have to do with the assertion that extreme Calvinism leads men to atheism?

We believe that a strong proclamation of the God of Scripture is the only basis upon which to answer atheists and their cavils against the Christian faith. Giving in to them and affirming the humanist doctrine of free will is not the way to win the battle. We believe there is nothing gained by hiding the Bible's plain teaching of the sovereignty of God simply to pacify the humanist who is in active rebellion against God's sovereign power in the first place. A God who would create and yet not maintain control over His creation is hardly a God worthy of defending against atheism.

Next it is said that Calvinism undermines the motive for evangelism. Despite the popularity of this accusation, it is false. Those who evangelize out of concern for man's free will rather than out of obedience to Christ and His command, do so for the wrong reasons, and will soon be disillusioned as men reject their message and bring persecution against them.

This particular objection is most troubling to me personally. I have seen its falsehood first hand. For many years I have led volunteers in passing out Christian literature and witnessing to people who are attending the semi-annual General Conference of the Church of Jesus Christ of Latter-day Saints in Salt Lake City, Utah. We are the only group who is in attendance at every single Conference. We have talked to Arminians who wonder why we bother, since "those are the hard cases anyway." Yes, they are the hard cases. And if I believed for a second that it was up to their "free will" and a grace that cannot change a heart, cannot renew a mind, I would never set foot outside that place again. But I do not believe in free will, nor do I believe in a grace that is a mere helping force and not the renewing power of God. That is why we keep going. That is why we see "hard cases" come out of Mormonism. When you believe that there is no power in heaven or on earth that can stop the Holy Spirit of God from drawing one of His elect to Himself (including the will of the creature!) you can preach the truth with boldness and trust God to save His people.

Indeed, the decline in American evangelicalism that manifests itself in the substitution of programs, drama, coffee bars, and anemic preaching that avoids a call to repentance can be laid directly at the feet of Arminianism, *not* Calvinism. When you have to worry about "offending" the almighty creature you have to start using non-biblical methods of "evangelism," and inevitably it is the evangel that suffers. But it is the gospel that speaks to man's true need, and it is the gospel that saves and results in changed (not slightly modified) lives. And the gospel of Scripture is the gospel of the Reformation.

Finally, it is asserted that Calvinism undermines the motivation for intercessory prayer. This, too, is false. Indeed, we turn the accusation around on Arminianism: if the Holy Spirit is already convicting every man of sin as best He can, and if God is already "giving His all" to save a particular person, why in the world pray for that person? What good would it do? The Arminian God can't save the person you are praying for without their help to begin with. Why intercede with a God who is incapable of doing anything more than offering a plan and then leaving the result to man?

Intercessory prayer is, by nature, Reformed. That is, it recognizes the sovereignty of God and His ability to change the hearts of men! Every such prayer is a tacit recognition that the biblical doctrine is the Reformed one. As is often said, our prayers are often far better than our professed theology.

What Now?

Chosen But Free presents what it calls a "balanced view" of divine election. We have seen that it does nothing of the sort. It presents Arminianism under the guise of "moderate Calvinism." The majority of its argumentation is aimed directly at simple Reformed theology, and its arguments against Arminianism are actually arguments against process theology and open theism. It can't argue against Arminianism since that is its core profession.

We have proven in this work that the redefinition of terms inherent in *CBF*'s presentation must be rejected. The attempt to turn Arminianism into Calvinism involves using words in a manner that is utterly self-contradictory, such as speaking of men who are not "so dead" that they cannot respond, or of believing in "irresistible grace on the willing." Further, we have seen the arbitrary nature of the assertion that Calvin did not believe in limited atonement, and hence all true Calvinists are "extreme Calvinists." The entire framework of the book has been removed by simple factual investigation and argumentation.

But the single most important issue that we wish to communicate to the reader is this: *CBF*'s attempts to defend Arminianism through the use of Scripture fail, consistently. On an exegetical basis *CBF* does not pass the most cursory examination, let alone an in-depth critique. The reader has seen examples of eisegesis in every single chapter of *CBF*. Surely the strength of Reformed theology is its biblical basis, and the weakness of Arminian theology is its philosophical basis. The

Reformed position begins with Scriptural truths. The Arminian position begins with philosophical necessities, and we have seen, over and over again, the result of forcing philosophical presuppositions into the text of Scripture. When one can turn Romans 9:16 and John 6:44 into affirmations of "free will," obviously the text itself is not driving the interpretation.

A person who believes in *sola scriptura* (Scripture alone is the final and only infallible rule of faith for the Church) and in *tota Scriptura* (one must believe *all* of Scripture, not just parts) must wrestle with the issues raised in this book. A person who cannot provide a contextually-based, fair and honest interpretation of such passages as John 6:37-45, Romans 8:28-9:23, or Ephesians 1:3-11, *must* face this fact and be willing to abandon long-held and maybe even cherished traditions. We firmly believe that only the Spirit of God can give to a person the heart-felt desire to be in subjection to *all* the Word teaches.

The Potter's freedom is precious to the Christian, for it is the very basis of salvation itself. Our sovereign Creator is free to be the good, holy, merciful, loving God that He is. It is our prayer that the reader of this book will know this truth not just in the mind, but most importantly, in the heart.

Notes

1   *Chosen But Free*, p. 131.
2   Ibid.
3   Ibid., p. 133.
4   Ibid., p. 133.
5   Ibid., p. 134.
6   Ibid., p. 135.
7   Ibid.

Scripture Index

More Praise for THE POTTER'S FREEDOM...

C. H. Spurgeon once said that "there seems to be an inveterate prejudice in the human mind against" the doctrine of predestination. A brief review of Norman Geisler's disappointing book, *Chosen But Free*, confirms the rightness of Spurgeon's judgment. But however uncomfortable is the doctrine of God's sovereign freedom to our rebellious, finite minds, this much must be said: it is indisputably biblical. For this reason and more, James White's *The Potter's Freedom* is to be welcomed.

    —J. Ligon Duncan III, Ph.D.; Minister, First Presbyterian Church, Jackson, MI; Adjunct Professor, Reformed Theological Seminary

In *The Potter's Freedom*, Reformed Baptist scholar Dr. James R. White has done the church a great service by exposing Dr. Geisler's faulty work and by positively providing an exegetcally sound, historically accurate, and theologically precise apology for Reformed theology. White's work is readable to the layman, worthy for the seminary, and will become a classic refutation of supposed "moderate Calvinist" views today which are usually a misinformed Arminianism.

    —Dr. Fred A. Malone, Author, Pastor of First Baptist Church, Clinton, LA; Southern Baptist Founders Ministries Board Member

We live in a dangerous era with regard to Christian literature. Many dear believers assume that any book in print has come out of a serious attempt to discern the truth by wrestling with Scripture and trying to fairly understand the thinking of the great Christians who have wrestled with the same doctrine in the past. Sadly today, no matter how unfairly one misrepresents the classical understanding of biblical truth, one can often find uncritical readers. Few in this day of lukewarmness for truth, are willing to do the painstaking work of refuting such works of distortion. By God's grace, Dr. James White has used his considerable gifts in this essential arena. We are delighted to see his work, *The Potter's Freedom*, expose the work of Dr. Norman Geisler, titled *Chosen But Free*. Scholars of the debate about free will and God's sovereignty immediately see that Dr. Geisler's book is a simplistic defense of Arminianism, notable only for the audacity of calling Arminianism "Moderate Calvinism" and historic Calvinism "Extreme Calvinism." Indeed, any who have read Jonathan Edwards' *Enquiry into the Freedom of the Will* will assume Dr. Geisler is hoping his readers have never carefully read this definitive destruction of Geisler's concept of human freedom on which

(continued on next page...)

his whole work rests. Dr. White patiently exposes Dr. Geisler's work to the broader evangelical world, noting Geisler's complete unwillingness to wrestle with the exegetical, theological or historical argument of historic reformed thinkers. Indeed I am sure that Dr. Geisler, with his distinguished work in the field of apologetics, would be embarrassed of any Christian apologist who evidenced as little knowledge of the opposing world view challenged, as he himself has shown of the knowledge of the biblical defense of reformed orthodoxy. Dr. White also provides his readers with a careful presentation of the truth from Scripture, and the importance of this truth for the Christian life. After reading Dr. White's careful work, the reader will clearly see Dr. Geisler as the emperor with no clothes, whose arguments cannot stand serious scrutiny. We pray by the work of the Spirit, readers of *The Potter's Freedom*—and Dr. Geisler himself—will come to see the truth of the only true God, who is sovereign over all things, especially the salvation and damnation of men.

    —Dr. Jonathan Gerstner, Author, Pastor, Baltimore, MD

With great penetration of argument, and in a manner reminiscent of Luther demolishing Erasmus, James White grinds the Semi-Pelagianism of Dr. Geisler to fine powder—not in the spirit of triumphalism, but knowing that all Arminianism is as hostile to the true gospel as it is friendly to a reviving Roman Catholicism.

    **—Maurice Roberts, Editor, *Banner of Truth* Magazine,
Edinburgh, Scotland, UK**

In his characteristically thorough style, Dr. White reveals that Norman Geisler's offensive against Reformed soteriology in his book, *Chosen But Free*, is based on a peculiar and spurious philosophical theory, rather than on solid biblical exegesis. In *The Potter's Freedom*, Dr. White rolls up his sleeves and does the exegetical work that is lacking in Geisler's book. The result is a marvelous defense and affirmation of what Dr. White refers to as "the free and proper kingship of God."

    **—Buddy Boone, Radio Program Director, WHVN, Charlotte, NC;
WCGC, Belmont, NC; WAVO, Rock Hill, SC**

Lest any reader be misled, this book is not really about Norman Geisler. Nor is it even about the good doctor's miscomprehension of the nature of providence. Rather, it is primarily about the person, character, and prerogative of the Sovereign God. In that regard, James White has rendered us all good service.

    —George Grant, Author; Pres., Bannockburn College, Franklin, TN

When Martin Luther wrote his *Bondage of the Will* in response to Erasmus' *Diatribe on Free-will*, he pointedly addressed Erasmus in the Introduction, declaring that the book "...struck me as so worthless and poor that my heart went out to you for having defiled your lovely, brilliant flow of language with such vile stuff. I thought it outrageous to convey material of so low a quality in the trappings of such rare eloquence; it is like using gold or silver dishes to carry garden rubbish or dung." Sadly, as exhibited by Norman Geisler's *Chosen But Free*, Erasmus was not the last learned man to use his tremendous literary capacities for such ignoble purposes. But God often uses assaults upon gospel truth as the occasion for mighty reaffirmations of the very truths under assault. I thank God that He has done just that in the publication of James White's excellent book, *The Potter's Freedom*. It is a comprehensive refutation of Geisler's Frankenstein-like creation, which he names, "moderate Calvinism." White makes a clear, compassionate and compelling case for the historic Christian faith (nicknamed evangelical Calvinism) that is Biblically saturated, exegetically sound, and theologically as straight as an arrow. I believe it will prove to be historically significant and am confident that it will not be met with a competent response. I heartily commend this fine work to all lovers of the cause of the Triune God and of His Truth.

—**Bill Ascol, Chairman of the Board, Southern Baptist Founders Ministries, Shreveport, LA**

James White's book, *The Potter's Freedom*, is as clear a presentation of the Reformed doctrine of salvation as I've ever read. He writes with an engaging style and ably defends his views from scripture. More importantly, he takes on one of evangelicalism's major Arminian apologists, Norm Geisler. In the least, Dr. White demonstrates repeatedly and thoroughly that Geisler's supposed "moderate Calvinism" is nothing of the sort. I am reminded here of the story of Alexander the Great confronting one of his soldiers who had not lived up to his duties. The soldier's name happened to be the same as the great general's. Alexander simply told him, "Either change your name or change your character." White essentially gives the same advice to Geisler: you have a right to believe what you want, but you have no right to call your views "moderate Calvinism." White has also demonstrated that Geisler has little basis to argue that his view—whatever it is called—is grounded in scripture. What Geisler is is a moderate Arminian or a "secure" Arminian. What he is not is a Calvinist—in any sense of the term.

The issues raised in this book are enormous, touching the very heart of the Protestant faith—a faith that finds its roots in Reformed thinking.

That so many evangelical Protestants today are ignorant of such roots is a sign of the times: we are moving closer and closer to a thoroughly anthropocentric worldview—a worldview that is devoid of both answers and comfort and, in fact, is beginning to look more like humanism than Christianity. But spiritual maturity—both individually and communally—begins with the progressively Copernican discovery that we are not the center of the universe! At bottom, White's book makes a magnificent contribution in this regard, for it exalts Jesus Christ at every turn, and affirms the Potter's absolute freedom to perform his will.
   —Daniel B. Wallace, Ph.D., Professor of New Testament Studies, Dallas Theological Seminary

In *The Potter's Freedom* James White has given us a fresh and heavily exegetical defense of the biblical doctrine of salvation. White wrote his excellent review of the biblical underpinings of the Reformed Faith in response to Norman Geisler's *Chosen But Free*. White's evaluation of Geisler's arguments is thorough and his ability to dismantle those arguments will be greatly appreciated by those who love their Calvinistic heritage. Nevertheless, White, in his refutation of Geisler's position, maintains a spirit of Christian graciousness throughout. Though this book was written for the purpose of debate, its thorough treatment of the prinicpal texts, on which the doctrine stands or falls, may serve as a textbook for those who are just coming to understand the doctrines of grace. Here in one volume is a thoughtful and well-written presentation of those truths. The English of *The Potter's Freedom* is clear and non-technical which should make it of value to those who are unfamiliar with the language of theologians.
   —Dr. Joe B. Nesom, Southern Baptist Founders Ministries, Jackson, LA

In his defense of Reformed theology, James White provides a refreshingly accurate and objective representation. White delivers a blow-by-blow refutation focusing *solely* on the exegesis of key passages, avoiding philosophical assertions, while Dr. Norman Geisler leaps out of his area and swims in unfamiliar waters in his treatment of Reformed theology.
   —Edward L. Dalcour, President, Department of Christian Defense

We decry the subterfuge of politicians as they redefine time-honored words in order to convince the public that they really did not raise taxes or commit adultery. Their form of double speak has so permeated our culture that even the church has been infected. The theologian, whose task is to learn and communicate the truth, betrays his trust when he resorts to redefinition. Yet Norman Geisler in *Chosen But Free* redefines some of the church's time-honored definitions and is guilty of double speak, when he calls the Reformation doctrines of grace "extreme Calvinism" and offers a form of Arminianism as "moderate Calvinism." Under the title of moderate Calvinism, he explains away the chief tenets of Calvinism. As Luther served the church well when he wrote his classic *Bondage of the Will* in response to Erasmus' denial of the sovereignty of God in salvation, James White has served the church today in writing *The Potter's Freedom*. Mr. White exposes Geisler's philosophical methodology and his attempt to redefine many important biblical concepts while giving a thorough Biblical defense of true Calvinism. If you have read Mr. Geisler's book you must read this response. If you want to learn more about the great Reformation doctrines (total depravity, election, particular redemption, effectual calling, and perseverance of the saints), you need to read this book.

> **—Joseph A. Pipa, Jr., Ph.D., President, Greenville Presbyterian Theological Seminary, Taylors, SC**

One ought not be surprised by the recurrence of error—it has always been the plague of the church. It is expected that false men will arise to trouble those who proclaim the truth. When, however, the opponents of sound doctrine come forth from within the professing church, we shake our heads and wonder, and we pray that the Lord will raise up a defender of the faith once delivered to the saints. That prayer has been answered with the publication of James White's *The Potter's Freedom*. In the face of attacks upon the sovereignty of God and His grace, Dr. White has provided the church with a careful and painstaking rebuttal of the most recent popular attempt to dethrone God and exalt man. It is replete with excellent exegesis and sound theology, and demonstrates clearly that Scripture unambiguously teaches God's *sovereignty* in the salvation of sinners. White's book should be recognized as a major contribution to this discussion. Let us pray that the Lord will use this work to exalt His own glory and restore to many professing Christians a sense of wonder at the power of the grace of God.

> **—James M. Renihan, Ph.D., Dean, Associate Professor of Historical Theology, Institute of Reformed Baptist Studies at Westminster Theological Seminary in California**

More endorsements are available at the author's *The Potter's Freedom* web page, located at the www address: **http://aomin.org/TPF.html**

Do you have comments? Please address them to:

Alpha and Omega Ministries
PO Box 37106
Phoenix, AZ 85069

For faster response, contact us via email:

xapis@aomin.org

Visit our web site at:

http://www.aomin.org

...for information about Mormonism, Jehovah's
Witnesses, Roman Catholicism,
General Apologetics, and listings of debates,
tapes, tracts, etc.

About the Author

JAMES R. WHITE, MA, Th. M, Th. D, is director of Alpha and Omega Ministries, a Christian apologetics organization based in Phoenix, Arizona, and is an elder in the Phoenix Reformed Baptist Church. He is also an adjunct professor with the Golden Gate Baptist Theological Seminary. He is a critical consultant for the Lockman Foundation on the New American Standard Bible Update. He is married to Kelli and has two children, Joshua and Summer Marie.

The Mission of Calvary Press

The ministry of Calvary Press is firmly committed to printing quality Christian literature relevant to the dire needs of the church and the world at the dawn of the 21st century. We unashamedly stand upon the foundation stones of the Reformation of the 16th century—Scripture alone, Faith alone, Grace alone, Christ alone, and God's Glory alone!

Our prayer for this ministry is found in two portions taken from the Psalms: "And let the beauty of the LORD our God be upon us, And establish the work of our hands for us; Yes, establish the work of our hands," and "Not unto us, O LORD, not unto us, but to Your name give glory" (Ps. 90:17; 115:1).